Tied With Heartstrings

True, encouraging stories of
joy and grief from adoptive
and foster families

Compiled by

Marian D. Reinford
and Emily D. Martin

CHRISTIAN LIGHT PUBLICATIONS
Harrisonburg, Virginia 22802

TIED WITH HEARTSTRINGS
Christian Light Publications, Inc.
Harrisonburg, Virginia 22802
© 2013 Christian Light Publications, Inc.
All rights reserved.
Printed in the United States of America

Cover and Inside Design: David W. Miller

ISBN: 978-0-87813-739-8

Dedication

We dedicate *Tied With Heartstrings* to all parents
and children who have felt the tug and the security
of being wrapped in "heartstrings of love,"
and especially to families built through
adoption and foster care.

Table of Contents

PART 1

With Longing Hearts
The Spirit of Adoption

PART 2

Knitting Hearts Together
Bonding Through Love

PART 3

Wounded Hearts

Binding Up the Wounds

———————————

THE PAIN OF PREJUDICE

THE PAIN OF SPECIAL NEEDS

PART 4

Our Unprotected Hearts

When Love Brings Pain

PART 5

Understanding Hearts

Lift Up Their Hands

PART 6

With Grateful Hearts

Trusting God With the End Results

Acknowledgements

We give thanks first to our heavenly Father who showers us daily with blessings, for always being there for us to meet our needs, and for making this book a reality.

Also, we give thanks to our dear husbands, Roy and Malvern, along with our children and extended family and friends who have supported and encouraged us.

We especially acknowledge Marian's daughter, Anya Kauffman, who in many ways was the third compiler in this project; our fellow writers who helped convey our message; and the CLP staff who shared our vision for *Tied With Heartstrings.*

Fred Miller, chairman of CLP's Book and Tract Committee when we started this project, was a great encouragement to us. When we presented the idea of *Tied With Heartstrings,* he told us he had been praying for ten years for someone to write about the challenges and blessings of adoption, and he felt this was God's answer to his prayer. Fred's birth mother passed away when he was very small, and he is very thankful for the wonderful second mother God gave him. When our project turned into something much bigger than we first envisioned, we were especially grateful for Fred's long-term commitment, compassion, and patience.

Leon and Martha Yoder also have been very supportive and helpful in finishing the project. We are deeply grateful for Martha's interest and time as she spent many hours helping us redesign the book. Working with her proved to be a blessing.

We greatly appreciate the early editorial work by Kristy Earl.

And a big thank you to Carol Peachey who gave the manuscript a final polishing and worked with the graphics department on design and layout.

David Miller designed the layout and assembled the pieces. We appreciate his skills and thank him for his excellent work in making this an attractive book.

Thanks, too, to Ann Custer who painstakingly typeset the book and worked with proofreaders and editors to make final corrections.

Preface

Our children are so very special. Each one is unique, a creation of God, a dream come true for us! We are their parents. They belong to us. Strings of love bind their hearts to ours. As the years pass, these heartstrings intertwine so securely that it is virtually impossible to sever the bonds that love has produced. Even after our children leave our homes, heartstrings of loving thoughts and prayers follow them.

Tied With Heartstrings is a compilation from many different writers whose hearts are wrapped up in these strings of love. Adoptive mothers wrote the majority of the entries, but adoptive fathers contributed also. We are delighted to include articles written by adopted children, now adults, telling about adoption from their viewpoints.

The burden of this book was conceived during a CLP Writers' Conference. Several months before the conference, we met an adoptive family who was looking forward to their thirteenth child. As their story unfolded, our hearts reached out to them. Zealous to serve God in any way they could, they had pursued fostering as a means of sharing their Christian home with needy children. The two preschoolers they fostered blended well into their family and became a blessing and joy. A few years later, these two children and their two older siblings all became available for adoption. Since the two younger children were already bonded with the family, the parents agreed to adopt all four of the children.

At first, all seemed to go well. But after the adoption was finalized, they noticed changes in their home. The two older adopted siblings had learned things in their former homes that now spread like measles among other children in the family. The boys and girls became indiscreet with each other. This behavior spread to include their oldest biological son. Though he was not a Christian, he had always been trustworthy before. Disobedience, sneaking, blaming, and lying occurred frequently.

The older adopted daughter constantly accused the parents of being partial, saying they favored and trusted their biological children above the adopted ones. The mother, especially, felt overwhelmed and completely at the end of her rope. Though the church people offered much advice, often it was not practical. These parents felt very much alone. Finally they tried secular counseling for the children to deal with the sexual exploitation that had occurred. But they weren't sure it was the answer. The constant vigil was wearing the parents down.

We tried to encourage them, to lift up their hands. But after the visit, their story continued to trouble us. We prayed and pondered much for this family and other families who felt just as overwhelmed and alone. We knew their church family did not mean to be critical and unsupportive, for the brotherhood had done much to reach out and help them.

We wondered, *How can we all learn to empathize and help more effectively? Is there a way for adoptive families such as this to find the support and help they need within our own circles?*

Then at the CLP Writers' Conference in 2003, Ruth Hobbs spoke about a powerfully influential book. Years ago, this book had enlightened many to the terrible evils of slave trading. It also showed how God worked through the compassion of caring people. *Uncle Tom's Cabin* started from a burning burden in Harriet Beecher Stowe's bosom and ended with changing a nation. Ruth challenged us to share the burdens in our hearts and to help change our world into a better place.

We sisters (both adoptive mothers) discussed our burden with Brother Fred Miller from Christian Light Publications. He encouraged us very much, saying he felt there was a real need for a book such as we envisioned.

Although we felt unworthy and inadequate, knowing our own failures and shortcomings, we continued to sense God gently prompting and directing us on.

We began by gathering addresses, phone numbers, and other information from adoptive families all across our nation. As information came in, we were delighted and amazed to discover a large number of adopted children in our conservative Mennonite churches.

Many wrote their personal stories, telling about their families and the blessings and challenges of adoption. Some children entered their adoptive families with hardly a ripple or any extra effort on the parents' part. Such bonding was not much different from bonding with children coming into the family by birth. Other foster and/or adoptive parents told how God miraculously worked out impossible details with happy results. They shared experiences of loving support from fellow believers.

But there were many heartrending stories as well. During the parenting process, some felt virtually alone, almost to despair. They told of foster/adoption challenges that we knew little or nothing of. Some found solutions as they leaned heavily on God to show them the next step. But some have not yet found solutions. They still cry for help.

As the articles came in, our understanding broadened and our empathy grew. We recognized many places where we had failed. But we found that there is hope. There are answers. God delights in building, rescuing, and restoring. His plan is to use His children to be hands, feet, and hearts in this big mission. God has designed us to be here for each other.

Nine years have passed since our first responses from adoptive parents.

We are praying for God's direction on what to do with the stories, pictures, and resource information not used in this book. We are very grateful for each one's contribution. We are especially indebted to all of you who shared your lives with us, even to the point of being willing to open old wounds, so that others could find hope and healing.

Marian D. Reinford and Emily D. Martin

Publisher's Note

Tied With Heartstrings is a compilation of accounts written by adoptive and foster parents for those involved in, or interested in, fostering or adopting children.

Those of you familiar with *For This Child We Prayed* may wonder why CLP is publishing another adoption book. In that compilation, parents shared how they became involved in foster care or adoption.

In *Heartstrings*, on the other hand, parents relate personal accounts of challenges they faced, lessons they learned, and blessings they experienced in ministering to lonely children. The writers of the pieces in this book acknowledge their dependence on our heavenly Father who has adopted us and all of His children.

Emily and Marian, the biological sisters who compiled this book, have ministered to children long enough to learn firsthand about the difficulties and delights of foster care and adoption. In addition to encouraging families already ministering to children by foster care and adoption, the purpose of this book is to inspire others to become involved also. To help keep excited would-be parents from becoming unrealistically optimistic, however, *Heartstrings* makes it clear that foster care and adoption are not for the fainthearted.

We trust the Lord will use this book to "lift up the hands which hang down, and the feeble knees" (Hebrews 12:12) and to provide renewed purpose and joy to those ministering to children in the name of Jesus.

May these pages help us understand and support foster and adoptive parents who serve children in this way.

If you wish to communicate with any of the writers, you may contact the compilers, preferably through email, at heartstrings@emypeople.net or by mail:

Emily D. Martin, 195 Main Stem Rd., Pantego, NC 27860
Marian Reinford, 155 Main Stem Rd., Pantego, NC 27860

Introduction

Adoption

Dallas Witmer

Parents anticipating adoption should look forward to bringing a child not of their own flesh and blood into a relationship equal to that of a child by birth.

In this they become like their heavenly Father, who has "chosen us in him . . . having predestinated us unto the adoption of children" (Ephesians 1:4, 5).

Many children await adoption today. While murderous abortion has greatly reduced the number of children available for adoption in the western world, the world still teems with children in need of homes. Every Christian parent's heart should go out to them, just as God's heart goes out to the lost souls He longs to adopt.

Since the fall of man and the entrance of death into the world, God has had two methods of bringing children into the home: by birth and by adoption. One is as legitimate as the other. Given the Bible examples of adoption, and God's use of the term *adoption* to illustrate our acceptance into His family, how can we question God's approval of adoption, or that God moves some parents to adopt?

Who Should Adopt?

Parents who are as convinced that God is bringing a particular child into their home as they are that He gives particular children by birth, are qualified to adopt. This sense of the Lord's leading can come in various ways, but it is similar to how we learn the Lord's will in other issues. Is this love and compassion given by God, or is it just a passing whim? Will we be able to offer this child the love, nurture, and support that he or she needs? We consult with others who know us well to see whether they think we should adopt.

Adopted Children Are Chosen Children

We are seldom confronted with a moral obligation to adopt quite like the moral obligation to love and support the children we beget. Hence, we adoptive parents have the privilege and obligation to seek counsel, and to finally *choose* the child or children whom we will welcome into our homes. God used this truth to illustrate His own choice and predestination in bringing us redeemed sinners into His family in Christ. "He hath chosen us in him . . . having predestinated us unto the adoption of children" (Ephesians 1:4, 5).

Lessons From Bible Adoptions

The mark of true sonship is not natural birth, but obedience, as shown by Esther in her relation to Mordecai.

Adoptive children are loved and regarded as equal to birth children. "As Reuben and Simeon, they shall be mine" were Jacob's words in Genesis 48:5. Biracial adoption is honorable, as evidenced by the fact that Ephraim and Manasseh were the offspring of the Hebrew Joseph and his Egyptian wife, yet Jacob blessed them and included them in the inheritance he granted his biological sons (Genesis 48:5, 6).

Godly parents honor adoption as transcending birthrights and emotional ties. Both Moses' and Samuel's parents could have felt otherwise, but allowed God to work His will as they gave their children up to God.

But as grown men and women, we put loyalty to God and His people above family loyalties, adoptive or otherwise. Moses followed God's leading in later life to identify with the Israelites from whom he had been removed as a child.

Adoption does not absolve one of responsibilities for known needs in his birth family. After Samuel had been raised in the house of Eli and became a judge in Israel, he returned to Ramah where his father Elkanah was from (1 Samuel 7:15-17).

Stresses of Adoption

All relationships have their stresses, each of its own kind.

Adoptive children sometimes blame their problems on their adoption. They may reason, "Since I was adopted and I have this problem, I must have this problem because I am adopted."

Parents can help prevent this stress by emphasizing early on that adoption is just as legitimate as is birth in becoming a part of the family. While no two children are in every way equal, no one is less equal because of how he came into the family.

Other stresses can be as varied as the children themselves and the circumstances of their adoptions. We cannot possibly deal with all of the stresses here. Adopting children who are old enough to resent, or even resist, adoption can present special challenges. Adopting children who know birth relatives living nearby can present another set of difficulties. Many "special needs" children become available for adoption, and it takes "special" parents to deal with special needs.

Blessings in Differences

The different genetics of adopted children can be a real blessing. In a home where both parents tend to be scatterbrained and have passed this weakness on to all their birth children, they might be pleasantly surprised to find their adopted child well organized and collected, remembering to follow through with each job after everyone else has become distracted.

On the other hand, if the adopted child is less gifted, or has characteristics that tend to irritate, parents must work with the challenge and not blame it on the adoption. Avoid comparisons that would hurt either your adopted or your birth children. Remember that the Lord allows every difference and difficulty with a mind to bless His people

The melding of different temperaments in adoption can be more like marriage than like childbearing. Just as the couple who loves each other finds ways in which their different personalities and temperaments can complement each other rather than cause friction, so resourceful parents will learn to encourage and discipline each child's peculiar set of characteristics so that all contribute to the harmony of the home, rather than to friction.

Understanding Love

Love is a choice, whereas *feelings* of love are simply emotion. Love is a commitment that may not always be convenient. Adoptive parents may become alarmed when they realize that they don't feel the same toward their recently-adopted child as they do toward another child who has been with them since birth. But upon closer introspection they may realize that it isn't that they don't love him. It is just that they are now feeling the inconveniences of their commitment.

Birth children test our love as often as do adoptive children, but in different ways. Remember how you felt when your newborn birth child kept you up all night, or when your strong-willed child refused to get over his attitude for days? We may have felt resentment and impatience for awhile. Our feelings were really about inconvenience, not commitment.

With our adopted children, the tests of our love may be different, but not substantially so. Their coming into our home at an older age may seem like an intrusion, and their disruption of routines may be harder to accept, and so they may affect us differently than the cuddly newborn. And in our weaker moments, the genetic differences may test our love.

At such times adoptive parents should review their reasons for adopting and reassure themselves that they are as committed to the adoption now as they were then. They will soon realize that they care as much for the child as ever, and would not want to think of losing him. And then they should confess to themselves, that yes, they still love him. They may not feel the same right now as they did back then, but that might only be because they are now able to more realistically evaluate their commitment. Feelings of love will grow stronger as they adjust to the new realities of life. Love is not all honeymoon. Love grows with time and shared experiences, so long as the commitment is there.

The Unique Love of Foster Care

While we expect our relationships with our adopted children to eventually become as stable as those with birth children, we must be prepared to give up foster children who enter our homes with no promise of permanency.

Were Moses and Samuel traumatized by being shifted to foster homes at an early age? If so, did their trauma devastate or mature them? We can imply from the Scriptures that in both cases they were loved in their new homes, and that both were able to use their disrupted home life to their spiritual advantage.

But how did Moses' mother and Hannah prepare their mother hearts for the separation they knew was inevitable? We may assume that not just any parent could have been chosen of God to raise a child for a few years and then let him go.

Most of the foster children we take in will not be such key figures in God's plan for history as were Moses and Samuel. But God's grace is as abundant for interrupted parenting now as it was then.

Why did Moses, "when he was come to years, refuse to be called the son of Pharaoh's daughter; choosing rather to suffer affliction with the people of God, than to enjoy the pleasures of sin for a season"? (Hebrews 11:24, 25). Evidently a lot of good was done by his parents in the few years they were allowed to nurture him.

Foster parents should not consider themselves failures, should the men or women they fostered as children choose differently than Moses did when they "come to years." But let none think, either, that the love, fairness, truth, and responsibility with which they treat the foster children in their care will have no effect. Too many testimonials suggest the contrary.

Hold the Ideal

Tremendous good can come from both adoption and foster care. That some have failed to raise godly children is no reason for despair. Parents have failed with birth children as well as with adopted or foster children. Adoption is Biblical. It is even idealized in the Scriptures. As with any noble endeavor, however, adoption and foster care present unique stresses. Parents should undertake these challenges, as they do marriage and child-bearing, with a strong measure of realism and assurance of the Lord's leading.

We choose to love. It is as possible to commit one's self to love those not born to us as it is to love those who are ours by birth. When our love is tested, we may need to remind ourselves that the Lord brought us together, and that we are committed. While that assurance remains, we need not be bothered by the rise or the ebbing of feelings of love. But even those feelings become more stable as we share life's experiences together.

Many blessings of adoption and foster care can be enjoyed and cherished now. Each child by birth, by adoption, or by foster care, makes its unique contribution to our homes here and now. But surely the rewards of faithful parenting will be even greater in the future. The more children we have, the more we rejoice to see each one choosing to walk in the truth, becoming God's adoptive child as well as our own. And as with birth children, our adopted and foster children who become God's children can go with us to Heaven.[1]

---

1   From *The Christian Contender.* Adapted and used by permission.

PART 1

With Longing Hearts

The Spirit of Adoption

"Someday I would like to take in foster children. Please let that be Your will for me. I have such a desire to take in hurting children, to help them heal, and to show them love."
—Prayer by Emily Martin as a teenager

"Alone, so alone," cry the children of night,
"Alone," cry the children, "and dark!"
"None here to hold us, none here to mold us,
Alone on life's sea we embark."

Oh! The doubts and the fears of the motherless ones;
They march in such infinite numbers
From one end of earth and around to the other.
Such small ones, yet heartache encumbers.

Let us go to the byways and highways of sin
And gather the children of night.
Bring them to Jesus, the all-loving Saviour
And show them the way to the light.

—Naoma Lee

The Prayer of
Two Hearts

Emily Martin

Every good gift and every perfect gift is from above,
and cometh down from the Father of lights. —James 1:17
Ask, and ye shall receive, that your joy may be full. —John 16:24

Read John 16:16-33

*S*omeday I would like to take in foster children, I wrote in my diary as a teenager. *Please let that be Your will for me. I have such a desire to take in hurting children, to help them heal, and to show them love.*

My big sister Marian had a library full of stories of unfortunate children who had been salvaged. In my quest for reading I devoured them. Books like *No Language But a Cry* gripped my heart. That particular book was a true story of a horribly scarred little girl who wouldn't talk and could barely even walk until after a therapist had helped unlock the door to her past and her pain. When she was a baby, Laura's parents had literally fried her alive in a frying pan. Because neighbors reported the bloodcurdling screams, she was rescued and lived. But since over half of her body had second degree burns, she spent the next three and a half years in the hospital. She then was transferred to a Catholic institution as a tiny crippled girl who found the world too awful to deal with. She was seemingly without speech—without joy—nothing but a vegetable-like existence. Together the nuns and the therapist gently coaxed her out of the lonely prison of herself. Her first words were spoken at fourteen years of age. The story finishes with triumph as a radiant Laura learns to trust again and devotes her life to caring for children.

I want to work in an orphanage, I dreamily added to my journal, *or travel to a third world country to rescue street children. There's so much I'd love to do!*

Life is too short to realize all of a girl's dreams, but unknown to me, God was preparing me. After teaching school for three years, I married the man of my heart. I delighted in being a new wife and hoped in due time to be a mother of many. *Maybe we can have our own children's home,* I thought.

Malvern shared my vision—especially after we had been married for a number of months and there was no promise of a little one on the way. As I cried into my pillow and longed for a baby, my plea became, *If not a baby, Lord, at least send us some little children.* We inquired about adoption and foster care. It was a goal we worked toward and longed and prayed for daily, then hourly, as the longing intensified. When our prayers were answered after two and a half years, it seemed God was smiling upon us.

Our first two little boys came in the arms of social workers. They were two and three years old with large, expressive brown eyes. That evening, Malvern and I sat smiling at each other across the dimly-lit living room, each rocking a little boy. At last our hearts and arms were full!

Ricky, the two-year-old, adjusted faster than Alex, who was a year older. The next day as Alex sat crying for the familiar and begging for "Mommy," little Ricky leaned up against him and asked in his sweet baby voice, "Wada matter, Alec?"

"You know!" Alex said, and pushed him away.

But it took only a few days until both felt secure with us. As new foster parents, it was a very happy time for us. In one month's time it was as if they had always been calling us Mommy and Daddy, filling our home with childish chatter and sunshine. "Oh, Mommy," one would say, "I need a hug!" Or "When is our daddy coming home?" It was like music to my ears.

Ricky was an especially huggable, lovable little boy with an optimism that seemed to say life was indeed an adventure worth living. Though he was naughty at times, punishment brought good results. Alex, just as lovable, was affectionate and sensitive. Like open sponges, they soaked up the teaching we tried to instill. They were our boys. We couldn't have loved them more.

A well-meaning aunt tried to explain to me that she couldn't believe we loved the boys quite like we would our own. "That's how it was for me," she confided. "I loved my nieces and nephews so much that I couldn't imagine loving my own children more. But when my first daughter was born, I realized it was just different. This one was mine!"

"Precisely!" I told her. "That is exactly how I felt about my nieces and nephews, but since Alex and Ricky came, there is no comparison. They are ours! We are enjoying them completely." And we did.

Thought for the Day

Foster children and adopted children become our own
just as surely as those born to us.

Alex

Ricky

In Answer to Our Prayer

Emily Martin

If ye shall ask any thing in my name, I will do it. —John 14:14

Read John 14, particularly noticing the promises for answered prayer
in verses 13 and 14.

*P*eople warned us to not get too attached to our foster boys. "Just think if they would have to leave," they said. "You're setting yourselves up for heartache."

"Isn't it every child's birthright to be loved?" we asked ourselves. "Besides, how could we possibly parent children without being attached to them?" We chose to love totally and wholly. If ever they would leave, then God would have to help us face that heartache. "But," we reasoned, "surely God loves these little boys even more than we do. Wouldn't He want them growing up in a Christian home?"

Each court day we attended with interest and a certain amount of apprehension. Our social worker freely shared details of the case. "Reunification of birth-families is always the first plan," she explained. "But as time moves on, permanency for the children becomes more important. Even though the father's love for Alex and Ricky is evident through the cards and letters he sends to them, he is in prison with a ten-year sentence. Considering the length of his term and also the nature of the crime for which he is serving, reunification does not seem probable.

"The main focus at this time is the birth mother," our social worker continued. "You know that in the two years her five children have been in foster care she has failed drastically in meeting the requirements we have

6

set up for her. Either she'll need to do better, or her parental rights will be terminated."

On several occasions we had met Alex and Ricky's birth mother. She had long, honey-brown hair, exactly the color of Ricky's, and a child-like simplicity. We had tried to build a relationship with her, remembering that the boys had belonged to her first. When we were together, she smiled upon the boys, commenting on how cute they were in a general sort of way. Yet she didn't appear to be pining over them or especially missing them. She didn't send cards or letters, rarely kept her visits, and as a general rule was not measuring up to the requirements the Department of Social Services was asking of her.

"If the birth mother's parental rights are terminated," the worker explained, "we will likely terminate the father's rights as well. Ten years is too long in a young child's life to wait. We need to move forward with this for the sake of the children. We're very pleased with how happy and well-adjusted Alex and Ricky are in your home. Certainly as their foster parents, you'll have first chance if adoption becomes an option."

Adopt Alex and Ricky? Keep them for always? Perhaps by the next court day real progress would be made toward that goal! Our hearts sang, until several weeks later when the phone rang.

"Mrs. Martin," Ms. Rosalyn's voice sounded strained and sad, "I hate to tell you this. We had a staff meeting here at DSS, meeting with the children's lawyer and guardian ad litem, and we are now considering returning all five children to the mother, including the two youngest boys. This would be on a temporary basis, as a trial to see how it goes. We do this sometimes as a sink or swim proposition. Either the parent makes it, or it is obvious that she won't. Then we proceed with the termination. The unfortunate part is that if the mother does gain custody—even temporary custody—she will likely take the children across the state line into Virginia where she now lives."

"But if she proves unfit and the boys are taken back into foster care, they'll be in Virginia. Does that mean they wouldn't come back to us?" I asked in a small voice.

"That's right. If she proves unfit and the boys are put back into foster care, they would be under the Department of Social Services in Virginia. It's very doubtful that they'd come back to the jurisdiction of our county. I'm so sorry. I know what this means to you and the boys."

Our poor little boys! Their birth mother was virtually a stranger to them. What if they would be taken from her and placed with more strangers? Would they become just statistics, adding to the numberless damaged children in the foster care system? How devastating! *And what about eternity? How will this decision affect where they will spend eternity?* I felt as if I were on an emotional roller coaster. *Is this what our friends meant about getting too attached to foster children?*

We prayed earnestly and often, begging our friends and family to join us in prayer. We knew we needed to pray that God's will be done, but we were so hoping it was His will for the boys to stay with us!

Court day arrived. We were sitting in the courtroom waiting for the boys' case to come up when a kind-faced gentleman in a suit and tie came up to us. "Excuse me," he began politely. "Are you the foster parents of the two minors, Alex and Ricky Spring?" When we acknowledged we were, he continued, "Would you mind stepping out a bit? I would like to have a word with all the foster parents of these five children."

He led the group of six adults into a small consulting room and offered us seats at a brown conference table. Nervously, I twirled the handle of my purse. We had left Ricky crying and Alex looking worried in that immense courtroom. I hoped they would be okay. Of course the social workers would make sure nothing bad happened to them. Curiously we turned our attention to the kind-faced gentleman.

He began by introducing himself. "My name is Jeff Baynor.[2] I am a lawyer of Hyde County." Then he asked each of us questions about how the children were doing in our homes and what effect we felt this experiment would have on the particular children that each of us was caring for.

After we all had a chance to voice our negative feelings about the situation, he explained further. "I am in a difficult position. As a lawyer, in nearly every other case in Hyde County, I represent the children. My

---

2   Not his real name

heart is with the children. I represent them in court and look out for their rights. But it so happens that in this case, someone else was assigned to these children. And since the mother could not afford to hire a lawyer to represent her case, I've been appointed for her." He readjusted his papers in front of him. Finally he continued.

"Twenty minutes ago I had a private talk with the children. When I questioned them, the little boys were very adamant that they did not want to go back to their birth mother. The littlest one kept crying and saying over and over, 'I just want to stay at this here house where I is!'"

We smiled and blessed Ricky's little heart. "But," he continued, "when questioned, the older children would all choose to return to their birth mother. That is normal, since younger children bond more quickly and surely with foster parents than these older children would, particularly since all three of these have been moved often and have been in a number of different foster homes. But still . . ." The lawyer sighed deeply.

"Can you sense my predicament? I'm supposed to be representing the mother, but I cannot see that it is in the best interests of the children involved. It seems to me that the experiment will surely fail, and the children will be the ones who lose the very most."

Oh, how we agreed with him!

"So here is my proposal. Perhaps Lonnie, who is twelve and the oldest of the five, could handle this experience the best. Surely better than the little ones. I will ask the judge to allow Lonnie to return to his mother for a trial period of four months. At the end of that time we'll reevaluate the situation."

Our hearts were singing when we left the courtroom an hour later! The judge had agreed to Mr. Baynor's proposition, and Alex and Ricky were still ours. We hugged them tightly and went out to celebrate. Our God was truly looking out for us! How we wanted to praise Him! How good He was to us!

Thought for the Day

Is our God's hand shortened in any situation?

God's Planned Additions

Marian Reinford

It is not the will of your Father which is in heaven,
that one of these little ones should perish. —Matthew 18:14
Read Matthew 18:10-14

"Marian, we found just the two little girls for you to adopt. We saw them in Indiana last weekend!" my friend Savilla announced with sparkling eyes and a big smile. "They would fit into your family just perfectly. The oldest is six years old and a natural little mother to her dolls. She rocks them and sings to them. I really think she'd be wonderful with Dawn also. The youngest is everybody's sweetheart. We stayed with their foster parents last week, and they told us the girls were coming up for adoption."

My heart did a funny flip-flop and my smile mirrored hers. "Could I please have the foster parents' names and number so I can give them a call for more information?"

Eagerly, we all talked about the girls on our way home from church. Anya, almost seven, was the most excited about having more sisters. She loved Dawn, who was two years older than she, but Dawn was handicapped with cerebral palsy and was as limited as a six-month-old baby. Maybe now Anya would have some sisters to share her work and play. Dale, almost fifteen, and Alan, thirteen, were happy about more sisters also; maybe they would be relieved of helping with the household chores.

A few days later we were speaking with the girls' social worker. "Yes, we do have two girls available for adoption," she said, "but they come with two brothers, and we'd like to keep them together."

"They do? How old are the boys?" I asked, my head almost spinning. *Four more children. Can we handle such a big bite? That would double our family!*

"Mike is nine and Chuck is seven. With Chris, age six, and Melissa, age four, it will be a handful, but we really feel families should be kept together."

"We'll give this prayerful consideration and get back with you," I told her. "Thank you for the information."

Roy and I talked it over with both of our parents. They seemed to feel it was a big responsibility, but if the doors opened and we felt it was God's will, they would support us with their prayers and love.

Two weeks later found us in our station wagon with our son Dale, our parents, and others bound for Montana. They dropped us off in Indiana, where we met the children, the social worker, and the girls' foster parents. We said our good-byes to those heading for Montana, and we went to a lovely park for a picnic with the social worker and the children. A picnic in a park was a wonderful place to connect with them. Chris and Melissa were bubbly and smiling, and the boys worked

Melissa, Chuck, Chris, and Mike

hard at being perfect little gentlemen. When they all ran down to watch the baby ducks by the water, my husband and I discussed the children with the social worker. We had so many questions. The social worker shared with us details of the children's lives as we watched them play.

Back at the table, Mike mumbled to Chuck something about us being their new parents.

"Who will be your new parents?" I asked, smiling.

With shining eyes and a big smile he pointed at us and announced, "You!"

On the way back to the office the four children sat together in the back seat, trying to figure out how to divide three apples between them. Mike congenially said to Chuck, "You and the girls can have them. I'll be okay." My heart warmed at his unselfishness toward his younger siblings.

That evening we caught the Amtrak train and rode east toward home again. Our minds were spinning, our hearts tender. *Four lovely children with eternal souls! What potential for good or bad! Is God asking us to reach out and make them part of our lives? We need to think and pray about our decision. Not only will it affect their lives, but also the lives of our birth children. When we stretch too far, our weak spots show up, and we want to be able to meet the needs of all eight children.*

Several days later my mother said, "They seem like such nice children, but I feel sorry for the mother who had to give them up!"

I explained that they had been relinquished voluntarily because their mother wanted to get married and her fiancé didn't want the children.

A week or two later we found out we were expecting another addition to our family by birth. What did this all mean? Should we abandon the idea of adoption? We decided to discuss this new turn of events with the children's social worker and see what she thought. If they had other prospective adoptive parents for these four children, maybe that would be our answer that we shouldn't adopt them.

"Hello, this is Marian Reinford. We're the ones who stopped by to see the sibling group of four children who need a home."

"Yes, we're so happy to hear from you!" Her voice sounded warm and welcoming. "We're wondering what you're thinking by now."

"I have a few questions. Do you have anyone else you are seriously considering as adoptive parents?" I asked.

"We have no one else. We're so happy about your family that we aren't looking farther. With Dawn, your handicapped daughter, you already have experience in dealing with special needs children. You also have a farm, which we feel is an ideal place to raise children."

"What about the two issues we discussed before?" I asked. "We have no savings, and as a church we don't promote higher education. Will that be a problem?"

"We think the basic things you have to offer—a Christian home, church, school, and farm—far outweigh these other things," the social worker assured me. "Our church has a mission in Africa. We send thousands of dollars there every year to keep missionaries at those churches. Over the last ten years we've had a number of converts, but none who stayed true to God. If you could help just one of these four children find God and be a true Christian, think of the impact on his life and the lives of his children."

"Yes, that's true," I agreed thoughtfully. "But we want *all* of them to find God and be true Christians. We want *all* of them and their children to be in Heaven someday."

"Yes," she said quietly. "That is also what we want for them—to grow up to be happy, responsible citizens and to learn to know God."

How could we turn our backs on the challenge before us? What would Jesus do?

When we discussed our situation with the social worker who was doing our home study, she nodded brightly and said, "A new baby is the best thing for your family, if you can handle it! Having a baby will help bring the two sets of children together. The new baby will be 'our baby.'"

We prayed earnestly many times for God to show us His will. If He wanted us to do this, He would need to work it out. We realized if we took on such a big responsibility, the extra stress might cause us to lose the new tiny one we were expecting.

A few weeks later we received a call from Indiana. "Are you still considering adopting the Clark children? Something came up in the boys' foster home, and they need to be moved as soon as possible. We'd rather send them right to your home instead of making them adjust to another foster home. Would you be able to come get them in the next few days?"

So our decision was finalized quickly. Since our car was still in Montana with the travelers, we went to Indiana by Amtrak to get the boys. Our son Alan, with the help of friends, did the farm chores and took care of Dawn and Anya.

We met with Mike's special education teacher to discuss his books and what he was learning. We were happy to hear of Mike's progress and thanked his teacher for a job well done. As we were leaving, Mike's teacher remarked pleasantly to the social worker, "Well, I think you found the perfect parents for Mike!"

The social worker smiled and nodded. "It was our pick out of twenty-five!"

Later I gently challenged her on what she had said. "You told me earlier you had no one else you were considering, and now you say we were your pick out of twenty-five!"

Roy and Marian Reinford family, 1989

She nodded slowly and answered, "No other interested couple came so close to being able to meet their different needs. We all felt you were the family for them."

So we accepted that God had opened and closed the right doors because He wanted them in our home. What a confirmation it was for us later, when times were difficult, to remember that God was walking this path with us. God never promised it would be easy. Is anything worthwhile ever easy? He knew the struggles ahead—physical, emotional, and spiritual—and yet He worked it out.

When we didn't know where to go for advice and help, He was always there every step of the way, rejoicing with us during victories and sorrowing over our mistakes. What a God of love we serve!

About fifteen years later a friend of mine asked me, "If you had it all to do over, would you adopt again?"

I pondered the question a minute or two . . . the hills and valleys we had walked, the rivers we had crossed, the mountains we had climbed . . . I felt tired and old. But then I thought of eternity, not only for our precious children, but for *their* children and, if the Lord tarried, their grandchildren. I looked at her and answered from the bottom of my heart, "How could we say no? We can't make decisions for our children, but we can give them the opportunity to find God and truth!"

Thought for the Day

God's will never leads us where His grace cannot keep us.

Roy and Marian Reinford family, 1996

Sisters, a Gift From God

Anya R. Kauffman

A friend loveth at all times, and a [sister] is born for adversity. Proverbs 17:17
Read Proverbs 17:1-28

A lonely childhood was mine. With two brothers, six and eight years older than I, and a sister two years older who couldn't walk or talk, I felt many times like an only child. My mom and dad were good at doing things with me and including me in their projects, but the void was still there.

If only I had a sister my age! Could anything be more wonderful? School didn't offer much consolation. When I started first grade, the only other students in the classroom were boys. Oh, for a sister!

At last we heard the news. Two little girls, ages four and six, needed a home. "Oh, Mom, can we get them?" I pleaded.

Another phone call came. "These two little girls have two brothers as well. We would like to place them as a family." The days of lonely sadness were fast diminishing in the background as I envisioned the wonderful, sibling-filled days to come.

Mike and Chuck came first. I was delighted to be the self-appointed guide to their new life on the farm. Six weeks went by quickly, and then Chris and Melissa arrived (See "God's Planned Additions").

My intense desire for companionship was fulfilled. Sisters would never have to go home at night. They would never stay for a week, then leave for some far-off place. We would always share each others' lives! Our first session of playing doll included an elaborate feast Chris and I prepared of lotion and powder for our dolls to "eat."

Of course the newness wore off in time, and the normal sisterly spats of "Your turn; no, your turn" arose. To make it more challenging, there were three of us, so it would often be two against one. Of course it was very hard to predict who the one forlorn person would be at any given time!

We three were especially delighted, though, when the phone call came from the hospital six months after the girls arrived: "You have a baby sister!" For seven years I had waited for a baby sister; now God decided to bless me with both— sisters close to my age, and also a baby sister!

Although there were some negative factors in learning to share and to blend, the positive far outweighed the negative. The days of boredom and loneliness receded to the far distant past. I always had someone to play dolls with, or a pretend game

Melissa, Anya, Debi, Chris

we called "Big Girl." I had someone to share secrets with, to giggle and talk with far into the night! I had someone to share the mundane chores of peeling potatoes and washing dishes and caring for our special sister . . . and someone to sing with while we worked.

Even today, there is always someone who understands who I am and how I feel. Of course! We're sisters!

Thought for the Day

Sisters are the ones who know us by heart
and love us for who we are.

Our Babies!

Jewel Carter

O give thanks unto the LORD; for he is good. —Psalm 118:1
Read Psalm 118:14-21

I leaned back in the seat with a sigh of relief. At last we were up in the air and on our way. The last weeks had been hectic right up to the last day. The night before we had planned to leave, we received our state approval for adoption. And then to add more tension, at the airport we found that there were snowstorms in Chicago and that we might have to postpone our flight. I felt I couldn't stand to wait even one more day. We had worked so hard and had counted on leaving December 4. Would we be delayed again?

No! We were on our way! We marveled at how God provided for us one step at a time, even if it was at the last minute.

I chuckled to myself as I thought of the glimpses of apprehension I had seen in our parents' eyes. Stopping to think about it, I couldn't really blame them. Here we were, two young people only twenty-two years old, and married for less than two years, heading for a country torn by war, infested with disease. Who knew what snakes and wild animals it held?

Adoption paperwork had caused us to grow wiser in the legal world. We had studied books and magazines, both Christian and secular, to get tips on how to parent. Also, we had listened to and observed the parenting of others. We had plenty of dreams and ideals, but we lacked experience.

I could imagine that I would feel similar to the way my parents felt, if my future children did something like this. Hopefully I would have the wisdom of our parents not to discourage them from following the path God had for them.

Our boys! Our babies! It was hard to believe that in Liberia, Africa, twin babies were waiting for us. Ours! I could hardly comprehend it.

Born eleven hours apart in a small hut deep in the bush, the twin boys had been laid at their dead mother's side and expected to die as well.

What had their mother been like? I thought of the love she must have felt as she labored all those many hours to bring twins into the world. I wished I could thank her for filling my heart—and, Lord willing, soon my arms—with these two precious babies I had not yet seen.

Their kind aunt had climbed through a window and rescued the twins. She had spent what little money she had to pay taxi fare to take them to the city for medical attention. Other incidents that we had been told drifted through my mind as the long hours of travel slowly drifted by.

Finally, our plane landed for the last time. It was dark when we arrived in Liberia, and as we walked down the steps, we were met by a blast of tropical heat. Inside the airport was a sea of black faces, loud voices, and an English dialect we could hardly understand. It was a relief to see the familiar face of one of the missionaries. We gratefully accepted his help!

The ride to the mission headquarters seemed long, although it was less than an hour. But at last we were meeting our babies for the first time. Craig took Brady and I took Brett. I was delighted when Brett gave me a shy smile. I loved his sweet, brown chubbiness. We traded babies then, and I was surprised at how much lighter Brady was. I could feel his skinny ribs, and his legs were so thin. Every breath came with a rasp, but we were told it was much better than it had been earlier. With his breathing problem, he had had a much rougher start in life than his brother. I cuddled him close. Who cared if he was skinny and sick! I was determined to do my best to fill out those scrawny arms and legs.

Our months of waiting were over. We had them in our arms at last. Our babies! It was still hard to comprehend!

Thank You, God!

Thought for the Day

Motherhood is a miracle of love. When the long journey of labor is over and we hug our babies to our breasts, delightful ownership floods our being. Of a surety we find them to be ours.

Brady and Brett

Who Loves the Children?

Jewel Carter

But Jesus said, Suffer little children, and forbid them not, to come unto me: for of such is the kingdom of heaven. —Matthew 19:14
Read Matthew 19:13-26

We had been in Liberia six months when the civil war that had been raging in the country for years reached the city where we were living. When the missionaries evacuated to another nearby African country, we were able to take our twins with us. We were still not able to take them back to the States. Not even in the midst of a crisis would the officials relent and let us take them home.

Nearly three months later we returned to a city torn by missiles and riddled with bullets. In the meantime, there had been international intervention, and a shaky peace had been established.

For a time I stayed close to home, unsure of how safe it was to go out on the daily walks I liked to take. But assured by my husband and friends that it was safe, and dealing with restless toddlers in a walled compound, I soon began taking the boys on walks again. I was met by more curious stares and questions than even before the war. The Liberians must have wondered why a white woman wanted two of *their* babies. Faced with desperate poverty, hunger, and ignorance, they were often too willing to give up their own children. And now with the recent hatred and killing, love and compassion seemed even more of a mystery to them.

One day as I was coming out of the gate pulling the boys in a wagon, I heard the chanting of childish voices. Glancing up the street, I saw an almond tree with its branches filled with small boys. One boy called out a question, and a chorus of voices shouted out a reply. I was too far away to understand what they were saying. Not paying much attention, I turned up a side street. Before long I heard the pounding of young feet behind me, and I was soon surrounded by boys. As we walked along, I asked, "What were you saying up in that tree?"

They stopped and stood silently, looking shyly down at their slippered feet. Finally one boy offered, "Charlie Boy would say, 'Who loves children?' And then the rest of us would say, 'Jewel loves children!' "

Startled, and not sure that I had understood right, I asked him to repeat what he had said. I was humbled as the boys told me again what they had been saying.

They walked a little farther with me and then scampered off to find something else to do. But I was deep in thought. I had a reputation I needed to live up to! This was the opinion of these young boys, but what was God's opinion of me? Did I have in my heart the love Jesus had when He said, "Suffer the little children to come unto me"? Was I allowing Christ's love in my life so that I could reach out and love children of any nationality, color, or race? Could I bring them into my heart and home so they would truly become my children? Wasn't that the basis of adoption— loving children without prejudice and racism—just loving them for who they were, regardless of handicaps or scars or the emotional hurts they may have experienced?

Thought for the Day

O God, help me to have a special love for ALL children, that I may be worthy of the compliment paid by innocent boys!

I Was a Stranger

Joanna Nevenschwander

I was a stranger, and ye took me in . . . Inasmuch as ye have done it unto one of the least of these my brethren, ye have done it unto me. —Matthew 25:35, 40
Read Matthew 25:34 – 40

The night was dark, the atmosphere around me warm—very warm and oppressive. It took a few seconds to gather my thoughts. I knew the atmosphere was hot and suffocating, but why did my chest and heart feel so heavy? Then it came back in a rush. I glanced at the clock which showed 2 a.m. and then at my husband by my side. He was breathing deeply, lost in slumber. *Here we go again—another night of unrest*, I thought. Many nights my husband and I would slip down beside our bed and seek God's guidance and wisdom, but just now the battle was mine alone. I needed to come to rest with the decision we had made and feel it was blessed by our heavenly Father.

The facts continuously circled in my mind. After seeking God's direction and counsel from trusted acquaintances, we had stepped into the great venture of adoption. After seemingly endless hours of preparation of the dossier, it was complete, and in our hands was the referral of a little boy. His picture hung on our refrigerator—a very sober little boy looking over his crib rails, waiting for some family to give security and meaning to his life. But were we that family? Could we meet his needs—possibly his *special* needs?

23

My husband had traveled overseas to meet his new son-to-be. As he walked into the orphanage, there stood the sad little boy, securely restrained in the corner of his crib. Never once did he look into his new daddy's face or show any interaction or social exchange. My husband left the country sick at heart, wondering if we could meet the obvious needs of this child, yet not feeling right about refusing him the love and security he so evidently needed.

This was the struggle: Was God giving us this extreme feeling of apprehension to keep us from getting into a situation that we were incapable of handling? Or was the devil blocking a child from being introduced to the Lord Jesus through the influence of a Christian home?

Slowly I climbed out of bed, trudged down the steps, turned on a low light in the kitchen, and stepped over in front of the refrigerator. There he was again. Should we or shouldn't we? On the counter lay my Bible. I reached over and opened its pages. Could it give rest to my troubled soul? So many times before we had hoped for a direct answer, but the answer had evaded us. The pages fell open to Matthew 25. "I was a stranger, and ye took me in . . . . Inasmuch as ye have done it unto one of the least of these . . . ye have done it unto me." My heart leaped. "Lord, this is Your answer! I'll gladly love and care for this child if by my service to him I am, in essence, doing it for You! Whatever You ask me to do, You will also supply the grace and wisdom for the task."

I found great peace in the coming months. When apprehension loomed above me, these quiet words brought reassurance: "As ye have done it unto one of the least of these . . . ye have done it unto me"!

Thought for the Day

God uses His Word to confirm His will.

Who Will Show Jesus to Him?

Name Withheld

The same came therefore to Philip . . . and desired him, saying,
Sir, we would see Jesus. —John 12:21
Read Hebrews 2:9-15

Silence hung between my husband's recliner and my rocking chair. We were deep in thought. The house that had surrounded childish chatter, peals of laughter, and loud wails all day now quietly sheltered our children in their beds.

After roller-coasting through uncertainties about our foster child's future, my husband and I now faced the decision of adoption. It was not a simple choice. Even at his young age, the child showed signs of explosive anger and rebellion. Adding gravity to the decision was my suspicion that learning disabilities would complicate his life. My mind's eye scanned the path that lay before us, but try as I might, I could not see for certain that light glowed at the end of the tunnel.

I can still hear my husband's thoughtful words that broke the silence, "I keep wondering . . . who will show Jesus to him? If we don't, who will? Will anybody?" His questions were loaded with love for a little boy who needed a permanent home.

"There is no fear in love; but perfect love casteth out fear" (1 John 4:18). Our love was not, and is not, perfect; yet it did dispel the fear enough to bring us the answer we sought. *Yes, we will show Jesus to him.*

Years later, adolescence intensified our adopted son's struggles. Now as I pray over a son who struggles to control his anger and is still tempted by rebellion, I often ask my husband's question again: "Who will show Jesus to him?"

By God's grace, we will!

What will the outcome be? We are not certain. Showing Jesus is our part. The results are God's part—combined with our son's decisions. We're not sorry we tried. We have come to understand that showing Jesus to others always brings glory to God, regardless of the results.

Thought for the Day

Show Jesus to someone who is struggling
to cope with what life has offered.

Adopted Child

Christine Diller

But ye have received the Spirit of adoption, whereby we cry,
Abba, Father. The Spirit itself beareth witness
with our spirit, that we are the children of God. —Romans 8:15, 16
Read Romans 8:12-17; 1 Corinthians 1:18-31

"Don't adopt," some say. "Sometimes it doesn't work out. Adopted children can bring a lot of heartache."

I thought about this. We wanted only God's will. I opened my Bible and started with the story of Moses. Then I looked some more.

Finally, I understood about adoption. The whole plan of salvation is a plan of adoption. I am the adopted child of God. I was born again into the family of God. When I became a child of God, He didn't say, "I can't take any chances with her; I'm afraid she'll cause Me a lot of heartache. She's so young and immature. Does she really know what she wants? Look here. I can see up ahead where she'll veer from the path. She'll disappoint Me. I just can't accept her. She's too much of a risk."

God gives every person a chance to enter into His family. He doesn't look at pedigrees and credentials. In fact, He's looking for the lowly and the humble. He loves to help those who are least likely to succeed. Sure, some of us will turn on Him. That doesn't change His love.

We decided to adopt. We wanted to be like our heavenly Father. We wanted to find a needy child who wasn't born flesh of our flesh. We wanted to take this child into our hearts and love him or her as God has loved and adopted us.

Thought for the Day

We love God because He first loved us.

A Cup of Cold Water

Julia Brubaker

*And whosoever shall give to drink unto one of these little ones
a cup of cold water only in the name of a disciple, verily I say unto you,
he shall in no wise lose his reward. —Matthew 10:42*
Read Mark 9:35—41

*I*n the daunting task of raising adopted or foster children, we may sometimes feel as though we are wasting our time. It is especially hard when we know they may eventually be taken away from us.

While attending pre-service training for becoming a foster parent, I found out how transitory many of the placements are. I struggled a little with this. Did I really want to pour myself into a small child's life only to later experience the heartbreak of seeing the child return to a less-than-ideal situation?

One of the trainers said something that has made all the difference to me. She said, "Even if you have a child for only a few months, you can give him a few months of stability and loving care. At least he will have the memory of how things *can* be and he will know what it is to be loved—something he may otherwise never experience."

I also think often of the old saying, "It is better to have loved and lost than never to have loved at all." If I did not believe in the truth of that saying, I could not continue doing this work, with all the parting it entails.

I believe that anything worth doing in life is worth some risk.

Some people tell me they could not do foster care because they could not give up a child to whom they had become attached. Others seem fearful of all the risks in raising adopted children. However, there are also

risks with raising birth children, and most of us have them anyway! There are never any guarantees that life will be as smooth and easy as we would like it to be, no matter who we are or what we do.

"I was a stranger, and ye took me in," Jesus will say to His followers on the Judgment Day. Of course there are risks involved in taking in "strangers," but such acts of service are essential to true Christianity. Jesus also said that a cup of cold water given to "one of these little ones" will be rewarded.

May we give those cups of cold water freely and generously, knowing that God sees and the child feels our love.

Thought for the Day

Small acts of service will make a difference,
not only in time, but in eternity.

Our Very Own

Mary Ellen Rivera

*Wherefore thou art no more a servant, but a son; and if a son,
then an heir of God through Christ.—Galatians 4:7*
Read Galatians 4:4-7

Our family was so excited! We could hardly wait until the school day was over so we could go pick up our precious baby boy. We had prayed and waited for this day, and now it had finally come!

God has blessed us with three precious biological daughters. Each one is a gift from God, and we love them all dearly. The time came when we had to face the fact that we would never have another biological child. Our hearts ached for more children, especially for a little boy to love and to be Daddy's little shadow. We prayed much about it and decided to try adoption. God answered our prayers and gave us a precious twenty-one-hour-old baby boy to love. What joy he brought our little family! He was our son—our very own son! He was every bit as special as our daughters were. Three years later we adopted a brother for him. God had given us another precious son to love and cherish and be our very own.

Some people do not seem to understand adoption. They differentiate between biological and adopted children. Well-meaning people ask, "How many children do you have of your own?" We know what they mean, but we do not like that question. They were all our own. It was just that three were biological and two were adopted.

I recently came across an adoption creed that says it so well.

Not flesh of my flesh nor bone of my bone,
But still miraculously my own.
Never forget for one single minute,
You didn't grow under my heart, but in it.[3]

Adoption is a wonderful thing. Many of these children will not have the opportunity to hear about God and be raised in Christian families if we do not open our hearts and homes to them. God accepts us as His sons and daughters, regardless of who we are. He loves us and pours out many blessings on us. It is the same for the children we adopt. Sometimes we may be heartbroken by the paths they choose, but at least they had an opportunity. The choice of what they want to do with that opportunity is theirs.

Not only adopted children choose the wrong paths; many biological children do too. Our hearts broke when our oldest son died at the age of twenty because of loving the pleasures of this world. Even though we went through that experience, we would not discourage anyone from adopting. God gave us our son for twenty years. We have many precious memories and some memories that are not so pleasant, but we never regretted that we gave him a chance. We will always love him and still miss him very much.

Thought for the Day

Take time for your children today.
They grow up and are gone so soon.

---

3   The Answer (to an adopted child) by Fleur Conkling Heylinger

The Spirit of Adoption

Roger and Joy Rangai

For ye have not received the spirit of bondage again to fear; but ye have received the Spirit of adoption, whereby we cry, Abba, Father. —Romans 8:15

Read Romans 8:15-21

My wife, Joy Maria, was adopted into the family of David L. and Edna Miller. She was eight years old at the time. Dad and Mom Miller were both past forty-nine years old. Despite their ages, and although this was a late start to introduce a child into a family, Joy adapted well to her new home. Her story could well be listed among the successful adoptions.

The reason it was successful was certainly not that she had a trouble-free childhood. There were many problems to deal with. In fact, her very early years were quite stormy and rocky. Some of those memories still linger today. They are difficult to shake off. Indeed, if Joy had not been rescued by a caring Christian orphanage and later adopted into a loving Christian home, her life could well have been disastrous.

It is my conviction that foremost in the success of her adoption was that she experienced the heavenly adoption. "Therefore if any man be in Christ, he is a new creature: old things are passed away; behold, all things are become new" (2 Corinthians 5:17).

Joy also connected immediately with her parents when they first met. That closeness is still alive today, and it is very important to her. After all, her parents provided the very things she longed for and anticipated in a home, fulfilling her longings to belong, to love, and to be loved in return.

Joy had to deal with authority in her life. A loving authority figure was absent in her earlier years before adoption. She was then living with her grandmother, and she never really learned to know her birth parents. She thinks the other woman who came to visit occasionally may have been her mother. We do not know why her parents rejected her. We do know that her grandma's house brought on her many kinds of abuses, including some grievous sins and misconduct. In fact, their poverty-stricken environment may have been largely due to sinful living.

My heart is pained to think that there may be many children living today in that condition in the same kind of society that Joy was rescued from. We praise God for the wonderful healing that she experienced. Please pray with us that this healing process will continue. Let us pray as well for the many children who still need to be rescued.

If we want to be useful in God's kingdom, we must learn not to dwell on unfortunate pasts. Rather, let us look ahead and see His loving hand leading and guiding us on to a brighter tomorrow and to a blissful eternity with Him in Heaven.

Yes, Joy is an adoptee. But we are both adoptees—just in a different way. It happened when we accepted Jesus into our hearts and were adopted into the wonderful family of God. The similarities that this heavenly adoption has with earthly adoption is very refreshing indeed!

The Rangai Family

Thought for the Day

There is hope for adopted children.

When the Cloud Stands Still

Sharilyn Martin

Wait on the LORD: be of good courage, and he shall strengthen thine heart: wait, I say, on the LORD. —Psalm 27:14
Read Numbers 9:15-23

I picked up my Bible and sighed as I noted the date on the calendar. *Another week almost gone—and still no word from the agency about travel dates!* I paged to the Book of Numbers and tried to read the next chapter. I found this a rather boring book, however, all about tribes and temple duties and the like. My mind wandered. *Will our caseworker call today? What else should I be doing?*

The adoption process had subjected us to the most erratic schedule I had ever experienced. Stressful days of hurried phone calls and Fed-Ex documents were interspersed with anxious days of waiting and wondering. Today looked like another day of waiting, yet I knew the next phone call could send me back into panic mode. *I'm so tired of this! If I just knew what to do next, I'd do it, but all I can do right now is wait!*

As I forced my mind back to the Book of Numbers, I found my answer in Chapter 9, verse 18: "At the commandment of the LORD the children of Israel journeyed, and at the commandment of the LORD they pitched: as long as the cloud abode upon the tabernacle they rested in their tents."

35

Was it hard for the Israelites to wait? Did they anxiously watch the cloud and wonder how much longer they would have to camp before arriving at Canaan's borders? Yet God had ordained each waiting period, "whether it were two days, or a month, or a year" (verse 22), for He was in the cloud. He provided for them and taught them needed lessons while they waited. And He also made it clear when it was time to travel on.

The cloud is resting today. God knows how long the wait will be, and He will show me when to move. This thought was a great comfort to me in the days ahead. Perhaps it will encourage you, too, as you wait for the thing you desire.

Poem for the Day

The Guiding Cloud

A cloud led Israel on their way
Across that barren, desert land,
Though why it stood so long at times
They didn't always understand.

The cloud is resting on your life;
Oh, when will God reveal His will?
If you could only see the way!
But now the cloud is standing still.

Though you, impatient, wish to find
Just what tomorrow holds in store . . .
God wants to be enough for you
Before He grants you something more.

And He may show you while you wait
A miracle to bless your soul—
A word of truth from Sinai,
A healing serpent on a pole.

And you may find your needs supplied
In ways not known to you before—
A gush of water from a rock,
And manna lying round your door.

As surely as 'tis right to move
When God reveals to you His will,
So it is right to tarry while
The guiding cloud is standing still.
                    —Sharilyn B. Martin

From the Other Side

Elizabeth Mullet

But this one thing I do, forgetting those things which are behind, and reaching forth unto those things which are before, I press toward the mark. —Philippians 3: 13, 14
But Zion said, The LORD hath forsaken me, and my Lord hath forgotten me.
Can a woman forget her sucking child, that she should not have compassion on the son of her womb? **yea, they may forget, yet will I not forget thee. Behold, I have graven thee upon the palms of my hands.** *—Isaiah 49:14-16*
Read Isaiah 49:8-16

"Oh! What a darling!" I gazed down at the perfectly-formed baby girl in my arms. A few minutes before, the doctor had come in and announced, "I need a nurse to hold this baby."

Since our hospital wasn't in the habit of delivering babies, our only baby warmer was an antiquated one that took half an hour to heat. Until then, human warmth was the best alternative.

The doctor was still caring for the baby's mother, but the grandmother stood nearby. "Let me see her," she requested, gingerly lifting aside the blanket flap to gaze for a moment at the tiny face. Then she turned away.

What was going on? Most grandmothers would be acting delighted with such a healthy, beautiful infant. They might even be requesting a chance to hold the grandchild themselves. But not this one!

I also noticed there was no man in attendance and no comments about letting "Daddy" know about the birth. My antennae went up.

I had two good friends plus a brother and sister-in-law who had adopted children, and I knew the scarcity of adoptable babies. I wondered, *How does one find out if a mother would be willing to let her child be adopted? How insulting it might be if I would ask, only to discover these people just happen to be private, undemonstrative people!*

I wracked my brains for a question that would reveal the mother's intentions without hurting the grandmother's feelings.

"Does your daughter have a name picked out for the baby?" I finally asked.

"Not that I know of." The answer was short and to the point.

By now it was high time for me to get back to my patients. The warmer was ready. Regretfully, I laid the little girl in her toasty bed.

As I gave medicine, I kept trying to think how I could discover the answer to my question. Suddenly I had it! Back down the long hall I trotted.

"Does your daughter plan to breast-feed the baby?" I queried in the most professional voice I could muster.

"Well, she doesn't even plan to keep her unless she changes her mind," replied the grandmother. Oh joy! I had my answer!

"Do you have plans made for the baby?" I questioned. When the answer was negative, I continued, "Would you like us to make arrangements?"

When she said yes, I lost no time in finding Dr. Jones and asking him if it would be okay for me to contact someone about adopting the baby.

"Sure, go ahead," he replied affably.

When my brother Don answered the phone, I got straight to the point. "Do you want a baby girl?" I asked.

"Of course," he replied, just like that. Not "How old is she?" or "What does she look like?" or "I'll have to ask my wife," just "Of course!"

When Doctor Jones found me waiting for him the next morning, he started laughing. "Do you know I have had four calls about that baby during the night!" he chuckled.

I was aghast. "How do you decide who gets her?" I wondered.

"I guess whoever gets a lawyer first." He shrugged.

After a quick phone call, I took off running, but when I reached the lawyer's office a couple blocks away, his secretary looked regretful. "He left just two minutes ago," she said.

More phone calls. Every lead I followed turned out to be a dead end. Lawyers were either in court for the day, off fishing, or impossibly priced. I was tired from three twelve-hour nursing shifts in a row. But how could I just give up?

At last I talked with a relatively local lawyer who was agreeable and willing to take the case. Even though he didn't know much about adoptions, he was interested in that kind of thing, he explained. Later in the afternoon I drove the twenty-five miles for the papers he had drawn up and hurried back to the town of Belhaven.

Dr. Jones was just finishing up at the office and came over to the hospital where I handed him the papers from the lawyer. He, the director of nursing, and a notary public walked down the hall to the mother's room and a few minutes later came back with a document stating that the baby was to be adopted by my brother Donald and his wife Rhoda, and that I was granted temporary custody until they could receive her. Baby Kelly Rose would be discharged the next morning. Driving the sixteen miles home, I was so happy I felt like I would float off the earth.

Only a few close friends were told of the arrangements until the next morning when I quietly slipped into a women's gathering with the babe in my arms. Then what rejoicing!

It was almost a month before Don and Rhoda could come for their new daughter. Remembering how hard it had been for me to part with a baby I had once cared for in Belize, I reminded myself to control my emotions. But this wasn't the same at all. Don and Rhoda, along with their other children and baby Kelly, lived at our house for a month while they worked on the adoption papers. Then they moved half a mile away as they waited some more. Next they moved to Rhoda's parents' home two hours north for a month before finally returning home to Wisconsin. So the transition was gradual. Besides, Kelly was my new niece and part of our family. So I could spend time with her whenever I wanted to.

I pity the birth family who did not have the joy of interacting with such a precious baby. Although Kelly's biological mother claimed that her pregnancy was the result of an act against her will, at least she had hidden her pregnancy until her family couldn't force her into an abortion. She had loved her baby enough to give her life.

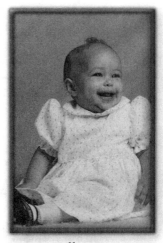

Kelly Rose

As I consider Kelly's pale-complexioned birth mother with her blue eyes and straight blonde hair, I wonder if she could have looked at my niece with her lovely, honey-gold skin, kinky hair, and big, beautiful, dark eyes and not associate her with the traumatic time of her conception. She had a hard choice to make, for even if she had been determined to raise her daughter, her fanatically prejudiced family would have certainly disowned her. How sad I could feel for her! But her loss was our gain.

And when she remembers, may she take comfort in knowing that her daughter is treasured in a loving Christian home. I am most certain that God placed dear little Kelly Rose into our family to fill a void that would have remained empty without her.

Thought for the Day

Sometimes it is necessary to put away the past
and live today for the future.

Created for His Glory

Joanna Neuenschwander

I will bring thy seed from the east, and gather thee from the west;
. . . bring my sons from far, and my daughters from the ends of the earth;
even every one that is called by my name: for I have created him for my glory,
I have formed him; yea, I have made him. —Isaiah 43:5-7
Read Isaiah 43:1-7

*A*t last she's quiet. My body swayed in cautious rhythm as my husband slipped quietly behind the chair and together we looked at the sleeping form of our precious new daughter. We had just been through one of the most tumultuous, joyous moments of our lives. A beautiful, charming baby girl had been handed to us to claim as our own darling daughter. Just moments before she had been squalling at the top of her voice, fear written all over her little face. Every time she had the courage to look into my face, she would break forth into another series of screams. Now she lay quiet, except for an occasional sob that shook her little body with quick jerks.

She is just perfect! The head of black hair, the black eyebrows and lashes . . .

Behind the closed eyelids were the most beautiful dark eyes we had ever seen. Her flushed cheeks, red rosebud mouth, dimpled hands, and plump little legs signified a healthy and well-cared-for child. She was more than we had ever allowed ourselves to dream of.

Our minds slipped back to the events that had led us to this point. We remembered our family kneeling around our kitchen table each Monday morning, praying for the safety and well-being of their baby sister. In varying stages of maturity, each child had expressed his plea, from the three-year-old's, "Please give us a baby girl," to the twenty-year-old remembering the soul needs of the baby's biological family.

With a twinge of pain I remembered my own prayer. "Lord," I had pleaded, "if one of Your children is longing to have her child placed in a Christian home, please lead us to that child."

In this, our moment of joy, we paused to ask God to direct the mother and father who had made the painful decision of separation. This mother who had so gently laid down her newborn baby in a dirty paper mill had also seen the beautiful features of her treasured child. Had she gently stooped and tenderly kissed those soft little cheeks before turning and walking away forever?

Lashae and big brother Jarrell

Nothing we could have done could have merited the favor of being placed in our pleasant circumstances, nor were this baby's parents responsible for being thrown into a godless environment. Possibly we could show appreciation for their sacrifice by loving and guiding their child to the Lord Jesus. Who knows but that in eternity God's plan will have been fulfilled for this child, in spite of her birth into a society that refused to recognize God as the Creator of human life.

Thought for the Day

God has a sovereign plan for every human life He creates.

Whose Son Is He?

Debi Graybill

Fear not therefore: ye are of more value
than many sparrows. —Luke 12:7
Read Luke 12: 1-12

hanks for your prayer support and letting me be honest with you. I am pretty confident that your family will be able to adopt my baby. Please don't ever give up the plans to provide a loving and wonderful home for a child who needs it.

Eagerly I gazed at the screen on my phone. These texts were so reassuring! I read on.

Realistically, your family is who I want to give my baby to. I know you will be an excellent adoptive family. You both will make it your own.

Good night my sister, my friend, and soon-to-be mother. I love you. When I got the sonogram not only was Coulson kicking. He waved at me and the people in the room. We had so much fun watching his hand and arm go in a perfect wave every time we talked to him. It was adorable. You are so blessed to be able to raise him and see all his adorable first moments.

Hurry and come. I expect the baby to be born very soon. I want to make sure you are here. I want you to be the first person he sees.

Many had been the texts and emails passed between Connie and me over the two months before "our" baby was to be born. There had been deep discussions about religion and family life and ethical views. Because of the time zone difference, we had talked late into the night. She had shared freely details of her life, her fears, and her goals. She told me why she wanted us to be the parents of her unborn baby, and I admired her willingness to sacrifice her own deep feelings for the good of her child.

Now the time had come, or so we thought. Excitement and a tiny bit of apprehension rang high as we met Connie and her mother Susannah at the airport for the first time. As we realized that the baby wasn't appearing as soon as we had thought, we rented a car and booked in at a nearby motel.

Even though we had finally met in person, Connie and I continued to converse by cell phone. That evening Connie sent me this text: *Why would meeting you change anything? It made the reality of things hit, but it just solidified and confirmed what I thought about you two. I was glad to see the love and joy you two have in one another. You both will be wonderful parents. Truly you and Phil are wonderful. I love you both and couldn't ask 4 better care 4 my baby.*

During the next six days we were in Susannah's home a lot. Phil fixed her mower, ceiling fan, and trim work around her front door. He caulked the showers and read books while I bonded with Connie and Susannah. I went along for Connie's prenatal visit, baked cookies, and looked at pictures. We played games together. One evening we took Connie and her seventeen-year-old brother to a Cabela's store forty minutes away. On the way home, her brother wondered if he could ask us some personal questions, such as, "What is the difference between Christians and Mennonites?" This led to an animated discussion of what God wants from us as Christians. We talked about the Amish and traditions. Their questions made me stop and actually think about why I have chosen to be where I am.

Coulson Phil was born at 3:49 p.m. on December 23, 2009. Birth is an incredible miracle. After witnessing the birth, I remember thinking, *If this dear lady decides to keep this darling baby, I really can't feel too bad after seeing what all she went through.* At the time I didn't realize the test God had just up the road for us!

The nurses gave Coulson to me to hold first. Connie said that made it easier for her to think of him as my baby and not hers any more. He was

SO PERFECT. Later when I handed him to Phil, we marveled together. We felt distinct ownership. I then showed him to Susannah and Connie. Earlier Connie had said she didn't want to hold the baby at all, but I wanted Connie to hold him so she could have closure on the situation. I didn't want her mourning later that she never even got to hold him. We were not there to kidnap her son. It was a choice only Connie could make, and she was the one who would live with her choice. Later Connie and her mother each took turns holding him. Connie crooned over and over, "Such a cute baby. You are so-o-o cute!"

Although Connie had given permission for us to take Coulson with us to another room, and the nurses tried hard to find a room for us, there wasn't an empty room to be found. Our other options were to leave the baby with Connie or in the nursery and go to a motel—or else we could stay with our baby in Connie's room. None of the options looked very good, but we decided to just stay in Connie's room so we could at least be with the baby.

For the first day and a half things went well. We took complete care of the baby. Phil came and went and Connie slept a lot. When she was awake, she made little comments to Coulson about what a good mommy and daddy he had. I felt incredibly grateful to her for the gift she was giving us.

I knew she had some contact with TJ, the baby's biological father. But I also knew she didn't trust him to be a good father for her baby. That's why she had chosen adoption. When I realized she was having contact with TJ after the baby was born, I started feeling very uncomfortable and afraid. I held Coulson a little tighter, loved him a little harder, and rocked him a little longer.

Connie cried a lot the next afternoon. Phil was sleeping and I was holding the baby, so I sat on the edge of the bed and rubbed her back. Helpless to know how to comfort her more, I returned to the rocking chair and started to sing. Her sobs increased. I sang some more. It was amazing how song after song came to me. The songs seemed to comfort Connie. She quieted down and fell asleep. Phil and I took turns holding and loving the baby. His future was so unsure.

The next morning, Connie spent a lot of time on the phone. She made a comment about feeling torn. She said TJ wanted to take her and the baby out for a Christmas dinner. I told her if she had any intentions of keeping on with the adoption, there was no way she could go with him. She admitted that if she did that, she was scared she'd never come back. I told her I thought TJ could come see the baby, but it needed to be at her mom's house or the hospital, and she needed someone else to be with her at all times. I reminded her that TJ did not want to support her or the baby, and that he didn't even want to sign the birth certificate because then he would be obligated to pay child support.

After a bit Connie asked us to leave the room. She said TJ would be at the hospital in forty-five minutes and since TJ was not approving of the adoption, she thought it would be better for him not to meet us. She agreed with me that a social worker needed to be there and called for one. Because she didn't want to handle TJ alone, she said she would ask for a nurse to remain with her until a social worker could arrive. Unfortunately, our caseworker was in Oklahoma for Christmas, and couldn't come.

We sat in the waiting room in hopes of seeing TJ, but finally gave up and decided to go eat. I was doing really well emotionally until we got through the cafeteria line with our food. Then I realized it was actually Christmas Day and I was far away from home, eating some pathetic cafeteria Christmas special. I thought of the rest of my family together eating my mom's good cooking. "Silver Bells" was singing cheerily across the speaker system. It was too much. I sat down at our table in tears. Missing Christmas for a darling baby to call our own was one thing. But missing Christmas, plus maybe not getting our baby after all, overwhelmed me.

It was good for Phil and me to cry and deal with the reality of the situation. Finally the thought hit me that God had a reason for bringing us here. I looked up through my misty tears and saw the other people in the cafeteria. Several gentlemen were sitting all alone, looking as sad as we felt. What was their story? Why weren't they at home with their families? After that, it was a little easier to look people in the eyes, tell them Merry Christmas, and give a few words of comfort and cheer.

After we finished eating, we returned to the waiting room. Every time an African-American or Indian-looking man happened by, we'd wonder, "Is that TJ?" Then there he was. We knew right away he was TJ. He looked just like Coulson and was happily talking on his phone, saying how alert the baby was. As we scrutinized him, he glanced our way, but there was no sign of recognition. He left. Finally around 5:00 p.m., Connie's mother and two sisters came.

When Susannah arrived, she went straight up to Connie's room. She came back in tears. She said that Connie was packing to go home with her boyfriend. We waited awhile, and finally Connie and TJ and the baby appeared. Connie was on a cart for transporting patients, and they headed toward the exit. Eyes averted, they made as if to pass by us when I called, "Hey, wait! I want to give you a hug." They stopped, and I hugged Connie. I kissed the baby and handed Connie a little gift I had for her.

We walked away with our hearts breaking in a million little pieces. *Is this part of the adoption journey? Why do people risk the chance of such heart-wrenching pain?* my heart was crying. I remember Coulson's beautiful blue eyes looking so intently up at me while he was drinking his bottle. Such trust and love. I couldn't help but feel that I had let him down.

Connie's mom took it almost as hard as we did. She said through tears, "It's like watching her jump off a cliff."

Connie's sister added, "With a baby in her arms!" They all liked us very much, and they had wanted us to have the baby. They knew that as long as Connie was with TJ, he would cut her off from her family. So Susannah was losing a daughter and grandchild, and we were losing "our" darling baby. We knew this was not at all what Connie really wanted. Her emotions were so unstable that I knew there was no way now that she would stand up to TJ and follow through with the adoption. In her heart she knew she was not making a safe decision for her baby. But right then she didn't have the strength to carry it through. Saying good-bye to her baby looked too big—even bigger than her fear of TJ.

We said our tearful good-bye to Susanna and her daughters and left to make arrangements to fly home.

We still have contact with Connie and her mother. We know that she changed Coulson's name and that she eventually left his abusive father and moved home to her mother which made life much safer for the baby. In this we see God answering our prayers for him. Connie sends us pictures, and we can watch him grow.

Coulson will forever be in our hearts and will always be our "firstborn." He was a little bit of Heaven brought to earth to us for two special days. We can pray for Coulson. Maybe God showers special blessings on him because of our prayers. We still feel God led us into this adoption. We hope the seeds we planted with Coulson and his family will sprout and grow.

Thought for the Day

It is not in our place to write the script for our journey in life. Our part is acceptance and faith. We are so thankful we can trust "our first son" to an all-wise God for an unknown future.

Our Precious Gift

Debi Graybill

Rest in the LORD, and wait patiently for him. —Psalm 37: 7

Read Psalm 37: 3-8, 23-27

"It's your lucky day!" The message on my phone was from the adoption facilitator. "We just heard from a girl who is due in ten days." My heart raced at the thought. *Might this really be the baby God has for us to call our own?* It looked a bit daunting to even try again. We had been matched with seven babies before this, and each match had fallen through, leaving us with broken dreams and empty arms.

At this time we were also considering a sibling group of five. How we wanted to know God's will for our lives!

A week later, the facilitator contacted us, wanting to know if we were ready for a birth mom conference call. Though apprehensive, we decided to move ahead and try again. How I dreaded the first call to a birth mother! Thankfully, it went very well. I learned she was about our age, and this was her fifth child. She explained why she felt adoption would be the best option for this baby. She asked us to be there for the birth if at all possible, and so we tried to plan ahead without letting our hopes and emotions get too involved.

Kaitlyn and I enjoyed texting each other over the next several days. We discussed baby names, dreams, fears, and family life. She texted, *When the lady from the agency asked me if I want to talk to more families,*

I didn't hesitate in telling her no. I knew you were the angel I had prayed for.

Five days later we received the message that we needed to head to Kaitlyn's area.

Darkness, fog, and thick sheets of rain presented a dreary welcome into Kaitlyn's local town. I nervously anticipated meeting our baby's mother. *How many times have we been through this?* My stomach was in knots. *We want a baby so much, but are we just being naive and gullible? Will we be disappointed again?*

It was 10:30 p.m. when Kaitlyn stopped by our motel to meet us. She was petite and blonde. Her honest blue eyes met mine, and instantly I liked her. I peeked into her car where her three youngest children were snuggled cozily under blankets.

We spent the next two weeks bonding with Kaitlyn and her children. One day after spending time together she texted me, *Jacob says he wants to go live with you, because he likes you so much.* It was exciting to think about what our little boy might look like. I was blessed to observe Kaitlyn mothering her three children. Her life revolved around them. I was reminded of an earlier text from her, *I love him as much as any of my other children, but I know I can't provide for him . . . so I will love him enough to let him go!*

We tried to keep her upbeat as we waited patiently for the birth. An encouraging text she sent me during this time was, *I wish there was a way I could reassure you that I won't take this away from you! I know it must be hard to be on your end to never know. But YES! I am still 100% sure. If he ever decides to be born, that is!!*

Since Kaitlyn was from a very small town, and many did not know of her pregnancy, she asked that we would present ourselves at the hospital as friends, rather than as Josiah's new parents. We recalled those first special hours with Coulson, the first baby we couldn't keep, and with Kamryn, the last baby, where we had our own hospital room to bond with the baby before the parents changed their minds. If we really were going to get this baby, I wanted to hold him and love him and feed him. How could we do this as casual friends?

And then Josiah Michael was born! I had the honor of cutting the umbilical cord, and although Kaitlyn held him first, she was quick to hand him to me. Soon he was carted away to the nursery. We were awestruck by our little son! He had a head full of dark brown hair and a sweet little rosebud mouth. He was perfect in every way! It was so hard to just admire him through the nursery window.

Kaitlyn asked us if we would be willing to run an errand for her. We knew we would be gone several hours. It was tough to leave. Twice before, we had left the baby at the hospital with the birth mom, and each time, she had changed her mind. While we were gone, I received a text from her saying, *Me and Josiah are having a conversation!! I was telling him how lucky he is to be going to such a wonderful place with so much love!! He's glad too!! He doesn't talk a lot tho. He must get that from Phil.*

The first night was a real test for us as we left to go to the motel. Kaitlyn had confided to me that she would enjoy spending the first night with Josiah alone, as this would be her only night to spend with him. "Lord, please, please don't let her get too attached to her baby, our baby!" was our constant prayer. But we needed to add, "Your will, Lord, be done."

The next day we were able to be with Josiah just a little. Kaitlyn signed herself out of the hospital early so she could go home to be with her other children. Since Josiah needed to stay one more night in the hospital, and we were to be posing as casual friends, he stayed alone.

In the morning Kaitlyn sent this sweet text. *You are not dreaming. Welcome to the wonderful world of motherhood!!*

We were very happy when we could go to the hospital and help pick up our little prince. Kaitlyn and her other children followed us to the motel, and we took some very special pictures of her and her children with Josiah. Sweetly she asked them if they wanted to hold "Phil and Debi's baby" which they were delighted to do. Tenderly she helped them. She held Josiah close and smiled at the camera, then with undaunted strength, she handed him back to us, gathered her children, and drove away.

We were overwhelmed by the gift she gave us, and by how bravely she gave it.

The next Sunday morning we were still at the motel, waiting for the interstate compact to go through when I heard the familiar ding of my cell phone. It was a message from Kaitlyn. *Happy Mother's Day, Debi! I used to be the best mommy in the world and now I have competition . . . but I don't mind one bit! I hope you have an amazing day. You deserve it!*

Josiah

Almost a year has passed, and Kaitlyn and I are still friends. She loves the pictures I send of Josiah and our family and wants to hear about his life. Kaitlyn will always be Josiah's birth mother and care deeply about him, but he is our son. We have the delightful privilege and responsibility of being his mom and dad.

It is amazing that through all our failed adoptions, God had a sweet baby already picked out and waiting for us. So if we would have actually been able to adopt Coulson, Kimberly, Kenlee, Kendalie, Kelsie, Kerry, or Kamryn, we wouldn't have our sweet little Josiah today. I can hardly imagine that!

Phil, Josiah, and Debi Graybill

Thought for the Day

The Lord never asks us to give up something,
unless He gives us something better in return.

—Elisabeth Elliott

Willing to Give

Sarah Kraybill

You're ours, sweet child! You're ours!
But somebody's heart is breaking today
With utterless words that she cannot say.
Somebody's baby is far away . . .
But I hold you within my powers.

You're mine, little girl! You're mine!
But in somebody's arms there's an empty ache,
And in somebody's heart there's a void I helped make,
And a sorrow that somebody's mind cannot shake . . .
But I cuddle you, and my eyes shine.

I love you, dear baby, so much!
But somebody loves with a piercing pain;
Somebody's tears fall as thick as the rain,
And somebody's thoughts run an endless train . . .
But I laugh as your small fingers clutch.

How can I smile when somebody's sighing?
How can I laugh when somebody's crying?
How can I rejoice when in the making . . .
Somewhere, somebody's heart is breaking?

She loved you, dear child, so very much
That she gave up the feel of your trusting clutch;
She gave up the shine of your deep, dark eyes;
She gave up the thrill of your lusty cries;
She gave you up to a better life
That was free from starvation and war-torn strife.

And it's only because she was willing to give
That there is a chance that you might live.

And I am now privileged beyond all other
Because I am now her darling's mother.
Now I am the one to look in your eyes
And thrill at the sound of your hunger cries;
Now I am the one to hold you tight
And soothe you to sleep in the quiet night;
Now I am the one to tickle your feet,
And laugh at the smile on your face so sweet.

But how can I smile when somebody's sighing?
How can I laugh when somebody's crying?
How can I rejoice when in the making
Somewhere, somebody's heart is breaking?

But child, if I really want you to live,
Then I, like your mother, must also give.
I give you up to the One on high
Because I know He is always nigh.
I give you up to His ceaseless care
With a confident heart, for He's always there;
I give you up for your entire life,
And ask Him to keep you from sin and strife,
From the wrongs of the world, and the snare of things,
From the heartache and hurting that evil brings.
Oh, child, I'm weak, and so very small . . .
I ask Him to be your all in all.

So, dear little girl, we two together
In a common bond—I and your mother,
From the depths of our hearts are willing to give
Because, sweet child, we want you to live.

—*Sarah Kraybill*

To my sweet little niece, Janita Kraybill, adopted from Liberia, July 2005

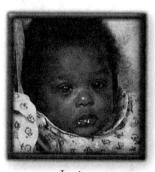

Janita

It Might Have Been Different

Crystal Van Pelt
an adoptee

We love him, because he first loved us. —1 John 4:19
Read 1 John 4:7-21

As I listened to the song *The Sign on the Highway*, tears filled my eyes. It gripped my heart to think how very nearly I could have been the daughter killed in a tragic accident, how nearly it could have been my mother weeping to realize she would never see my smile again. And yes, also weeping because she had not taught me differently about God, salvation, and the way to Heaven.

As you may guess, my mother did want a better life for me—better than she had herself. I'm glad she chose to put me where I would have a chance. Then God brought another woman into my life, a mother to teach me of Him and His requirements and His rewards.

Through adoption, and then Mom marrying a widower, my family grew by leaps and bounds. I was blessed with six brothers and a sister and, later, many nieces and nephews whom I love dearly. Why? Why did God choose to give me so much? Why me out of all the needy children? I realize it was nothing I deserved. God chose to give me a chance to learn of Him. Will I make Him my choice?

I wonder about other things. Why does God not give more children the chance I have with a Christian home and family? Is it because we limit His working in our lives? Do we have reservations? True, adoption and/or foster care is not for everyone, but maybe it is for you.

Pray about it! I have one memory that goes back as far as I can remember. It is of a little old lady who must have been my great-grandmother or great-great-grandmother praying with me when we went to visit with her. Surely if she prayed *with* me, she also prayed *for* me and my future. Did God hear? I'm sure He did. He will hear your prayer today also!

Thought for the Day

God can mend broken hearts,
but we must choose to give Him all the pieces.

Legacy of an Adopted Child

Author Unknown

Once there were two women who never knew each other . . .

One I do not remember; the other I call Mother.

One gave me a nationality; the other gave me a name.

The one gave me the seed of talent; the other gave me an aim.

Two different lives shaped to make me one.

One became my guiding star. The other became my sun.

One gave me emotions; the other calmed my fears.

One saw my sweet smile; the other dried my tears.

The first gave me life; the second taught me to live it.

The first gave me a need for love,

The second was there to give it.

The one gave me up—'twas all she could do,

The other prayed for a child, and God led me to you!

Thank You, Lord, for Your special way,

Of bringing children and parents together . . .

Who need each other.

—Penny

This poem, signed, "I love you, Mother" was given to me by our adopted daughter, Maria, and has been very special to me. —Elizabeth Yoder

Bind us together, Lord,
Bind us together with cords
That cannot be broken.

Bind us together, Lord,
Bind us together in love.[4]

PART 2

Knitting Hearts Together

Bonding Through Love

"There is a beauty particular to adoption—
the mystical joining of souls
that in retrospect seems foreordained."
—William McGurn,
an adoptive parent

He's Ours

Brenda Weaver

Whosoever shall confess that Jesus is the Son of God,
God dwelleth in him, and he in God. —1 John 4:15

Read 1 John 4:14-24

"*I*s he a Fresh Air child?" Strangers have asked me this question on numerous occasions, wondering if our son was part of the Fresh Air program that gives inner-city children a taste of life with a country family for several weeks each summer.

I was asked this question in the grocery store, while our son jumped off and on the shopping cart . . . at a playground while he whizzed down a slide or dangled over a spring-mounted riding toy . . . in the library while he pulled my skirt or darted just ahead of my grasp. Invariably the question would arise after the viewer had observed my head covering, our fair-skinned, conservatively-dressed family, and our darting, babbling, vivacious, chocolate-colored son.

I have always been glad to pat his tight curls, give him a quick squeeze, gently touch his arm, or put my arm around his shoulders and answer, "No, he's ours." (I will admit that sometimes his behavior made me wish to run and hide rather than answer questions with a smile!)

Ours. Does the word, coupled with my reassuring touch, chase warm circles around Eddie's heart, as it does mine? *Ours.* He is not vacationing in the fresh air of the country, away from a home in some polluted city. No, he is here for good. He's ours. He belongs.

Belonging is the essence of adoption. I marvel, knowing that I am also an adopted child. God the Father looks at His beloved Son, communicates with His Spirit which resides in me, and proclaims, "She's ours." Oh, blessed thought that bonds my soul to the heart of my adoptive Father! I belong.

In many ways we convey belonging to both our adopted and our biological children. If someone asks, "Which children are yours and which are adopted?" reply graciously, "They are all ours." Decide today to never call your birth children "ours" in a way that makes your adopted children feel excluded. Be certain they know they *belong*.

Thought for the Day

Belonging builds a bridge to serenity and eternity.

Eddie with sister

Mystical Normalcy

Regina Derstine

*And we know that all things work together for good to them that love God,
to them who are the called according to his purpose. —Romans 8:28*
Read Romans 8:31-39

I think *adoption* is a rather colorless word to describe an event that is so marvelous. Because of the amazing circumstances of my life, I feel inclined to analyze the process we call adoption.

Two years ago, when Kendra, Diego, Alexandra, Felix, and Arianna, a sibling group of five foster children, were brought to our house and left here, it felt as though we had company. I was worried about dessert for Sunday dinner and took great pains to make strawberry delight, which none of them appreciated or even recognized. The children didn't even want to taste it because it looked strange to them. They cried over their mashed potatoes and gravy and wanted ice cream!

Parenting these children looked like a tremendous amount of work all of a sudden, and I felt completely overwhelmed, overworked, and stressed out most of the time those first few weeks.

Then something exquisite began happening. Seven hundred and thirty days later, I have the same amount of work, but my heart is completely changed within me. Instead of company, these children have turned into my family. I have the same mother instincts for them as I have for each of my biological children. The same sadness overwhelms me at another report of misbehavior in Sunday school, and the same gladness fills me when we finally master the multiplication table or maneuver our way through a tough emotional problem. Now they fight over the strawberry delight and look forward with anticipation to our Sunday dinner mashed potatoes.

At first we viewed each other with distrust and fear; now we look at each other with eyes of trust. They trust that I will always have their meals ready for them, their clothes washed, and be waiting to meet them after school; they trust that I will not hurt them

The Derstine family

or enjoy seeing them punished. And I trust that they love me and are happy to be called my children. I will never try to sever the ties with their biological mother; it seems the more we allow them the freedom to know her as their biological mother, the more they can allow me to be their "real" mother.

Sometimes in our cruel, jaded world we think there are no such things as miracles, but the adoption process truly is a miracle. As William McGurn writes, "There is a beauty particular to adoption—the mystical joining of souls that in retrospect seems foreordained—but the beauty lies in the normalcy of it all. We feel the same sense of awe and wonder as other moms and dads; we buy the same toys and bore our friends with the same repertoire of stories."[5] May each of us find beauty in the mystical normalcy of it all!

Thought for the Day

No cord or cable can draw so forcibly, or bind so fast, as love can do with a single thread.   —Richard E. Burton

---

5   Used by permission.

No More a Stranger

Joanna Neuenschwander

O the depth of the riches both of the wisdom and knowledge of God! how unsearchable are his judgments, and his ways past finding out! —Romans 11:33

Read Romans 11:21–33

What a busy summer! Today had been no exception. *How*, I wondered, *do moms juggle their schedules and still meet the emotional and spiritual needs of their families?* My life seemed to be a constant rush of preserving the garden produce most liable to rot next. Then there were the scheduled and unscheduled duties of farm life. Tonight, once again, the children scurried off to the dairy parlor. Turning to my three-year-old son who remained, I asked, "Do you want to go to the farm and ride your bike, or would you like to stay home with Mommy?" He decided a quiet evening with just Mom looked more inviting.

As my eyes surveyed the kitchen, I saw evidence of a family calling this place home. A bowl of sweet corn sat waiting to be cut off the cob. On the counter lay a package of graham crackers, a sticky knife, and an open can of peanut butter. Through the laundry room door I viewed several baskets of laundry waiting to be folded.

In the center of my untidy kitchen stood my little son, his skin tanned to a handsome brown, black hair framing a cherub face (See "I Was a Stranger"). I seized the opportunity and called him to my knee. As he jumped up, I gave him a big bear hug and said, "I'm so glad you're my little boy. What would I ever do if I didn't have a little boy like you?"

In this intimate moment, he seemed to have a glimpse of insight that I had thought him incapable of. With serious black eyes he looked into my face and asked, "What did my name used to be in Vietnam?"

I assured him that Mommy and Daddy had named him his given name while he was still in Vietnam. Sensing his need for security, I hugged

him again and said, "You used to live in Vietnam, but you didn't have a mommy or daddy, and God knew you needed one. God knew that we needed a little boy, so he sent Mommy and Daddy all the way from America to Vietnam to get you. Now you will always live with Mommy and Daddy and be their own little boy, and we will take care of you."

In his sweet innocence he leaned his little face closer to mine and said, "Now when I get big and you start to get little, I'll take care of you!"

This was the boy who seldom expressed pain, who expressed his insecurity by repetitious behavior, who seldom verbalized, and who we hadn't been sure was meant for our family!

Thought for the Day

"God moves in a mysterious way, His wonders to perform!"

—William Cowper

Faith, Commitment, and Love

Harry Lee Nevenswander family

(composed of excerpts from e-mails written by Jarrell's sisters, Janae and Krissie)

Let us therefore come boldly unto the throne of grace, that we
may obtain mercy, and find grace to help in time of need. —Hebrews 4:16
Read Psalm 103:11-17

"There waits for me a glad tomorrow, where gates of pearl swing open wide . . ." Jarrell's brave, sweet voice rang out across the auditorium of our church. Grown men faltered and reached for their handkerchiefs, but the eight-year-old sang joyfully on, not missing a word. "Some day, the dark clouds will be lifted, and all the night of gloom be past; and all life's burdens will be lifted. *The day of rest shall dawn at last!*"

Our little brother, Jarrell, had arrived from Vietnam in 2002 to join our family. How joyfully we had welcomed him! How we looked forward to watching him grow! (See "I Was a Stranger," and "No More a Stranger.")

However, in April 2009, at the age of eight, Jarrell was diagnosed with acute myloid leukemia. He suffered much from the side effects of chemotherapy—headaches, achy joints, nausea, and vomiting. Sometimes he was so weak he even needed help to walk to the restroom.

We cried as we watched our little buddy wrestle with his misery. And sometimes we smiled through our tears at his unique humor. One evening as he was drifting off to sleep, Mom heard him murmur, "So sick I am .

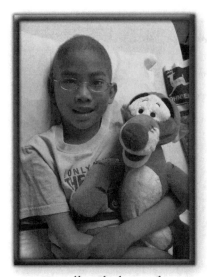

Jarrell in the hospital

. . so sick I feel . . . I wish, I wish . . . I wish I'd heal." Another time, Mom looked over to see Jarrell's bald head bent over his lunch tray, gingerly pulling out a piece of hair—not black hair, but a long blonde hair. With a twinkle in his eye he commented, "One of the cooks down in the cafeteria must be taking chemo!"

Even after several months, we could hardly believe cancer had invaded our family. Often I would awake with a start at night and whisper, "I can't believe this is happening to our family—to Jarrell! He's such a dear little guy and has filled the empty spot in our family with giggles and jokes and countless paper creations. God knew we needed to have our hearts softened by this happy little boy. Why would He take him from us? I just don't understand!"

On nights when Jarrell had a hard time going to sleep, Mom sat up until the wee hours of the morning rubbing his legs and reassuring him. "Mom," he confided one night, "I'm just scared all the time." Poor boy! He was dealing with fears any of us would have—fears of pain and death and the unknown.

One Monday morning during this time, God gave us a beautiful reminder of His unfailing promises to His children. A bright, beautiful rainbow arched across the western sky. To us it looked like it stretched and shimmered all the way to Akron. That evening we had another shower and sure enough! The sun came out again, blessing us with another rainbow. What a beautiful way to start the week!

In September, Jarrell became gravely ill, battling pneumonia, pain, fever, and a high heart rate. Weary and heartbroken, we stood helplessly beside him and watched him fight for each painful breath.

Tossing in agony, he often beckoned from his bed for Mom and Dad. "Will you please come pray with me? I hurt so bad." One night they heard his sweet soprano humming a song. "Come sing with me, Mom and Dad," he said. Bravely the trio struggled through the song. "I am bound for the promised land; I'm bound for the promised land. Oh, who will come and go with me? I am bound for the promised land."

Test after test, scan after scan finally revealed a rare and aggressive fungus which grows on decaying plant debris. In most cases the immune system quickly fights off the infection, but because Jarrell was neutropenic, the fungus had lodged in his body. Our parents called the whole family together to describe and discuss the heartrending facts. Mom's face was gray with apprehension and horror. The prognosis was not good. Ninety-nine percent of victims do not survive. Jarrell was only the fourth patient in this modern hospital to have been treated for this fungus, and none of the previous patients had survived. There was evidence it was growing in his sinuses, lungs, and kidneys. This fungus knows no boundaries. If unchecked, it would quickly eat through the nasal passages, and eyes, disfiguring Jarrell's beautiful face and body.

Two months later, Jarrell was a walking miracle. He had recovered from the surgical removal of a kidney and a lobe of a lung, and our subdued but jubilant family welcomed him home again. Daily Jarrell improved and we praised God for the modern-day miracle. His leukemia was in remission and the fungus was under control. Our hopes soared as he ran around with pink

Lashae and Jarrell the winter
before his death

cheeks, bright eyes, and a big grin. It felt to us like Jarrell's life had been given back.

During that winter, Jarrell continued to do well. He had a terrific appetite and was gaining weight just like we wanted him to. His color was good. He ran and romped and giggled and shouted just like a normal child. If he hadn't developed an infection that required hospitalization, we would not have known that the leukemia had returned. It tore at our hearts to know that in spite of rigorous treatment, his good health would not last and he would soon be gone. As we watched him tear through the house, we shook our heads and said, "There has to be some mistake!"

One night we watched the pictures from Mom and Dad's trip to Vietnam. We relived holding Jarrell for the first time, teaching him how to jump, watching his expression when he felt the wind for the first time, watching him discover new foods, seeing him open up and blossom emotionally and intellectually to the love and devotion showered on him. What a beautiful child! How we wished we could have him a little longer—could watch him grow up and become a man of God. We couldn't imagine life without his bright smile, hugs, giggles, and jokes.

The Sunday Uncle Joe preached about Heaven was one of the first times we had attended church as an entire family in many weeks. He said that Heaven is a place for children. In Heaven, there would be no chemotherapy, no pain, and no insecurity. It was a difficult but healing service for our congregation. And now, here we were, listening to Jarrell sing, "The day of rest shall dawn at last!"

A year after Jarrell was first diagnosed with cancer, his white blood cell count escalated again. We knew that his journey would soon be over. We struggled, trying to understand where the promises of God fit in with the crisis at hand. We felt defeated and discouraged by this experience.

Lashae's stormy tears, Anya's blank "it-hurts-too-bad-to-cry" look, Dad's quivering chin, Mom's bloodshot eyes, big sister's midnight sobs—all spoke of anguish too deep, too excruciating to bear. Jarrell was the life of our family. We had given him all we had from the day he was first referred to us. What would life be like without him?

Then on May 19, 2010, it happened, and very quickly. Jarrell had been having stomach pain and fever and had gone for a platelet transfusion that afternoon. Arriving home that evening, he seemed to get more comfortable in his own bed. But soon he jumped out and declared, "I'm getting out of this room. I'm bored!" He moved to the couch, and shortly after that, began to lose consciousness.

Dad called the family. A few minutes later, while we all hovered around him and let our tears fall on his dear cheeks, Jarrell slipped into glory.

For awhile we felt relief that Jarrell's suffering was over, but later came such pain. Scenes of his suffering filled our thoughts, even our sleep. Why had God let this terrible disease ravage this child's beautiful body, crush his spirit, and break our hearts? There is so much we do not understand. We ask the age-old question: Why do the innocent have to suffer so? However, in the midst of all this pain, we still believe that Heaven will more than make up for all the suffering here. "In His presence is FULLNESS OF JOY."

A note from Jarrell's mom, Joanna:

We view Jarrell's entrance into our hearts as the beginning of a beautiful masterpiece creatively designed by God. The outline of His painting was etched in faith, commitment, and love.

Faith—because we had to believe that out of the millions of orphans, God would choose the perfect child for our family. Faith also assured us that the One who was painting the picture would add all the right shades and hues to make it complete. Jarrell was unique. He faced insecurities, and his nature was sensitive.

Commitment called each family member to nurture and reassure through acceptance. We marvel how God so skillfully masked the blotches that we made while He was painting. We had varied opinions on the best way to mold and conform his tender life.

Love softened the sharp lines of reality.

As we daily watched God add the brush strokes to His masterpiece, we were intrigued with its developing beauty. Who could have so masterfully blended all the shades together but God? Then God laid down His brush while we waited in anticipation. We begged Him to keep painting, but His answer was this, "The painting is complete. One more stroke would mar its perfection."

Would we open up our hearts and home again to a little boy whose departure left us with such

Lashae and Jarrell

broken, bleeding hearts? A thousand times over—Yes! His life stretched our hearts and filled our lives with love. We long for the day when we will be again reunited and our family circle will be complete.

The Harry Lee and Joanna
Neuenschwander Family, 2010

With a sharp dagger of pain, I realize that his commitment of devotion as a toddler (to someday take care of me) will never be fulfilled. Right now I feel pretty small, and I could use a hug from a big boy like him!

It marks a year now that Jarrell left us. How we miss him! We continue to thank God for the special privilege of loving him.

Thought for the Day

God gives us the courage and strength to reach out with faith, commitment, and love.

The Tie That Binds

Emily Martin

For I was my father's son, tender and only beloved in the sight of my mother.
He taught me also, and said unto me, Let thine heart retain my words:
keep my commandments, and live. —Proverbs 4:3, 4
Read Proverbs 4:1-9

"You are all ours now, boy! Truly ours! No one can take you away!" My husband's voice was jubilant, and his smile spread from ear to ear. We were sitting in the airport awaiting our flight to Mexico City. The adoption papers were finally signed and safely in my satchel; all we needed were the immigration papers finalized, and we'd be heading home.

Three-month-old Darian looked up with a grin and stuck his chubby fingers in Dad's mouth. Malvern had been delighted with our new baby from the day we had met him at two days old. He had cuddled him and cradled him to sleep on his chest and fed him his bottle on our two previous trips to Mexico. But now there was an unrestrained acceptance that went beyond that first attachment. The papers were signed!

"My son . . . Darian Ray Martin. Hey, boy, that sounds good! Doesn't it?"

Babyhood passed, and the preschool years, when Darian followed Dad every chance he could. When our two foster boys left after four and a half years with us, we relished the permanency of four-year-old Darian's adoption even more. By the time he was eight years old, Dari was adept with equipment, running the big forklifts and working with Dad at the sawmill after school hours and early mornings.

Darian

Dad understood, too, about the struggle with learning that Dari faced, as both father and son share the challenge of dyslexia. Dad was better with numbers, and Darian better with reading, but for both, running equipment was easy. And they both had inborn radar to show them which direction to go when they were driving. Companionable comradeship continued.

We had told Dari that we would like to take him back to Mexico, maybe when he was ten, so he could see where he was born and what it was like in the country of his birth. But when Dari was nine, Jill, a preemie, was born to us. Since there were big hospital bills, we couldn't go then. Maybe later. So we saved our money and prayed about it. We planned our trip for the summer of 2000, the year Dari turned fourteen.

One morning about a month before our trip, I found Dari sitting on the back steps. His face was a thundercloud.

"What's wrong, sonny boy? Is something the matter? Why aren't you at the sawmill?"

Darian and Dad

He shrugged. "I just don't fit anywhere. Where do I belong? It seems like I can't do anything right. I should've just stayed in Mexico." And he went on to share particular relationship problems he was facing.

I listened and tried to encourage him. "You do what is right," I challenged him. "You can't change the other person and control what he says or does, but you can respond rightly. And we are certainly glad you are our son and that you are not still in Mexico. Maybe you'll find some answers on our trip that will help you understand about your roots."

Malvern and I were looking forward to this trip. It would be special to take our children on the twelve-hour train ride across the beautiful, treacherous mountains, just as we had done years before, and to show them the little town where Dari was born. We would stay at the same mission house where we had stayed fourteen years before with Gustavo and Caroline Verdugo, except this time there would be thirteen of us instead of three.

We were not worried about meeting Darian's birth parents. His father was unknown, and we had been informed that his mother had left the town years before. We would just show him the town so he could feel what his life could have been.

Imagine our surprise when, shortly after our arrival, Caroline said, "Darian's birth father would like to meet him while you are here. I arranged that he could come visit tomorrow evening about seven, if that's okay with you."

"Dari's birth father! I thought he was unknown!"

"Oh, Poncho readily admits to being the father, and he would like to see Darian. He is a fairly well-to-do man in this town. He owns his house and a store. When the doctors came from the States this past year, Poncho had cataracts removed from his eyes, so we know him fairly well. He will be respectful and courteous."

Later we asked Dari, "How do you really feel about it. Shall we say no?"

He shrugged, "I don't know. I guess he can come if he wants."

The next evening we were all prepared for the visit, excitement and apprehension riding high. *What will he be like? How will it go? What will we say? Is it really best to go through with this? Will we be sorry?* It was all wasted worrying, for he never showed up. Dari seemed relieved and disappointed at the same time, and I wished this newly-known birth father had never said anything about coming.

The next day was very busy. We spent the morning at the ocean about forty-five minutes away and then helped out at the children's Bible school in the early evening. Sixty to eighty children with big brown eyes and eager faces stared with unashamed curiosity at our big family. Our children returned the stares and then happily helped pass out the crayons and papers, chattering to the children in English. The children answered in Spanish with smiles and crinkled eyes. Oh, the masses of children in each village! How I would have loved to take some home with us! Some were obviously poor, with pitiful clothes and thin little faces; others were better dressed, but all of them had the Spanish features I loved in Darian.

Dari quietly observed everything—the pitiful little houses that many lived in . . . the heat and the poverty . . . the loud blaring music from nearby taverns . . . the drunks staggering about . . . the jabbering in a language he did not understand . . . the many children milling about with very little supervision. His eyes followed a little black-haired boy with big chocolate eyes so much like his own. *What is he thinking?* I wondered. *Is he realizing how easily he could have been that little boy?*

That evening we arrived home late, and I was already preparing for bed when the message came. "Poncho is here! Do you want to come meet him?"

When I entered the room, the others had already met. I shook the stranger's hand. *Dari is tall and broad. This little man, claiming to be his father, is short and slight. It's hard to believe he is actually Dari's father. He does have a friendly smile—what I can see under that mustache. He seems a bit ill at ease, but he's trying to make conversation.*

"Darian looks like his mother," was translated to us. (I had often told Dari that as well.) "She was a beautiful woman. I have three other sons. One is *grande* like you." He looked at Dari and held his hand above his head. "The other two are small like me." Again he gestured with his hands.

"My oldest son is in college. Do you work hard? I do not want my sons to be lazy!" The conversation continued for fifteen or twenty minutes. Dari answered when spoken to. We took several pictures of them together. Before he left, Poncho hugged Dari, then he was gone.

That visit seemed to settle something for Dari. This man he had just met may have been his birth father, but he was not his dad. And although it had been interesting to meet him, that was all it was. His real dad was the one who had raised him. Never again have I heard him mention anything about not fitting in or belonging.

Thought for the Day

It's the everyday acts of love that bond us together.

Sharing Strengthens the Bond

Emily Martin

Hear, O my son, and receive my sayings;
and the years of thy life shall be many. I have taught thee in the
way of wisdom; I have led thee in right paths. —Proverbs 4:10, 11
Read Proverbs 4:10-27

"Dari and Conrad were in a bad wreck! Conrad called home, but he wasn't really making sense. Apparently Conrad hit his head, and we don't know how badly Dari was hurt." Malvern's voice broke.

A group of boys had gone to the nearby ocean on an outing. They had planned to fish during the night. Now they were on the way home. Conrad, a friend three years Dari's senior, had been driving with his cruise control set, and both boys had fallen asleep. The truck had veered off the road and hit a culvert. The direct impact had wreaked havoc on the little Nissan pickup, smashing the cab so badly that we could hardly visualize anyone coming out of it alive.

But they did. Both boys were wearing their seatbelts. When sixteen-year-old Dari came to, he was hanging upside down in the truck. His chest felt crushed, and the bone above his left wrist was protruding several inches through the skin. *Where's Conrad and what's this white powdery stuff in my eyes and hair? Must be from the air bag.*

About then a bystander mistook the powder for smoke and started attacking the windshield with a hatchet.

"Stop that!" Dari yelled. "Glass is falling all over me! Could you please help me out of this seatbelt instead?" The tightness on his chest was unbearable! A knife appeared through the broken window, followed by a hand and a friendly, intense face.

"Here, let me cut that seatbelt." After a bit of sawing and hacking, the belt gave, and down Dari crashed with a new wave of pain engulfing him. The helping hands grabbed his broken arm and gave a mighty tug.

"Stop!" Dari cried out in pain. "I'll get it." Grimly, he worked himself to the window. He jammed his broken arm in the dirt and grass outside the overturned truck to help give leverage and dragged himself out to the sunlight. Curious spectators gathered, sirens filled the air, and fire trucks and ambulances arrived.

Conrad sauntered toward him. "You okay? I called Dad and he told your dad. The ambulance will be taking us to the hospital, I guess."

When Malvern arrived at the hospital, Darian was unavailable. "Your son is seriously injured, although he is conscious and has been since his arrival. His arm is broken and will need immediate surgery. But first they are checking for internal injuries to his vital organs, as he keeps complaining of pain in his chest."

When Malvern and Darian's brothers were able to see him, he was in a great deal of pain. Malvern called and told me, "I'll just plan on staying in here tonight. Dari's really hurting. The surgery was extensive in his arm and wrist, and he's rather handicapped with just one arm to use. Also, even though they can't really find any major internal damage, he's so sore across his back and chest that

Malvern and sons

moving around at all really gets him. The boys will come home and one of them can bring you and the girls in tomorrow."

Malvern stayed at the hospital with Dari until he was released three days later. Each time Malvern talked of coming home, our big independent son begged him to stay. We offered one of his brothers, but Dari just wanted Dad. And as Dad ministered to his needs, the bond between them grew.

Two years later, the tables were turned. Malvern was in an accident resulting in a broken pelvis and crushed hip socket. Now it was Darian and his brothers who lifted Malvern from the wheelchair to the bed and in and out of vehicles during the two months he was not to put any weight on his legs. When he was able to start walking again, they walked beside him, supporting him in case he fell. And the bond grew.

Danger, disrespect, failure, and frustration have at times driven us to our knees in behalf of our sons, fasting together, praying with them and for them . . . out loud together, talking, sharing struggles. These things are not new. Countless other Christian parents do the same. It helps tie the heartstrings securely from child to parent as we yearn over our children.

One night at a youth gathering each young person was asked to name someone he appreciated and describe one attribute of that person. Names were given, along with attributes such as kindness and gentleness. We were told that when Dari's turn came, he said, "I'd like to say 'my parents,' and one thing I especially appreciate about them is how, no matter what, they don't give up on me." For Dari to say this in front of his peers at that time was very encouraging to us. It is not wasted, this love and effort we put into our children.

Thought for the Day

Let us do our best to tie the cords of love from our hearts to our children's and pray that they will feel the depth of our love.

Angel-Leah's Life Book

Carla Raley

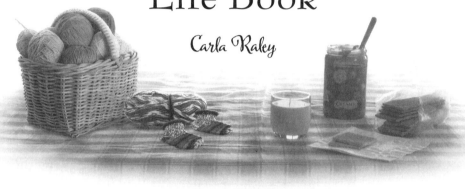

[The LORD] set my feet upon a rock, and established my goings.
And he hath put a new song in my mouth. —Psalm 40:2, 3

Read Psalm 40:1–11

Angel-Leah and I sat together on our couch looking at her life book. The longer she looked at the pictures of her birth family, the more she cried. With great, gulping, body-shaking sobs, she cried, "I want my mommy! I want my mommy!"

I didn't try to stop her. I just let her get it out. "Why couldn't I stay with someone I know?" she cried. She pointed to this aunt and that aunt. "Why couldn't I live with her?" Suddenly, seeing her birth mother's picture, she cried, "I forgot to say bye! Why didn't you remind me to say bye?"

"You did say bye, Angel-Leah. You said bye, then you blew kisses to her." That made her feel a little better, yet she continued to weep. Finally I put the photo album away and prepared her for bed. I dressed her in pajamas, and then I sat beside her while she sobbed. I explained more than I thought a four-year-old could understand. I told her that someday when she was bigger, she would likely see her mommy again. She asked how long that was—a few weeks? "No," I said. "A lot of years, until you are big like Max."

"That's too long!" she cried.

How could I explain hard facts that could not be changed? A judge had determined her safety and placement. I told her, "As soon as the adoption is final, we will write letters to your grandma and mommy. We can send pictures too."

That was good, but not enough. I read her a book and got her under the covers, and she started to cry again. I said, "Why don't you go to sleep and dream about being with Mommy?"

She said, "I don't want to dream it if it isn't real!" So I turned off the light, lay down beside her on the bed, and said I would sleep with her for awhile. Lying beside her, I prayed for wisdom. I felt so utterly helpless in the face of her grief.

Angel-Leah

I remembered the day she first came to us. We were getting ready for bed when we got the call about a two-and-a-half-year-old girl. An hour later, Angel-Leah came into our lives.

She was a precocious child, very verbal. The first thing she said to me was, "I'm wet, and you need to change me."

Surprised, I responded, "I think I can probably handle that."

She went to bed easily that night, and the next day she shopped happily with us at the flea market our small town has twice a year.

Soon, however, she realized no one seemed to be coming to pick her up. She walked around saying, "My nanny's coming to get me." Her eyes brimmed with tears and her lips trembled.

She was a much-loved child, but had been put in a very dangerous situation by her birth mother, which made her a ward of the state. Her biological family was upset over this situation, and many of them attended Child Protective Services meetings and court hearings regarding her case. I learned to know the family well over the next year. I did all I could to encourage them, and they often expressed appreciation for her good care.

As the final court hearing approached, it was apparent the birth parents would not get their little girl back. The goal changed from family reunification to unrelated adoption. We expressed our desire to adopt her, and the family was relieved that she would not be moved again to strangers.

In April of 2007, Angel-Leah's parents' rights were terminated, and a final visit with her birth family was planned. I explained to three-year-old Angel-Leah what was happening. She understood as well as a smart little girl can understand. When I went to pick her up after the visit, her mother gave her a final hug. Fighting tears, she walked backward out the door, her eyes cemented on the little girl's face. Angel-Leah blew kisses and giggled. It was very sad.

Months later, Angel-Leah told me, "I'm afraid it's all going to wash away!"

"You mean you're afraid you're going to forget everyone?" I said. She said yes. I promised her I would not let that happen. We went to Wal-Mart and bought a pretty pink photo album. I gathered all the pictures we had of her birth family, and we chronicled her life from the day she came to live with us until the present time. We had fun putting it together. Once it was done, I told her she could get it out every Sunday and look at it for a while, hoping that would keep her from becoming too obsessed with it. All the research I had done on adoption suggested having some kind of "life book." It was supposed to help with the process of grieving the loss of the first family, something that is very important for adoptees to do.

Still, I worried. Angel-Leah told me often that she didn't love me, that she only loved her birth mother. I assured her that it was okay for her to love her birth mother, but I hoped that someday she would love me too.

"Mommy," she would say, "when I grow up, I'm going back to my other mommy, and I'm never coming to see you again."

"That would make me very sad," I told her. "I love you and would miss you. Just think, if you never come back to visit, you will never see Luke again, or Mary Susannah, or the grandchildren."

She paused. Then she straightened her shoulders, saying, "I'm sure I'll never visit you again."

I said I was sorry to hear that, and let it go.

Then she came down with a raging ear infection which made her very miserable. I gave her medicine and I told her I would rock her until it helped and she felt better. We rocked in my trusty rocking chair until she fell asleep. I gently laid her in her bed. When she awakened several hours later, she found me and crawled into my lap.

After a minute she said, "Mommy? I guess I really do love you and my other mommy the same."

"I'm glad to hear that, Angel-Leah. I love you too," I answered.

After a really fun week full of visits from the grandchildren, she came to me and said, "Maybe when I grow up I *will* come back and visit you. Maybe I will even just stay here and not go live with my other mommy."

I reached down to hug her. "I'll be very happy with either of those decisions," I assured her. I felt like we had won a battle together.

Angel-Leah and Carla

Thought for the Day

Foster care/adoption is not all kittens and rainbows and butterflies, but hard work on the part of all. It's about great loss and great gain. It's about taking heartache and making a family. It's about taking the loss of first best (an intact first family) and turning it around to a new beginning, which is a specialty of God's!

The Same

Name Withheld

Neither is there respect of persons with him. —Ephesians 6:9
Give . . . that which is just and equal. —Colossians 4:1
He fashioneth their hearts alike. —Psalm 33:15
Read Psalm 33

"Don't look for problems," counseled an older adoptive father. "Just love the adopted child and train him or her the same as you would any other child."

We have adopted children in our family. Among our biological children are twins. When the twins were born, I was amazed to find out there were books, magazines, and clubs available just for parents of twins. *Is parenting twins really so different?* I wondered. When the twins were babies, I read some of the books and enjoyed the tips. As the twins grew, I began more and more to forget they were twins.

Twins do face some special issues. People aren't sure what your name is; you have to share more; and should you dress alike? Yet if being twins isn't constantly pointed out, it's just not much of a problem.

If a problem comes up that I think may be a twin issue, I may read up on twins again or talk to another mother of twins. Otherwise, they're just brothers who happen to be the same age.

Thinking about the twin issue has helped me clear my thinking about adoptive issues. Adopted children face thoughts and feelings none of the rest of us do, and at times we may need to hunt for different answers, but ultimately we love them and teach them and train them just the same as the rest of our children. In day-to-day living we forget they are adopted.

Thought for the Day

Lord, please help me love all of our
children the same today.
Help each child to know I love him
for who he is as an individual.

Look Alike

Anita King

He that is of a merry heart hath a continual feast. —Proverbs 15:15
Read Proverbs 15

*E*ven with our birth children, I never heard that our children looked like me. Two of them look just like their father, and the other looks just like my Grandfather Robison, whom I favor not at all. I was content with that. I didn't need a mini-me.

When our adopted children arrived, they were so cute that they got lots of comments on their looks, most of which they would have been better off not hearing! We also heard lots of comments about who each one favored. But I knew if my birth children didn't resemble me in looks, certainly neither would my children who were of a different race!

One day when we were traveling, we were seated around a large table at a restaurant when I noticed a man observing us closely. I was a bit embarrassed. Three in high chairs at one time can be a bit hectic. I wondered what this man was thinking. He came to our table before leaving and complimented us on our family. He thanked us for praying together and for our patience with the children. He took our bill and paid it with the comment that he was very blessed by our family that day. I, who am seldom speechless, was.

He shook our hands and then said to me, "They look like you!" Startled, I protested that he had to be stretching to see any resemblance. Turning to leave, he said, "No, Mom, they have your smile!"

So if ever you secretly wish your children would look a little like you, remember you can give them your smile! I am still convinced this man was an angel sent from God to give my wobbly confidence as an adoptive mother a bit of a boost.

King children, 2007

Thought for the Day

When you feel you have nothing left to give,
you can still give them your smile!

Crumbling Walls

Emily Martin

It is better to go to the house of mourning, than to go to the house of feasting:
for that is the end of all men; and the living will lay it to his heart.
Sorrow is better than laughter: for by the sadness of the countenance
the heart is made better. —Ecclesiastes 7:2, 3
Read Ecclesiastes 7:1-14

"A new special dress? I'm so happy for you! Just think, a baby of your own at last!" Heads turned as the sister in the bench in front of me beamed upon me.

I could feel my cheeks glowing, and my smile felt as if it would consume my whole face. I had waited years to wear a maternity dress. Finally I could wear one. It seemed to shout to anyone caring to notice, "A baby is on the way. Soon there will be a brand-new baby for this happy lady!"

"Do you have morning sickness? Have you felt movement? Can you sleep nights? What does the doctor say about . . . ?" At last I could answer the questions and enter into these womanly conversations in a way I never had been able to before. Of course I enjoyed talking about my baby. It seemed I thought about it all the time, and with each morning wave of nausea I reminded myself, "But just think . . . we will really have a baby! It is surely worth feeling sick." As movement began I was so very excited that I wanted to talk about it and share my joy.

But there was a damper on my happiness, for I had some very close friends who, like me, were mothers of adopted children, but had never experienced what I was experiencing now. When others gushed over me, especially when they stressed how wonderful a baby of our own would be, I ached for my friends. I could see the hurt flash across their faces as they turned and smiled bravely. All too well I knew the anguish they were feeling. And now it was as if I, too, thought that somehow their babies were not quite as special as one that might have been born to them. Somehow, I felt an invisible wall rising between us to block the sweet friendship we had shared. Alone at home, I cried. I longed for and missed the closeness we had felt as we had filled out adoption papers together and received our first children around the same time. We knew that adoption and foster care worked. I couldn't imagine loving a baby born to us any more than the three little boys we had already. I didn't expect to love this new baby more. But oh, I loved him already! And my very happiness had helped create the wall.

Then my baby was born prematurely and died. Even in our great anguish, I thanked God that if He was going to take one of my babies, it was the new baby and not my darling eighteen-month-old adopted son. The attachment we had to Darian was equal to the attachment for my birth child and more . . . for we had loved him longer.

As I lay in the hospital room recovering, I received a very special phone call. I could hardly understand the words at first, for the voice was choked with tears as my dear friend confessed her struggles and attitudes. "It seemed everyone kept acting like you had attained. I felt like that was saying I hadn't. But . . . oh, I never meant for you to lose your baby!" Her anguished sobs made it impossible for her to talk further. I cried with her and assured her that it wasn't her fault that our baby had died, and that I hadn't meant to act like I had attained. I assured her that I understood, and was very glad for the strain to be gone from between us.

A few days later another friend came to visit, and we freely shared the feelings she had struggled with. Tears washed away the frosty politeness that had grown between us. In losing my baby, the wall between my friends and me crumbled and disappeared.

In time God blessed us with seven more babies by birth. Praise the Lord, the wall has never been rebuilt. My friends are genuinely happy for me . . . just as I delight in the babies they have added to their families through adoption. And I can tell them from experience what they were quite sure they already knew: The joy I feel as I hug my newborn baby to myself is the very same delight and ecstasy and awe that I felt as I met each of my adopted children for the first time. When the sense of ownership kicks in, that is what sets this baby or child apart from any other child in the world. Imperfections become unimportant. We see our child through eyes of love and wonderment. *"O God, she is so unique, so amazing, so special! How can it be? Is she really ours?"*

Thought for the Day

The darkest clouds have silver linings.

Real Parents

Anita King

Then spake the woman whose the living child was unto the king, for her
bowels yearned upon her son, and she said, O my lord,
give her the living child, and in no wise slay it. But the other said,
Let it be neither mine nor thine, but divide it. —1 Kings 3:26
Read 1 Kings 3

ur family consists of adopted, biological, and interracial children. It has always been important that we convey that all of us are "real," no matter how many times people inquire if they are our real children, or if any of the children are real brothers and sisters.

One of our children's favorite things for us to do is to sit together in the evenings while I read out loud. One of their favorite books was *Zachary's New Family*. It has been quite a few years since I have read it. As I remember, Zachary was placed in a new home. The parents were ducks. He was a cat. He enjoyed life with his family, but he looked different and couldn't understand how he could possibly be loved, because he was so different. He decided to run away, and it made the family very sad. Someone convinced him to return home to them, and once again they were a real family.

This storybook was a springboard for many discussions. Why did our children have skin tones different from ours? Why did they look different from us? I felt that the children had a good understanding. We didn't want to focus on color and shape, but on hearts.

One evening little Julie was snuggled by my side. When the story was finished, I looked down at her big brown tear-filled eyes. She snuggled closer and said, "I am so glad that you are my real mother!"

My first thought was, *After three years I thought she would have understood. Does Julie think she was born to me?* Then suddenly my heart was overwhelmed with the message—*I AM her real mother! Maybe I am not her mother by birth, but the love I feel is just as deep and abiding as if she were born of my flesh.* REALLY!

Thought for the Day

I am their real mother!

Doubts

Jewel Carter

*I can do all things through Christ which
strengtheneth me. —Philippians 4:13*
Read Colossians 3:12-17

After more than three years of marriage and the adoption of twin boys, here I was, expecting a baby! Feelings of joy and delight conflicted with emotions of fear and apprehension. I wanted a baby, but we had just come home from a year and a half in a foreign country (See "Our Babies" and "Who Loves the Children?"). We were all in the process of adjusting to life in the U.S., and I felt very unprepared to deal with a pregnancy.

I wanted to have a biological child—someday. But right now it looked overwhelming. Besides, I had dreamed and thought adoption for so long that it was hard to change my thinking to something different. My husband and I felt strongly that adoption was not just second best. We adopted because it was something we wanted to do and had dreamed of doing. Infertility had only made it come sooner than we had expected, and I felt blessed to be an adoptive mother. I was happy about the coming baby, but somehow I felt guilty. I felt I was in some way cheating my boys.

I had heard so much about partiality. *What if I suddenly stopped loving my boys and loved my biological child instead? Or what if I loved my boys and not the coming baby?* She couldn't help it that she was born to us, any more than the twins could help that they were adopted.

I painted, in my mind, a glowing picture of a happily blended family where our adopted and biological children were very close. *But what if I wasn't able to make the realities of family life meet my lofty ideals?*

I knew my fears were growing more out of proportion by the day. A talk with my practical husband and a visit with a wise friend helped immensely to put things back into perspective.

My husband was unconcerned about loving one child more than the next. "God has given us each one of our children," he maintained, "and God will give us love enough to go around." We would trust God to help us one day at a time and not carry with us a fear of failure before we had even tried!

My friend advised me, "Expect your children to get along, but don't expect your adopted children to be as close to your biological children as they may be to each other. Your adopted children have had experiences that your biological children may have a hard time understanding. Let your children develop their own relationships. If they are close, that's wonderful! But don't try to force a cozy relationship they do not feel."

Brady, Lindsay, Brett

I began to realize it was not about what I could do personally, but what I allowed God to do through me in our home. Together, my husband and I can create an atmosphere of love and impartiality. We can guide our children's relationships, but we cannot force them to love and understand each other.

And now, almost a year after our daughter's birth, it is delightful to watch our children's relationship blossom. I love to see our daughter run up to her big brothers and give them a hug. It's nice to see the way they include her in their play, even though she messes things up for them. And I witness their delight in seeing each other again in the morning when they awake, or after they've been apart for a while. Someday it may be different. But we'll enjoy the present, and leave the future to God!

Thought for the Day

Don't try to hold God's hand. Let Him hold yours.
Let Him do the holding and you do the trusting.

—Hammer William Webb-Peploe

Partiality?
God Forbid!

Kathy Rohrer

My brethren, have not the faith of our Lord Jesus Christ,
the Lord of glory, with respect of persons. —James 2:1
Read James 2:1-10

When our foster daughter Meaghan came up for adoption, we were concerned about the possibility that it would be harder to feel love for the adopted child than our biological children. It was hard for me to admit that I might in some way be partial to a child simply because he or she was not born to us. But if we were going to take this on, we wanted to be sure that it would not be that way.

During the time we were considering adopting Meaghan, my husband Charles asked me, "Will we treat Meaghan the same way we do our biological children?" Charlie was our biological baby, and Missy was well on the way.

I answered, "Of course we will treat them the same."

Looking back over the past ten years since the adoption, I admit we did not always feel the same toward Meaghan as we did toward our biological children. She was a drug and alcohol baby and had been exposed to domestic violence. The effects of her abuse and neglect were clearly visible and contrasted with babies born and raised in a secure environment. We struggled to accept this, but as time went on, we found that feelings do not equal love. Love is a choice. And when we choose to love and choose to care, feelings are not far behind. Also we found that due to varying personalities and idiosyncrasies, it is not always easy to have "lovey" feelings toward our biological children, either. Again, love is a choice—a long-term commitment.

We all face temptations that are common to man, but God is able to deliver us. One of the ways we found help when we struggled with lack of love or partial feelings, was to openly admit it to others. This has been a blessing, and we can say confidently that we love all our children dearly.

God has given us adoptive parents a special charge. These precious souls, whom He has placed in our care, trust us for love and guidance. Let's be impartial and give them what they deserve.

Remember: We have been adopted into God's family, and He shows no partiality. God forbid that we do otherwise!

Thought for the Day

God doesn't call qualified adoptive parents;
He qualifies the called!

Bonding Through Love

Marian Reinford

For God hath not given us the spirit of fear; but of power,
and of love, and of a sound mind. —2 Timothy 1:7
Read 2 Timothy 2:3-15

Roger loved Aunt Becky. She lived next door, and his greatest delight, when his mother gave him permission, was to go and help her for an hour or two. She always seemed to have chores to do before she was free to play with him. But even the dishes were fun to do as Aunt Becky chatted about all the things they'd do and the fun they'd have once the work was done.

Running out to the old disabled Toyota in the backyard, they jumped in. Eagerly Roger rolled down his window and clicked his seatbelt. "Where are we going today, Aunt Becky?"

Grabbing the steering wheel, she smiled. "Let's see. Shall we go to the mountains where we can see elk, mule deer, and lots of other wild animals? We can see the fish swimming in the clear blue lakes and make snowballs high in the mountains!"

For the next hour Roger was in a state of bliss as he listened to one interesting story after another from this special aunt.

Aunt Becky also took the fears out of his early days of school. She was always ready to listen to Roger's joys and frustrations as he adjusted to his classmates and the discipline of school.

Years later when Roger was in his early teens, he had three buddies he considered his best friends. Their loyalty to him and to each other made him feel warm and included. The hours they spent together fishing, playing ball, and camping were multiplied since they were all within walking distance of each other. Sometimes they even enjoyed walking to the corner grocery store on their way home from school. Each week Roger was allowed to buy a treat for one dollar if he earned one hundred percent on his spelling test.

The newest owner of the store was Mr. Gazzari. He was still a little skeptical of these different, Bible-believing-and-practicing Mennonites. He'd watch the boys with a slight scowl as they made their choices for the day. The boys thought he was relieved when they left.

One hot sunny day in May, Roger yearned for a popsicle to cool off. His friends each bought one, but he had missed a word on his spelling test. As they were turning to go, he reached into the freezer and slipped one into his pocket.

Walking toward home, he pulled it out and quietly ate it. It didn't even taste good, especially after he saw his buddies lift their eyebrows to each other.

Sunday morning after the last amen, Brother Samuel announced that he had something he'd like to talk to the congregation about. His face was burdened and sad as he looked over the hushed, expectant crowd.

"Last evening I stopped at Mr. Gazzari's store on my way home for some ice cream. He was very upset and angry. He told me how he has watched the people from our church and wondered if we were as good as we talked, but now he knows the truth. One of our boys stole something from his store, and he never wants to see another Mennonite walk through his door again—not unless that boy comes back, apologizes, and pays for it. He said I should put the ice cream back and get out of his store. Brethren, where do we go from here? What shall we do?"

You could have heard a pin drop! Some of the boys flushed and cleared their throats. After a pause, one of the fathers spoke up, "Well I guess we fathers have some homework to do. Each of us with boys needs to have a heart-to-heart talk with his sons."

Brother Samuel nodded. "I think that sounds like a good idea. The brethren will meet Wednesday night after prayer meeting to decide anything further."

After church was over, Roger and his buddies found a quiet spot to discuss their new problem. "We don't want to tell on you, but we really feel bad that you did what you did. You need to tell," said Todd.

"And remember, we can't lie if we're asked outright if we know anything about it," Chuck added.

Roger felt a big lump in his throat. His face and ears felt hot. He really didn't want his friends to lie for him, did he? He couldn't talk, so he nodded and slowly started walking over to Dad's car. He had never felt this miserable and wretched since years ago before he was adopted. He still remembered the lonely, aching hurt he used to feel in his heart those first years of his life.

Aunt Becky came by the car and chatted a few minutes. She seemed to be looking at him searchingly as she talked, and her farewell was concluded with, "I'll be praying for you!"

Why did she say that? Roger felt hot all over again.

When Dad and Mom questioned Roger that afternoon, he declared his innocence. Dad seemed a little uncertain about what to say next, but he didn't press the point. "To feel good about ourselves and be at peace with God, we must always be honest, even if it's hard," he added.

Tuesday evening Aunt Becky came over to play croquet. Roger loved playing outdoor games, especially when Aunt Becky came. Tonight, though, Roger had a hard time getting into the game. The last several nights he'd had trouble sleeping, and nothing seemed to be going right.

Halfway through the game, Aunt Becky, seeing Roger's lack of interest said, "It's so warm today; would you rather just sit and talk?"

Roger nodded. Sitting in the grass under their favorite maple, Aunt Becky looked out over the fields, then into Roger's eyes.

"Roger, you seem unhappy these last few days; what's the matter?"

Roger just looked at her miserably, not saying a word.

"Do you know anything about what was taken in Mr. Gazzari's store?"

Roger dropped his head and started pulling up little blades of grass. All was silent. Aunt Becky breathed a prayer. She could sense Roger struggling. Was he angry or sad? Guilty, or offended to be a suspect?

Carefully, she probed, "Do you remember how unhappy you were when you came here to live?"

Roger nodded cautiously.

"Your eyes have the same look now as they did then—so full of pain! What is hurting you?"

Studying the grass, he shrugged his shoulders.

Aunt Becky noticed tears gathering in his eyes. "I love you so much, Roger. Ever since you became a part of our family, you've been special to me," she said, gently touching his arm. He quickly drew away, something he had never done before.

"Please, Roger, if whoever took something doesn't own up to it, none of us can go to Mr. Gazzari's store again!"

"Even if I did say I did it, can you imagine what people would say if they found out it was me?" Roger shot back, his voice rising. "Can you imagine how Dad and Mom would feel after all they did for me?" His face was red and the tears were coming faster. "There's no way I could say I did it. I can just see the look on Sister Jane's face and everybody else at school! Are you crazy?" Roger threw himself facedown on the grass.

Waiting until his sobs subsided, Aunt Becky touched his shoulder. "Please, Roger!"

Flinging off her hand, he sat up abruptly. "I said I can't, and I mean that. I can't; I can't!"

Aunt Becky's heart fell when she saw the intensity of his feelings. *Please, Lord, help me!* she breathed.

"Roger, people admire others who are honest, even if it hurts to be so. Stealing is wrong, but it's more wrong to add lies to it."

"But I can't. Nobody will ever trust me again; they'll say it's just because I'm adopted, and it's just because Dad and Mom aren't good parents. Maybe even my buddies won't be allowed to be my friends anymore. Why don't you understand me and see why I can't tell?"

"I do understand you, Roger; I know you're full of pain, anger, and fear. It will be a slow climb to build up your reputation again, but God will help you. Think of the testimony of the church with Mr. Gazzari and the community folks. Think of having your own heart clean before God."

"I can't do it!" stated Roger, emphatically shaking his head.

"Think of the weight it will lift off your parents' shoulders to see your honesty."

"I just can't," he mumbled, biting his fingernail.

After a long pause, breathing another tearful prayer, Aunt Becky looked lovingly at her nephew. "Roger," she said quietly, "look at me." As their eyes met, she begged, "Roger, I love you so much. Will you admit it for me? If I go with you?"

He studied her eyes for a moment. Dropping his eyes, he answered, "I did it. I stole the popsicle. I lied. Oh, Aunt Becky, you've always been there for me, and if this means so much to you and you'll help me make it right, I'll do it! I really do want to live right and to please God."

"I will help you, and God will help us both!" Aunt Becky rejoiced, tears of joy on her cheeks.

Thought for the Day

Bonding puts down roots of trust and love that
we can draw strength from during a crisis.

Bonding Through Birth

Marian Reinford

Now unto him that is able to do exceeding abundantly above all that we ask
or think, according to the power that worketh in us. —Ephesians 3:20

Read Psalm 23

*R*ing—*ring*—*ring*. The phone rang insistently as our sleep-
beclouded minds tried to awaken early Sunday morning,
December 31, 2006.

"Hello, Mom?" Excitement rang in our daughter Melissa's voice. "What
are your plans for today? I think I'm in labor."

Instantly my mind cleared. *Melissa's baby—our new grandchild—is due*
to be born soon. Is today the big day?

Our oldest son with his wife and eight children were visiting from one
thousand miles away, and we were all planning to go visit my sister's family
at a newly-planted church three hours away. Now what should we do?

"The others here are planning to go to Cedar Fork for the day, but I can
stay home. I'll just send my food along, and Aunt Becky will make out fine
for dinner."

"Oh, Mom, I wouldn't want you to miss out! Maybe it's just another
false alarm," Melissa stated bravely.

"But if it's not, I want to be here for you. You're still considering a home
birth?"

"Yes."

"Let me talk with Dad and the others. We'll see what we can make out."

Although Melissa had had her three previous babies in the hospital, the decision to have a home birth for their fourth baby had come one step at a time for Melissa and Delbert. A few days earlier, Delbert and I had sat around Melissa's bed in the hospital as the doctor tried inducing labor for three hours. As the drug wore off, the painful contractions stopped, and we all looked helplessly at each other.

"I'm not having this baby in the hospital," declared Melissa with finality. "I really think I would be able to relax better having the baby at Mom's house with her help, anyway."

Delbert looked a little concerned. "Remember, it takes almost two hours to come to this hospital, and this is the third time we've come. It's a long ride to come back."

"But I'm not coming back to have this baby, so we may as well go home. The baby's not ready, and we're not going to force the birth." Melissa got out of bed and started dressing. "Mom will help us when the baby's ready to be born, and we'll just wait until it is ready."

She looked at me entreatingly. "Won't you, Mom?"

I looked at Delbert, then back to Melissa. "You will birth your baby best wherever you're the most comfortable and relaxed. God will be with us wherever your baby is born."

"Okay, I'll go tell the doctor our decision and we'll go home," Delbert agreed. I admired the way he supported her.

On the two-hour drive home we shared together the pros and cons of home birth, possible emergencies, and so on. We all agreed to pray about it. I had helped at many births, but when it came to helping my daughters, sisters, and nieces, there was something more precious and special about it—also more weighty.

After praying about this birth, I sensed a peace about it. I felt ready to support and help Melissa in every way I could, looking to God to make this a wonderful experience and memory.

Debi, Melissa's twenty-year-old sister, was eager to stay and help take care of our handicapped daughter Dawn and Melissa's other children during the birth. Our visitors and the rest of the family left early for church and Debi, Dawn, and I left for Delbert's house.

We found three bouncing children with eager shining eyes awaiting our arrival. They bubbled about coming to Grammy's house where Mommy was going to get the new baby.

We soon realized it would be wise to pack up right away and head for "Grammy's house," twenty minutes away, for the birth.

At my house, Debi fed the children breakfast while we prepared the birthing room. Delbert and I read the directions for the emergency equipment, refreshing our minds so we'd know what to do if the need arose.

About an hour later, Delbert read stories to the children, snuggling together on the bed as Melissa quietly labored. I'll always treasure that peaceful, quiet scene of a loving family surrounding their mother.

Smiling up at me, Melissa remarked, "I'm so glad to be here with the children. They are so much happier and more contented this way."

Later, I told them I was going to my bedroom to pray about the birth. I felt a need for wisdom, and safety for mother, father, baby, and midwife. Debi took the children to the kitchen, and the young couple took quiet time out to pray together. We came back together, eager and strengthened for the birth.

Melissa remembers how she felt so loved and supported with no pressure to perform. Working together for one common cause and trusting God to help us in every way brought a treasured bond between us.

Soon Melissa was holding a beautiful, healthy baby girl. I smiled as she gazed into her daughter's large lovely eyes and crooned to her, telling her how much she loved her. Melissa was bonding to her baby, and the baby was basking in her love! I never tire of experiencing those magical moments directly after birth. But how extra special this was—witnessing my daughter bonding with *her* daughter! New love flooded over me for my daughter. Since Melissa had joined our family through adoption at four years old (See "Sisters, a Gift From God") we had missed this part of her life. Now, somehow, in watching her bond to her children, it was almost like God was giving us a special gift, a part we had missed.

Opening the bedroom door, a very pleased father invited the baby's siblings and Aunt Debi to gather around and welcome the newcomer. I tucked away treasured memories in my heart to enjoy again and again—memories of beaming smiles and everyone taking turns cuddling Shaina Marie.

Delbert and Melissa's children

Melissa had experienced some times of perplexing sickness with this pregnancy, which caused concerns for both baby and mother. As a family, we have shared the care of our handicapped daughter, Dawn, for over thirty years. It is ever before us that not all births and newborns turn out as we hope. This healthy, bouncy baby was a real answer to prayer and another confirmation of how God loves and cares.

We love each of our grandchildren dearly, and we find that the love we share with our children and grandchildren comes around full circle and blesses us.

Thought for the Day

One of life's greatest treasures
is the love that draws our hearts together.

Help to Honesty

Name Withheld

The way of a fool is right in his own eyes: but he that hearkeneth
unto counsel is wise. Lying lips are abomination to the LORD:
but they that deal truly are his delight. —*Proverbs 12:15, 22*
Read Proverbs 12

One of our boys was having a real struggle with being honest. It was worse after he had been in contact with his birth family for a time, where lying was a way of life. Darvin had given his heart to the Lord and wanted to do what was right, but time and again when caught in a difficult situation, he lied. He was becoming more and more miserable, and we were unable to trust him.

One day we sat down and pleaded with him to be open with us. We wanted to help him clear his slate. I wrote things down as he admitted to them. Yes, he had run into the trailer with the lawn mower. He had hit it, not *almost* hit it like he had claimed, and that was probably why it had a hole in the radiator. He had forgotten to add water to the mower, which may have been why it blew up. And he had been mowing in high gear instead of low, as he had earlier insisted. He had also taken his brother's stack of quarters, and he had lied before the whole family when he had flatly denied knowing anything about it.

There was more to the list. And yes, he was sorry for all of it, and he was willing to do whatever we thought best to clear it up.

We commended Darvin for being honest and open with us. We reminded him of the four steps to make things right when we have done wrong. 1) Admit it. 2) Apologize. 3) Take your punishment like a man. 4) Try hard to fix it. He had heard these four steps often before. We talked with him quite a while to decide on appropriate punishments and how he could help fix things.

That evening in devotions each of the children found verses relating to honesty and took turns sharing them and explaining their meaning. Then Darvin openly confessed his failure. He checked the list and made sure each lie was covered. He said he planned to pay back double what he had taken, and he would help pay for the damaged lawn mower. We all discussed what honesty is about, how God looks at it, how it feels not to be trusted, and also how it feels to not be able to trust someone you love. Then we prayed together.

It was a growing experience for everyone. Nobody thought less of Darvin for having admitted his failings. His winning smile appeared again—a welcome sight to all of us. Contentment and peace reigned.

Two weeks later, we ran into the same problem again. Twice Darvin took something and lied about it. We approached him privately. It took a great deal of coaxing until he finally admitted it. When we suggested he acknowledge his failure to the family again, he rebelled. He couldn't see how his dishonesty had anything to do with anybody else. He had taken care of it with the ones involved and felt that was enough.

We asked him to confess his failure to the family anyway, and he did so grudgingly. We talked about it for a while, then asked if each of the children would be willing to share with Darvin how it looks to them and say something to encourage him.

Darla: "Darvin, you know it's not the pack of peppermints that mattered to me. What mattered was that not only did you steal, but you lied to me as well. You told me that you wouldn't think of taking something from me since I had been your best big sister and all. Then for you to turn around and lie about it and not admit it until you had to—that hurts. I don't want you to be that kind of boy. I want to be able to trust you. Do you understand that?"

Russ: "It's like I read in Proverbs tonight. We need to hear instruction from our father. Dad and Mom want what's best for us. It's like they pointed out to you—when you do something wrong, if you come and confess it on your own, it's so much better. It wasn't the pocketknife you took that bothered me. If you had asked, I probably would have let you borrow it. But taking it without asking and then openly denying it is what bothered me."

Brad: "It's pretty tough having someone around you can't trust. I want to trust you, but if you keep lying, it makes it really hard."

Jenny: "I'll be praying for you so you can get victory over this problem."

Susie: "I know what it's like to take stuff and have to go back and make it right. I want to pray for you too that you can get over this problem."

Daryl: "I just keep thinking about how the Bible says, 'All liars will have their part in the lake of fire.' I know I don't want you to go there. I'll try to pray for you too so you can get victory over this."

This involvement of our other children made an impression that underlined what we were telling Darvin. They cared and wanted him to find victory. This caring and sharing gave Darvin courage to try again.

Editor's Note: While this article depicts one family's experience, it illustrates an approach to be employed only cautiously, if at all. Public humiliation can be devastating. Whether it yields repentance or rebellion may depend particularly on the brokenness of the parents.

Thought for the Day

Sometimes it helps to include other family members
to help solve a particular problem.

Ways to Show Love

Brookie Martin
a teen adoptee

The greatest of these is charity. —1 Corinthians 13:13

Read 1 Corinthians 13

Ways Parents Can Show Their Daughter They Love Her

1. Pray for her.
2. Give her a home.
3. Read the Bible together and pray together.
4. Provide a bed and food and clothes for her.
5. Sew dresses for her.
6. Make sure everyone obeys the rules.
7. Hug her.
8. Tell her how much they love her.
9. Do not yell at her.
10. When little, rock and hold her.
11. Teach her right from wrong.
12. Teach her to work.
13. When she disobeys, punish kindly.
14. Give her presents on special days.
15. Take time to talk about how she feels about things.

16. Try to keep the home a loving atmosphere where everyone is kind and loving to each other.
17. Tell her what you appreciate about her.
18. Take time to do things together.
19. If she is away, call and talk to her.

Brookie Martin
5 months

Ways a Daughter Can Show Her Parents She Loves Them

Brookie Martin
age 19

1. Pray for them.
2. Obey right away.
3. Talk respectfully to them.
4. Do not talk back.
5. Give them gifts just for love.
6. Do jobs extra well.
7. Help extra much when the work load is extra big.
8. Thank God for them.
9. Thank them for all the things they have done for her.
10. Make supper when Mom is tired, sick, or just because.
11. Do more than her share of the work.
12. Help make the home a happy place by not fighting with the other children.
13. Always speak respectfully about them when talking to others.
14. Be trustworthy by doing what they wish even when they aren't looking.
15. Share with them how she feels about things in her heart.
16. Tell them about her day.
17. Tell them she loves them.

18. Tell them what she appreciates about them.
19. If away from home, call home at least once if not two or three times a week and tell them how things are going and what she is doing.

Brookie, Shari, and Jill

Thought for the Day

Having a place to go is home; having someone to love is family; having both is a blessing.

—Donna Hedges

A Blue Pea

Name Witheld

I will praise thee; for I am fearfully and wonderfully made. —Psalm 139:14
When my father and my mother forsake me, then the LORD will take me up.
Teach me thy way, O LORD, and lead me in a plain path. —Psalm 27:10, 11
Read Psalm 27:1-5, 11, 14

"I wish I wasn't adopted!" Breanna declared.

"Me too!" her cousin Cindy added. "Why couldn't we be just like the rest of you? I hate all this emphasis on being adopted. I just want to be normal."

"You're not normal?" Ken asked with a grin.

"You know what I mean. I just want to be like everybody else."

"Me too," Breanna said. "So many times I feel like a blue pea in a pan full of green ones. It would be so neat to look like everybody else and to feel like I really belonged."

"But if you had been born here to Dad and Mom, you wouldn't even be you," Ken persisted. "Same way with Cindy. You would be some new creation. It took the combination of your biological parents to make the unique person who is you. So no matter where you were, you would still be you. To not be adopted wouldn't prove anything except that you would be somewhere else instead of here."

Ken smiled teasingly across the dining room table. "Anyway, Cindy makes just as good a cousin whether she's adopted or not, and what would life be like here without Breanna? I can't imagine. Nobody to milk the cow or feed the pigs or catch the mice for Mom! My other sisters are too sissy. I for one am glad you're adopted." Turning toward his sisters, he asked, "How about the rest of you?"

"Of course we're glad," Gail and Kari assured him.

"I don't even think about you being adopted," Kari added sincerely. "To me you belong here as much as the rest of us. I like adoption. I want to adopt several children myself when I grow up."

"Of course you like adoption," Breanna retorted. "But since you're not adopted, you don't know how it feels! Maybe if you were, you wouldn't think it was so great!"

"I guess I don't know how it feels," Kari admitted. "I just think of all those little children out there in pitiful situations and want to gather them in somehow. Especially if I couldn't have children right away . . . I'm sure I would want to adopt right off or do foster care like Cindy. You would too, Breanna, the way you love babies!"

"Yeah, I know I would," Breanna admitted. "I can hardly stand to think about the children out there. I get so frustrated that there's nothing I can do."

Quietly she pushed her peas around on her plate. *A blue pea? There really aren't any blue ones.* She toyed with her fork as her thoughts raced on.

If I was born to Dad and Mom, then I wouldn't be me! I never thought of that before! If I was their biological child, I would be someone else! I mean, if they had another biological daughter, it would be someone else. Not me. I would never have been at all if my birth mother had not conceived me. God used my biological parents to form me. It is the only way I could be me. God created me. I don't want to just not be. It was a new realization, and thoughts chugged endlessly through Breanna's brain.

Where would I be? Who would I be if I had not been adopted? Breanna thought about what little she knew of her birth parents. It wasn't very good. *What would my life be like if I wasn't here? I would not be in a safe, secure home. Mom and Dad wouldn't be my parents. Ken wouldn't be my brother. Would I even have little sisters? I wouldn't be going to the school I love.*

My friends . . . I wouldn't have my friends. I very likely would not even be a Christian. Would I know anything about God and Heaven and Hell? I would likely be living a life of sin, and in eternity . . . eternity lasts forever . . . what then?

Breanna looked up to see Cindy watching her face. "How about it, Bree?" she asked. "Being adopted isn't so great sometimes, I agree . . . particularly when we're feeling like blue peas. But not being adopted . . . Can you even imagine how that would be?"

Thought for the Day

We have all been lovingly created by a God who desires an intimate relationship with us. He delights in taking what others may consider ugly or a mistake and turning the whole situation into a beautiful blessing to those who choose to love Him and serve Him.

PART 3

Wounded Hearts

Binding Up the Wounds

"I felt the forces of good and evil in conflict over the soul of this child. If this child could never learn to give and receive love, she would be on the devil's side of the kingdom, for God is love."

—An adoptive mother

"And when he saw him, he had compassion on him, and went to him, and bound up his wounds, pouring in oil and wine." —Luke 10:33, 34

These Wounded Lambs

Name Withheld

He hath sent me to heal the brokenhearted. —Luke 4:18
It were better for him that a millstone were hanged about his neck, and he cast
into the sea, than that he should offend one of these little ones. —Luke 17:2
Read Jeremiah 17:5-14

So many innocent little lambs today suffer from shattered hearts. Many Christian families with hearts of compassion reach out and take them in, hoping to bring healing to their wounds. But no one knows just how badly damaged some of these little hearts can be.

Janelle came to her parents as a six-year-old. Smiling bravely, she embraced them as though she was delighted to have a mom and a dad. At first she was eager to please and tried hard to learn English. But oh, the turmoil that surfaced when the family began to realize how difficult it was to put all the broken pieces of her heart back together. Now Janelle's parents struggle with a teenager who appears very rebellious. Others looking on are quick to criticize, offering counsel even though they have no idea how badly Janelle's heart was broken before she was adopted. They blame her adoptive parents for being either too strict or too lenient, for not taking time for her, for not loving her enough, for not disciplining properly. But her parents have discovered it will take more than spankings, pleadings, and restrictions to erase the years of abuse and neglect that took place in Janelle's early life. Janelle's parents are heartbroken, too, when their efforts to help their daughter seem to cause only more pain.

Sadly, there are many such brokenhearted lambs, and many critics of the parents who are pouring out their hearts to help these children. Some of these children are adopted at an older age, after the sad circumstances of their lives have broken their fragile little hearts almost beyond repair. Some of them experienced firsthand the horrors of war and famine in other countries. Many of these older adopted children survived cruel abandonment or abuse from those who should have protected and loved them. Any and all of these situations can shatter a small child's heart.

But what about a child adopted from our own country and culture, perhaps an infant, who is merely torn away from the familiarity of the only home he has ever known? Even if this first home was not a good environment for the child, this disruption can crack and break a little heart in ways that no one understands.

A brokenhearted child may be placed with strangers who expect him to be grateful that they rescued him from his plight and gave him a good home. The adopted child may be unable to express his emotions or to take the broken pieces of his heart to his new parents for comfort and healing and security. He may learn to survive by hiding his wounds under a mask of charm or deceit.

When adoptive parents purposefully or inadvertently touch the tender, broken places and attempt to mend the problems, the child may instinctively recoil with what appears to be disobedience and defiance. Adoptive parents may be baffled and devastated when normal child-training methods drive these children to worse and yet worse behaviors. They may struggle on year after year, keeping their struggles hidden, until suddenly they have a teenager they cannot handle. Other parents are honest about the difficulties with their child from the start, hoping to find help. Sometimes would-be helpers who don't understand the struggle, pile more heartache and guilt onto parents who don't know how to help their troubled child. Parents dealing with adopted children who hide wounded hearts may give up hope of ever having a close relationship with the child. They may stumble on in depression and guilt, feeling reproached and misunderstood.

Yes, the broken hearts are many, and the path to healing is difficult.

Larry was placed in his eighth foster home by the time he was four. In each home, Larry's extreme behavior was too difficult for the foster family to handle. Each new foster family may have thought, *The other homes didn't do it right. We know how to make this child behave.*

Larry's ninth placement is a Christian home among the plain people. Friends looking on think that, finally, this is what Larry needs. Someone to really love him. Someone to discipline him. Someone to show him what good Christian home life is all about. But after living three years in this loving Christian home, Larry's problems have grown worse, not better. Larry's foster parents wonder how they can go on. The more they try to reach Larry's broken heart, the more terrible his behavior becomes. Do they have what it takes to help Larry? Is it worth the risk to the rest of the family?

Six-year-old Rosita's parents are finally finding answers after a very rocky road. Rosita has begun to experience the painful process of having her broken heart mended. She often flinches so violently during this process that she nearly drives away those who are gently touching her heart-wounds. Fearful of being hurt more, she fights for control. Her resistance and determination to protect the deep pain within seems almost inhuman. Rosita has discovered that urinating and defecating at unusual times and places takes some of the attention off her broken heart and gives her some control over her deeply hidden pain.

Rosita's mother Marie is at an extremely difficult point in the struggle—the darkest time just before the dawn. Just now, when she most needs the support of caring friends to help her hang in there until the breakthrough, Marie is forced into a lonely world of misunderstanding and criticism. Friends suggest that she should evaluate what she is doing to aggravate Rosita, provoking this bizarre behavior. They don't see what Marie sees. And they have no idea how much love it takes for Marie to hold and cuddle a child who might urinate on her at any time.

However, there is hope! Rosita's parents are learning how to relate to her in ways that minimize the fight and reduce Rosita's need for control. If Marie and her husband can truly "hang in there," Rosita will begin to understand that a mother's love is so strong it can love the unlovely and break through to the touchiest, most fearful heart. But how long can Marie endure without support?

Natalie's foster parents took her in because the Lord laid on their hearts a desire to reach out to others. She came to them with the typical charm and initial compliance of a child with attachment issues. But alas, nine months later, Natalie's extremely difficult behavior has driven them, after many prayers and tears, to tell their foster agency that Natalie must be out of their home by the end of the month. This Christian agency cannot find a single other family among their many licensed foster care homes who will take a child with such a history. Natalie is cruel to animals. She is physically aggressive, punching her foster mom in the face. She is angry at the newborn baby. She acts out sexually because of past abuse. Natalie is not safe to be alone with anyone or anything. Can you believe this broken child is only three years old? She will join the statistics as yet another child turned over to the state permanently.

One cannot blame Natalie's foster parents for deciding they cannot adopt her. But many people lack discernment when relating to children like Natalie and families who attempt to help heal their wounds. One family acquainted with Natalie's foster family was approved to do respite care for foster children. This family kept Natalie one weekend to give her foster family a much-needed break. When the respite family took Natalie to church with them, people who knew nothing of Natalie's problems commented, "Whose sweet little girl do you have?" "She seems very well-behaved!" "What a darling!" "Is she available for adoption? I want her!" These well-meaning people saw only the surface. They could not see the desperately wounded heart beating inside the pretty child who dazzled them with her brilliant smile and charming behavior.

Jonathan was adopted so young that one would think surely his adoptive parents are to blame for his behavior. How can a child remember what happened to him before he was two weeks old? Of course, Jonathan has no conscious memory of the terrible things he endured as a newborn and possibly even in the womb. These events seared themselves into Jonathan's emotions and still affect his thought patterns and behavior. Jonathan's chaotic existence before he came to his adoptive parents continues to tell him, *This world isn't a safe place. Adults don't like me. They cause me pain. I must fight!* And fight he does.

Added to the difficult circumstances of Jonathan's earliest existence, he developed a medical problem that caused him to endure intense physical pain as an infant. He encountered sudden emergency room trips, hospital stays, and several surgeries, all before he was a year old. When Jonathan's father walks out of a church service with his kicking, howling preschooler screaming, "No, Daddy, no, no!" those looking on think the problem is so easy to discern. Such disrespect and rebellion is obviously the result of a serious lack of discipline! Surely Jonathan's parents must not have spanked him enough when he was smaller. When they offer child-training solutions to the parents in the presence of a listening Jonathan, they only add to the anguish of his already frustrated and exhausted parents.

Those who have not committed themselves to parenting this wounded child and do not live daily with the results of his early trauma do not realize how hard it is for Jonathan to learn to trust adults who have so often taken him to big, scary places where he suffers so much physical pain. They do not understand that a child so young cannot tell the difference between pain caused by abuse and pain caused by medical interventions. But Jonathan's parents understand. As they learn how to help Jonathan, his broken heart will slowly heal.

We also have felt the pain of misunderstandings from those dear to us, but praise God, we are finding help for our own adopted daughter. And even though some close to us do not understand, we find support and encouragement from other adoptive parents and those who work with deeply wounded children.

Why have so few families been able to help these severely wounded children? And why have even fewer been able to understand and support adoptive families who are brave enough to begin the rough, painful journey of helping to heal a child's wounded heart?

Are we ready to take an honest look at our own hearts as we try to help these struggling children? Are we willing to look past the surface and go deep into the heart-wrenching pain that these children experience? Are we willing to admit when we fail? Are we open to whatever the Lord may show us about cleansing and binding up these wounds?

Look not on his countenance . . . for the LORD *seeth not as man seeth; for man looketh on the outward appearance, but the* LORD *looketh on the heart.* 1 Samuel 16:7.

Thought for the Day

A bandage on an infected wound is a deadly cover-up.
The daily cleansing is excruciatingly painful, but life-giving.

Cleansing the Wounds

Name Witheld

And when he saw him, he had compassion on him, and went to him,
and bound up his wounds, pouring in oil and wine. —Luke 10:33, 34
Read Luke 10:30-37

We have examined the wounds of these dear little lambs. We have pondered over the causes. Our tears have flowed with those of the heartbroken parents. And now, we ask some soul-searching questions: Can these children be brought to full cleansing and healing? Do we have hope to offer? Is there a way to get close enough to their hearts to bring cleansing without wounding them further? If the answer to these questions is yes, why are not more of these children finding cleansing and healing among our Christian homes?

Dear innocent lambs and weeping parents, there are answers. This sin-cursed world bears untold reaping for defying its Creator, but it is not in the heart of our God to ignore the suffering of the innocent ones without making a way for them to also be named among the redeemed.

It takes the oil, and it takes the wine. It takes a constant crying out to God for wisdom to know when to apply the oil and when to apply the wine. The wine cleanses the infection. The oil is soothing and restoring, but does not cleanse. Some have tried only the oil. Some have tried only the wine. Some have tried to come up with a balanced formula that works. It takes both the oil and the wine, sometimes more of the one, sometimes more of the other, applied to the heart according to the many varied wounds of the individual child. There is no quick-and-easy formula. The cleansing process is long and painful for both parent and child. But the resulting joy of healing and restoration is worth it all!

In many cases, the wounds that these children have experienced cause them to resist bonding to their adoptive parents. This is where the healing needs to begin. Lack of bonding produces an insecure, emotionally fragile child. Since we tend to look at these children from the perspective of how an emotionally healthy, securely-attached child would respond, we may think all they need is more love, more cuddling, more commendation, more gifts—more things to show *how much we care!* It is hard to fathom a child who actually resists love and nurture. We cannot see that as we are pouring our love into the child's heart, it is flowing right back out through the holes in the wounded heart. Or worse, infection has set in so thickly that love cannot penetrate it at all.

The love, the extra time spent with the child, the nourishing meals, the warm bubble baths, the singing and the rocking, the baby talk that does not demand a response, the unconditional acceptance, the warmth and delight, the hugging and the kissing and all the other things that mothers do for their babies—this is the oil. This is what the hurting child needs. And he needs it in very large doses, because so much of it will not be absorbed, and because of all he has missed in his early life. No matter the age of the child, he first needs this oil if he is to heal and be able to form a secure bond with his mother and father.

The need for this soothing oil is naturally recognized by most parents, especially when made aware that the child's negative behavior is caused by a lack of attachment. What is not so easy to see is how to apply the cleansing wine. Some parents have poured what they thought was wine into the wounds, not realizing that it was a burning acid, which has a use, but not for open wounds. Difficult though it is, many parents have come to realize that the normal child-training methods to which emotionally stable children respond well, have only caused more pain and damage when used on the wounded lambs.

Herein lies the great misunderstanding of those looking on. *What? You have given up on the Bible way? You have forsaken the tried-and-true methods of our heritage for worldly psychology? And you are reading their books, following their advice? If I'd have the child, I'd show you that love and discipline have all the answers . . .*

Yes, the world and its methods do present a real threat to us, and we must always compare what we hear with the principles of God's Word. Yet we admit we have not been able to help these wounded little ones by treating them like our normal children. By refusing to learn from others who have been able to help children with these kinds of problems, have we been missing the keys to healing that God would give us? Their years of experience and study can keep us from learning everything the hard way with our children, wasting precious years and losing many souls.

One key to healing is to help the child form a positive view of himself, while at the same time empathizing with his feelings otherwise. The wounded child often sees himself as bad, shameful, and unlovable and sets out to prove it to the ones who are getting close to him. Children have testified that this is the only way they know how to reconcile the terrible pain they have suffered. *There is something wrong with me. That's why these bad things have happened to me. Nobody can care about me, because I am bad.* Empathizing with the child is very, very important. If he says, "I feel like nobody loves me," a parent's intuitive response is, "Stop saying that! Of course you know we love you." But this only wounds the child yet more. He has revealed some of his deepest feelings, and the parent has not connected with them. Parents have been amazed at the difference when they instead tell the child in a loving, caring voice, "So you see yourself as bad. Hmmm . . . That would be really hard—to feel like nobody loves you. That makes me feel sad for you. I can understand why you think you're bad, considering all that has happened to you. But I want you to know that I do not see you that way. And I hope someday you will see yourself differently too." This gentle persistence often moves the child to trust his parents with more negative feelings that they can help him with, and it can be a wonderful step toward healing.

Another key to healing is to understand that if a child never forms close relationships with a mother figure, his ability to form any close relationship will be crippled. Unattached children have made remarkable progress when kept close to the parents, especially the mother, for their waking hours. As the child begins to relate well to his mother, she then helps him reach out from there, much the same as when an infant first stays only with his mother. The parents keep the child within their sight unless he is sleeping or in the care of another responsible adult who understands his needs. Others tend to interpret this focus on Mom as punishment rather than understand that it is vital to his healing. They may accuse the parents of being narrow-minded and cruel, of not giving the child a chance at normal life, but knowledgeable parents can stay calm and not let this deter them. When onlookers see the child beginning to enjoy being with Mom and learning trust, they will understand. And if they don't, the parents trust it to God who knows all things.

Perhaps the most difficult part of pouring in the wine is providing the structure and routine that these children need. An insecure, poorly-bonded child thrives in an environment where he is given basic activities that prevent him from having opportunity to harm others or destroy personal property. Any child is easily overwhelmed if given more freedom than he can handle. This principle is easy to understand when a one-year-old is left to do whatever he wants, but it is harder for parents to apply this to an older, emotionally unstable child who is old enough for others to assume he is able to handle more freedom. Parents have been blessed to see their child calm down and improve when they allow only toddler-style freedoms to a child with toddler-like behaviors. They keep the child closely supervised, never leaving him alone with animals or children. The child is not allowed to run and play at random, but given specific activities that provide limits for him to respect. As his behaviors show that he can respect the limits his parents set for him, they gradually give him more freedoms. When parents receive criticism for this, it helps them to consider it this way: Is it fair to the child to give him opportunity to do things that will hinder his healing, give him a terrible setback, or harm others? Enduring quiet stares or bold disagreement from those who don't understand is the sacrifice parents may need to make for doing what they know is best for their child and the only way to healing.

When parents pull the child closer and begin pouring in oil and wine, they may discover that at first, he fights as hard as he can. They learn ways of minimizing the fight, because a child cannot bond to fighting, exhausted parents who are filled with frustration and tension. This part especially goes against our natural parenting intuition. If we think in terms of a normal child, we think the child deserves punishment for such terrible disrespect and defiance. It helps to think, instead, in terms of a child with a wounded heart. Picture him as a toddler, remembering that emotionally he is at much the same level.

This is the wine—learning how to correct the child's negative view of himself, clearing his emotions of fears and distrust, bringing him to the point of trusting his parents enough that he is comfortable discussing his past with them, and creating a highly structured, therapeutic environment. Knowing when and how to apply the wine is the most difficult part of helping a child to heal. It is a subject so vast that it is far beyond the scope of this article. If you think this description fits your child, make a study of the subject. Talk to experienced parents and read books specific to your situation.

Is there hope for the wounded lambs? Yes, with God's help, there is! Are we willing to bear the pain, to give of our hearts when it never seems enough, to face misunderstanding and criticism, to devote ourselves to studying how to help these lambs, to be used as tools in the hands of the Good Shepherd—for the sake of one of His wounded lambs?

Thought for the Day

GOD is faithful. He will make a way of escape!
See 1 Corinthians 10:13.

Reach for Hope

Carol Peachey

Hope deferred maketh the heart sick, but when the desire cometh,
it is a tree of life. —Proverbs 13:12
Read Psalm 31:19-24

Many children adopted from foster care or from orphanages abroad have problems with bonding that baffle, overwhelm, and exhaust loving parents. If you are an adoptive parent who experiences intense rejection and lack of normal responses from the child you love so dearly and have committed to raise as your own, you may be dealing with what is known in the mental health field as reactive attachment disorder (RAD). The theory is that emotional damage occurs when a young child is deprived of normal bonding with a loving, protective mother. Each uprooting in the child's life and each traumatic episode (war, violence, severe neglect of physical needs, or rejection by the birth mother) skews his emotional development a little more.

Older children who become available for adoption these days seem to be more severely wounded than many such children a generation or two ago. As our world grows worse in its rebellion against God, the increased breakdown of marriage and families is perhaps making a bigger chaos of children's lives than it did years ago.

Foster care and adoption agencies can get overwhelmed and are often unable to meet the needs of these sadly dysfunctional children. When children don't bond securely with families who take them in, they may get passed from one new family or institution to another. This only deepens their difficulty in forming secure and meaningful attachments to anyone.

But the damage caused by this chaos is reversible. So if you have nearly given up hope that you can help this child, take heart! Answers are available. If you know where to look and what to ask for, your ability to bond with this child and provide what he needs to grow into a happy, healthy adult can be greatly improved. God brought this sad, needy child into your life; He will also provide a way for you to understand his needs and discover what helps him.

There is no instant cure; it's hard work. It may take every ounce of emotional strength you have, but the influence you can have on this wounded child's eternal soul will be well worth the effort. Some or all of what he lacked in the early years can be finally supplied by a consistently nurturing home that understands what is missing. God's heart weeps with your child's pain—and also with yours. Ask Him to lead you to accurate and godly sources of information to expand your knowledge of your child's problems.

Get up-to-date information to help you understand what's going on in your child's mind that induces him to respond so negatively to your love and your reasonable discipline. Your adoption agency or local social services agency may have useful information. Even better, they may be able to point you to other parents or support groups for families who are facing the same difficulties you are. Don't trust all the extreme, unverifiable data you might find from secular sources. Find other families who have walked in the shoes you are now wearing, who can give you personal support from their own experiences. Find out which resources helped them the most.

What a relief to discover that your disturbed child is not emotionally handicapped beyond repair, irrevocably bad, or a born psychopath! You know your child well enough to understand that something inside is deeply wounded. The child simply seems *unable* to respond normally to your intense desire to love and care for him. When you realize the important components he has missed that hinder him from healthy bonding and a proper trust in your ability to care for him, you can better understand the resulting bizarre behavior.

Simply having your hope renewed can do wonders to improve the quality of life in your home. When the way no longer looks impossible, you will find the strength to keep on loving this difficult child.

Thought for the Day

How calmly we may commend ourselves into
the hands of Him who bears up the world!

—John Paul Richter

Reach for Knowledge

Carol Peachey

Give instruction to a wise man, and he will be yet wiser:
teach a just man, and he will increase in learning. —Proverbs 9:9
Read James 1:2-6 and 3:13-18

*I*f possible, find out all you can about what happened to your older adopted child before he came to you. Some adoption agencies are very willing to share as much information as possible, and this is helpful. Knowing what happened to your child as a newborn, as an infant, and as a toddler, may shed great light on the things that trigger the negative responses you see now. If you can talk with former foster parents or orphanage caretakers, you may get valuable information about the damage that was done to your child's emotions long before you became the parent. The more you know about your child's past, the better equipped you'll be to supply the missing ingredients to his emotional security.

You may find a good attachment therapist helpful. I have one very firm caution here. Not every therapist or agency who says they deal with attachment issues do so knowledgeably. And not every counselor follows Biblical methods and philosophies. *Any useful therapy for the problem must be directed toward helping the child bond with his new adoptive family, primarily the mother.* The mother or both parents should be involved in each and every session. If a therapist or agency seeks to work with your child alone, your antennae should go up. In order to heal, your child needs to bond with *you*, the parents who have adopted him and committed their daily lives to him, not a therapist who sees the child briefly once a week or less. Any therapist who purports to be able to help your child better without your presence is probably not helping the bond between you and your child to grow and strengthen.

You, as the child's parent, are the best human healer of your child's heart. But you can glean many valuable helps from those who have studied how children bond with their parents and have had experience working with families who face bonding difficulties. Lean on God for answers, and let Him lead you to godly counselors who are qualified to teach you how to manage the emotional roller coaster many older adopted children put a family through.

Thought for the Day

Use your gifts faithfully, and they shall be enlarged;
practice what you know, and you shall attain to higher knowledge.

Seeking Counsel

Name Withheld

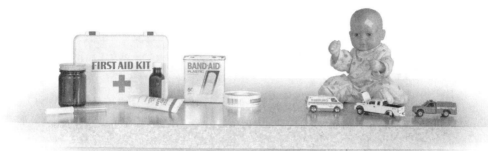

Pleasant words are as an honeycomb, sweet to the soul,
and health to the bones. —Proverbs 16:24
Read Proverbs 16:16; 20-24

G od is our source of help in any trouble. Often He directs us to people with experience and wisdom. The following ideas I gleaned from a family counselor who was herself an adoptee, and who had worked for years with adoptive families. These pointers helped me deal with my adopted daughter's frequent episodes of rage and physical violence.

- When my 14-year-old was raging out of control, I learned to see her in my mind as a screaming, upset infant in my arms rather than the perceptive adolescent she was in calmer moments. My counselor asked me, "What would you do for a howling three-month-old?" The answers were so simple. I'd soothe, talk quietly, pity my poor baby's helplessness, and try calmly and methodically to find out what was causing the upset. I had to quit expecting my daughter to be capable of reasoning or controlling her rage when she was that agitated. The part of her brain that should have been able to regulate her intense emotions was undeveloped when compared with the rest of her very normal body and brain. The last thing Annie needed when her inner volcano erupted unexpectedly was a loud, fearful, agitated, restraining response from me.

- I learned that I could best teach my daughter how to stay calm if I modeled calm, objective responses myself. When she was pushing every sensitive button I had, testing my last nerve, I learned to take deep breaths and let them out slowly, releasing the tension in my body so I could respond in an even tone of voice, with nonthreatening body language. The counselor gave me an interesting tip: When Annie exploded in anger over some little trigger, I should sit on the floor and look her calmly in the eye without saying a word. The idea was that my defenseless physical position and eye contact would dissolve the threat my daughter felt when I loomed over her and retorted sharply to her tirade. The first couple of times I tried it, I was astonished and gratified to see my daughter's rage deflate within minutes.

- Annie needed me to be the calm, in-control, steady center that her scary out-of-control emotions couldn't move. She was helpless to rein in her terrifying violence when it came spewing out. She needed to know I wasn't helpless, like she, to control my responses. Once, in a calmer moment of rare insight, Annie told me, "When I get so out-of-control, I scare myself. I'm afraid of what I might do to hurt myself or someone else."

- I needed help to cope with my stress. During several years of intense struggle to help my daughter through her losses and her pain and her inability to bond fully with me, I gained weight, my blood pressure soared, and I developed chronic insomnia. I felt wired all the time—tense and afraid of what dangerous, violent thing my daughter might do next. Being single, I felt so alone and helpless in my troubles with Annie.

   I swallowed my pride and told my doctor the truth about what was going on in my home. Medications helped control the blood pressure and the insomnia and gave me the tranquility I needed. I was able to face the challenges of each new day with a sense of hope rather than terrible foreboding. Eventually, I was able to stop taking the medications, but I am grateful for the way they helped me cope during the most exhausting times of parenting. I may have fallen apart completely without that help, and been less able to be a good mother to my needy daughter.

- My counselor constantly affirmed my parenting abilities and the supreme effort I was making to help my daughter heal from her invisible wounds. By the time I found this family counselor, Annie was old enough to object strongly to accompanying me to counseling, and I couldn't force her to attend the sessions with me. The counselor agreed to see me alone about once every three weeks, anyway. She told me over and over again that parents are the very best healers for their wounded children, and that if she could pass her knowledge of bonding issues on to me, it would help my daughter too. And she was right. I'd travel the three hours to her office, feeling like an utter failure because Annie was in the middle of yet another alarming emotional crisis, and I seemed unable to penetrate her pain. After an hour with this kind woman, I'd drive home full of overwhelming love and pity for my daughter again. Somehow, this counselor helped me take the focus off myself and my hopeless feelings, and back onto my precious daughter's bottomless needs.

  She filled my tank to overflowing with new hope and resolve every time I met with her. She helped me see the parts of myself that were getting in the way of reaching my daughter. It was humiliating, but illuminating, to understand why my daughter made me feel so worthless and rejected. It wasn't her fault—it was my own unresolved issues! I learned not to expect Annie to fill my needs to be loved and respected and wanted. I could get those things from my loving heavenly Father and from other people in my life. Then I was able to pour them back into Annie, who simply had no resources of her own to give me.

- My counselor was not overtly religious, but her advice never went against Scriptural teaching. In fact, everything I learned from her about parent-child bonding gave me a deeper understanding of God and His supreme love for us undeserving human beings. By experiencing my daughter's continual rejection of my love, I learned how much I grieve God when I reject His loving discipline. I received strength to continue giving and giving and giving, even though I did not often experience the wished-for returns on my sacrifice. God gave so much to rescue me; how can I do less for my daughter, who, though nearly grown, is still struggling in painful confusion over the circumstances of her early life?

Thought for the Day

Patience is not passive; on the contrary it is active;
it is concentrated strength.

—Edward G. Bulwer-Lytton

The Cry and
The Answer

Ann J. Burkholder

Their soul fainted in them. Then they cried unto the LORD in their trouble,
and he delivered them out of their distresses. —Psalm 107:5, 6
Read Psalm 107:1-9

She came as a bouncy, sparkly-eyed little girl with a contagious smile. When I stooped to pick her up from where she was sitting on the steps that first memorable night in Liberia, she put her arms around me and laid her head on my shoulder. It was any adoptive mother's dream. *My new daughter accepts me! She loves me! She's calling me mama!*

We brought her home and she fit into our family as if this was what she had been waiting for. She played, she laughed, she sang, and she happily marched off to Sunday school like any normal four-year-old. She was sweet and obedient and responded well to discipline. When people asked how she was adjusting, we had only positive things to share.

Nine months later, however, after I had put my children to bed one afternoon, I fell to my knees at the sofa and wept . . . again. "O Lord," I cried, "what happened to our sweet little girl? Show me what I am doing wrong!" As the tears flowed and I cried out to God, my mind relived the months since our daughter's homecoming.

Our model child had lasted only a short time. While she was still presenting herself to the public as the most docile, obedient little girl, trouble was brewing at home. The storm clouds gathered slowly at first and then suddenly burst into a torrent that we didn't know how to handle.

Over and over again, I struggled with the question, "What lack I yet?"

Well-meaning friends said, "You need to love her more." Love her more? I was loving her in every way I knew how!

Others thought we needed to be more firm in disciplining her. "If a child doesn't respond to a spanking, you're not spanking hard enough," they said. Spank her more? We *had* spanked her—they had no idea how many times and how hard. "But any child will respond to pain." No, this one didn't.

And so again and again came the cry from the depths of my heart, "Lord, help me! Something is wrong with my child, and I don't know what it is! Lord, show me! What lack I yet?"

God is faithful. He answers the cries of a seeking soul. "Their soul is melted because of trouble. They reel to and fro, and stagger like a drunken man, and are at their wit's end. Then they cry unto the Lord in their trouble, and he bringeth them out of their distresses" (Psalm 107:26-28).

Through the book *A New Family for Semoj* and a talk with our social worker, God showed us, *You don't have this girl's heart. She has not yet claimed you as her family. She is not bonded to you.* This revelation led us to seek more information and advice, which turned into a deep study during the next year and brought us to the doors of an attachment counselor.

One by one, the lights came on and we began to understand what was happening. This poor girl had suffered profound neglect as well as the horrors of war. In her young life she had known so much pain that she had become calloused to it. She had experienced multiple changes in caregivers and did not have a true concept of who a mother is. When she put her arms around me that first night and said "Mama," she only meant that she had found someone new to take care of her, a pattern she was much too familiar with. She did not understand true love and closeness in human relationships, and she had no desire to please us after the newness of the relationship wore off and we tried to get close to her heart.

We had naively assumed that if a child has suffered lack of affectionate love and proper discipline, all she needs in order to heal is a good home life that provides this. We did not realize what terrible emotional wounds she had that needed to be cleansed and bound up before she could even begin to accept our love and nurture. Sadly, this naïveté is all too common.

Understanding attachment disorder continues to be an ongoing study as the Lord leads us into new experiences in our daughter's healing and growth. Contacts with new friends have greatly enriched our lives, and to them we say thank you. Thank you for sharing your experiences, which helped us to know that we are not alone in this. Thank you to those who have taken time to listen and encourage as I poured out my heart of pain and tears. Thank you to the father who just called my husband last week, at his wit's end with his son. When we share our burdens, it is one small way that our pain can be a blessing to others.

If you are considering adoption, learn all you can about helping an emotionally wounded child. Know the symptoms and warning signs— they are often contrary to what we might imagine. Parents can take pro-active steps to ease the transition when adopting a child. The way you handle the child in the first several months can help correct the child's wrong concepts and bring him to healing much sooner than a "wait and see" approach. Though attachment problems are more common in children older than a year old when adopted, any adoptive parent should be prepared. Rejection and trauma can be communicated to the baby as a newborn or, possibly, even in the womb.

If you see your child in our story, there is help! There is hope! Talk to other adoptive parents. Learn the skills necessary to help your child. The journey of helping a child like this is long, lonely, and excruciatingly painful, but the rewards are tremendous. Oh, the indescribable joy of watching our daughter go from trauma to healing!

"O that men would praise the LORD for his goodness, and for his wonderful works to the children of men! And let them . . . declare his works with rejoicing" (Psalm 107:21, 22).

Thought for the Day

When we are at our wisdom's end, God's wisdom is there for us.

The Pain of Rejection

Ann J. Burkholder

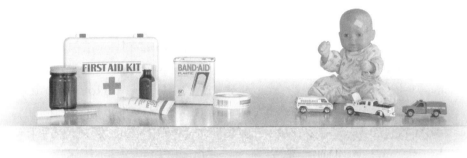

He is despised and rejected of men; a man of sorrows,
and acquainted with grief: and we hid as it were our faces from him;
he was despised, and we esteemed him not. —Isaiah 53:3
Read Isaiah 53

*I*t had been another long, difficult day with my daughter.

When we adopted her at the tender age of almost-four, she had already experienced far more suffering than anyone should ever have to face. She came into our home with a beguiling smile and a charming personality that hid all the pain and heartache seething underneath. Her heart was so wounded and scarred that when presented with a close relationship with me as her mother, she reacted in terror.

And so, after the initial newness wore off and the charm was reserved for strangers, I had many difficult days. No, difficult doesn't describe it. The Lord was taking me on the most painful, heart-wrenching experience of my life. I felt like all my dreams were crashing down around me . . . dreams of having a little girl by my side who would love to watch what I was doing and beg to help . . . dreams of helping her through preschool work. Now that I was married, I missed my old classroom and dear little students. A daughter at my side would fill that void. I had dreams of working in the garden together, of picking flowers, of reading stories, of drawing and coloring and painting and singing and strolling hand in hand . . . my daughter and me.

But she didn't want to be my daughter. She went to great lengths to avoid being by my side. She never followed me around the house or dragged a stool over to the kitchen to climb up and see what I was making. Preschool work turned into terrible contention. Gardening angered her because it didn't work unless she did it her way. She hated doing anything fun with me and resisted learning how to sing when I tried to teach her new songs, though she had a lovely voice for strangers. The extreme things she would do to resist the cozy, nurturing, motherly times with me left me confounded.

Rejection. That is what I was experiencing. Noah Webster's 1828 dictionary defines *reject* as "to throw away, cast off, refuse to accept, forsake." This is the silent message that was coming from her. "I don't want you! I am throwing you away! I refuse to accept you as my mother." The pain of rejection is one of the most difficult things in this world to face, especially when others were blaming me for having done something to cause her to reject me.

Many times I wrestled in agonizing prayer, pleading with God to search my heart and show me what I was doing wrong that would cause a child to act like this. Even though others who had experience with such children assured me it was not my fault, it was hard not to take the rejection personally. Why, why, why? Why would a girl want to give herself a bath in half an inch of cold water instead of letting Mom give her a nice warm bath? Why would she press her lips closed and turn away when I offered her candy, yet accept it with relish from anyone else? Why would she refuse to let me hold her and then go and climb into the laps of uncles and aunts and grandpas and even total strangers? Why would she refuse to eat food I gave her, yet have an endless appetite away from home, loudly asking for more and more and lavishly thanking the cook? Why? Why didn't she like me, if it wasn't that there was something wrong with *me?*

Facing this day after day was exhausting. I began slipping into despair, struggling with feelings of anger and repulsion toward this child who was throwing our family life into chaos. The emotional and spiritual strength it takes to pour your heart and soul into a child who gives nothing in return is enormous.

After one especially difficult day during a week of revival meetings, the sermon that night shed new light on the term "rejection." The title of the message was "If Any Man Draw Back" from Hebrews 10:38.

As I sat there and drank in the message, my thoughts raced, making applications to what I was facing with my daughter. "If any man draw back, my soul shall have no pleasure in him." *No pleasure* equals *repulsive*. That is strong language! One reason we were so concerned about our daughter's fear of close relationships was that if she never learned to trust an adult in a close relationship, she would not learn to trust God. I compared my relationship with her to God's relationship with His people. God finds no pleasure in those who do not want a relationship with Him; I found no pleasure in a child who did not want a relationship with me. Yes! God really did understand what I was going through! He faces it all the time, when the very souls He created, the people He dearly loves, reject Him!

My husband and I talked more about this at home that evening. He had pondered the same thoughts himself during the sermon. Here are some gleanings from our conversation:

In God's dealings with His people Israel, He faced rejection and "drawing back" again and again, to the point that at one time He would have destroyed them all, but Moses interceded. In the era of the kings, over and over we read, "And he did that which was evil in the sight of the Lord . . ." Finally, after sending many prophets to warn Israel, God brought serious judgment upon His people. Still, mankind struggled with sin and evil, withdrawing yet more from God.

At last God provided the ultimate solution: He came Himself in the form of a man to minister to these people. He reasoned that if people could see God among them and could talk to Him and hear His words, they would desire to draw closer to God the Father! So Jesus Christ came down to minister to the needs of mankind. But "he was despised and rejected of men." Yes, God's people, the religious people, drew back even from the form of God in person. They hated Him, they tried to outwit Him, and they wished Him dead. When the time was right, God allowed them to kill Jesus . . . not a quiet, simple execution, but crucifixion—the death reserved for the worst of criminals, the ultimate in rejection and shame.

It's true, Jesus had friends and disciples who believed in Him, but even they forsook Him when He faced such great rejection and agony. And the one who did follow afar off denied that He ever knew such a man. As the perfect Son of God, the rejection He faced was certainly not because of something He had done wrong.

"Amazing love, how can it be that Thou, my God, shouldst die for me!" Amazing . . . because God loved us before we were lovely. He loved us when we were rejecting Him! He loved us when we drew back from Him! He loved us before we knew how to reciprocate that love! Jesus came to earth *knowing* that He would be despised and rejected!

My husband had shared thoughts with me along this line before, but that night they touched me in a new way after my very difficult day. I pondered how my Lord had given His heart for me, pouring out everything in His power to help me when I was weak and sinful, and finally suffering the most shameful rejection and pain . . . all for me. Could I do anything less for Him, for an innocent child He created? My friends don't understand me . . . neither did His. Others contradict me sharply and say my conclusions are all wrong . . . they did this to Jesus too. I am pouring my whole heart and soul into doing loving things for my child, and she still hates me and rejects me . . . Jesus experienced this too with those He was trying to help.

And the final result of God's gentle, persistent love in the face of rejection is . . . redemption and healing! Restoration! Changed hearts, changed lives! That's the power of the amazing love of God! If God did it for sinful man, He can do it for my child, through me, if I let Him.

Healing . . . restoration . . . changed life . . . that's what my daughter desperately needs. And that's the work of our God. But He needs a tool. A human being. A mother for this child. He needs *me!*

I woke up the next morning with a new outlook on life . . . a new hope . . . and some new ways of handling my daughter's behavior. She had been using every power within herself to draw back from me; but since I am not divine, I cannot say when a human soul has reached the point of no return. I cannot take it into my own judgment to say that my soul can never have pleasure in this child. I resolved to do my best to keep her from winning the game of trying to keep her distance from Mom. Oh, the changes were painful! This meant holding her when she hated me, hugging her even when she made herself stiff and tried to get away, keeping her beside me after she had disobeyed instead of sending her to her room, even rubbing her back or kissing her when she had just done something purposely to anger me . . .

I confess, that wasn't easy. When someone is repulsive to you, do you feel like letting them touch you? Then is when I needed a vision of Christ's love and the rejection He faced, how He loved yet more and more when others rejected Him. And that love is still available to us today! His love looked past the rejection to something of value in us, and His love can do the same in my heart for my child. Because of what Christ has done for me, I can look past the rejection to something of value in my daughter.

We can have the power of God's love in our hearts, flowing through us to love the unlovely.

Thought for the Day

When you have someone in your life who is not
accepting what you have done for him, ponder the rejection
Christ suffered before we accepted His work for us.

Joy Cometh
In the Morning

Ann J. Burkholder

Weeping may endure for a night,
but joy cometh in the morning. —Psalm 30:5
Read Psalm 126, Psalm 30

The scene was simple: my husband at the table reading a book and sipping a cup of tea, our two-year-old daughter and three-year-old son at his side putting puzzles together, and our now almost six-year-old daughter beside me doing a page in her preschool book. Simple, yes. But after the turmoil of the past two years, I no longer took simplicity for granted. The peace, the smiles and laughter, the relaxed conversation, the absence of tension and conflict, the joy that could be felt flowing from heart to heart . . . not so long ago, these simple pleasures had been almost unheard of in our home.

Was it only the previous week that I had lain awake crying for most of the night? It all comes back to me so clearly . . .

During the past six months of seeing an attachment therapist with our daughter, things were changing ever so slowly. She was like a wildcat we were trying to tame. She would let us come close to her sometimes, then suddenly withdraw in fright and anger. But slowly, almost imperceptibly, she was changing. Then one wonderful day she suddenly began to open her heart to us like never before. From that day on, the improvement was astounding, to the point that our therapist said this can only be called a miracle from God. In all her years of working with children, she had never seen anything like it. How we rejoiced and praised God for His goodness!

But He had more dark valleys to lead us through. As our daughter began sharing the deep things of her heart with us, we faced new challenges. She confided in us that she had often been hungry at the children's home, had to get her own drinks if she was thirsty, and felt like nobody cared about her. She said the caretakers never held her, talked to her, or helped her if she was hurt. The climax of it all came when she began sharing her memories of the war. How our hearts bled with hers to hear her describe in horrible detail the things she had endured. I shuddered as I listened to one especially detailed description, realizing that she was describing exactly what she had done to her doll one day.

During the next several days, at the therapist's suggestion, our daughter spent a lot of time drawing pictures of her memories to help process her feelings. The finished drawings had dreadful detail that no child so young who has had no media exposure would be able to draw unless they had experienced it.

That night was my night of weeping. Late into the night I wrestled with a torrent of emotions as my mind went over the happenings of the last two years in light of what our little girl had shared with us that week. I began to see a picture of this child that I had never seen before, and her bizarre behavior suddenly made sense. She had experienced unmention-able suffering at the hands of adults, *and I was upset with her for being afraid of me and going to great lengths to avoid me?* During one experience, her disobedience to the rebel soldiers had saved her life, *and I was frustrated with her for how difficult it was for her to obey me?* She had endured terrible physical and emotional pain, *and we wondered why she didn't respond to the pain of spankings?* She had been grossly rejected again and again by people she should have been able to trust, *and I am repulsed by her rejection of me?* O God in Heaven, forgive!

I fell to my knees in weeping and prayer. As I cried out to God, I felt the forces of good and evil in conflict over the soul of this child. If this child could never learn to give and receive love, she would be on the devil's side of the kingdom, for God is love. But if I submitted completely to God's leading for us in helping this child to heal, she would be another soul for the Lord to win into His kingdom.

Finally in the early hours of the morning, peace and tranquility came over my soul and the battle was won. My tears subsided as the soothing balm of God's presence became very real to me. I was finally able to join my husband in bed, where he had been sleeping peacefully for several hours. The next day as we shared our hearts, we talked about how the experiences of that week were extremely difficult and emotionally painful, and yet so immeasurably precious.

We still have our "down" times. Our daughter's journey toward emotional healing is still in process. But then I remember the joys . . .

She shakes her head at Grandma's offer to hold her and says, "No, I'm going to Mama and she will hold me."

"Look, Mama! This warm bath is all full of your love!" I laugh with her as she points to the soap bubbles.

"I like your good food, Mama. It makes me feel happy inside."

"I'm not scared of you anymore, Mama. I don't think I want to go to a new mama."

"Will you help me with this, please?"

"Do you think I can help you pick strawberries when it's my birthday? Sometime I would like you to help me grow hot peppers in the garden."

And then there's the joy of this simple family time around the kitchen table.

Though these times are mixed with disappointing moments, when I ponder the joy we have been experiencing, I can see that, yes, our daughter is healing! Truly, joy cometh in the morning!

Thought for the Day

God can take what the devil meant for harm
and use it to bless our lives.

Accepting a Child's Past

Julia Brubaker

These are the things that ye shall do; Speak ye every man the truth to his neighbor; execute the judgment of truth and peace in your gates. —*Zechariah 8:16*
Read Proverbs 12:17-22

*D*avy[6] came to us when he was almost three years old. We were told that an adoptive family had been chosen for him, and he just needed a temporary home until his new home could be approved.

The time stretched to nine months, and Davy became attached to our family. He considered himself one of us, and we loved this blond, blue-eyed charmer.

Eventually, Davy began having visits with his adoptive parents. When they changed his name and told him not to call me Mom anymore, I felt uneasy, but decided I needed to let go so he could bond with them.

On the day I took Davy to his new home to stay, he begged to stay with me. We both cried as he clung to me, and I assured him I would come to visit him.

---

6   Not his real name.

I meant to keep my promise, for the social worker had recommended contact for the first while, and the new parents had agreed to this. But when I made efforts to visit Davy, they did not return my calls. After months of wondering and worrying, I happened to meet the mother in town and asked about Davy. She replied, "He's fine. He doesn't miss you and wouldn't remember you by now. A visit would just confuse him."

Through inquiry, I learned that the social workers and his birth siblings were also being held at arm's length. These parents seemed to want Davy completely to themselves, to forget that he had a previous identity and just know him as their child who would fulfill all their hopes and dreams.

It didn't work. Six months after Davy moved to his new home, his adoptive parents requested his removal. Their reason? He was not bonding with them. They admitted that he was depressed and was often on the verge of tears, that he had regressed in his toileting habits, and that he had to be coaxed out of bed every morning.

Davy returned to our home. I will never forget the look of sheer joy on his face when we were reunited. He shouted my name and ran to my waiting arms. I cried with relief that his long nightmare was over.

That was six months ago. We've had some rough days with Davy, but he is happy to be home. If he ever moves again, I hope his new family will understand and acknowledge his past. He's not just an empty slate, but a four-year-old with a history. He has a birth family and other significant people with whom he's had ongoing contact. All these are part of who he is, and it's good and healthy for him to remember them.

We are making a life book for Davy, a record of those people and events that helped to shape his life. He loves to pore over the pictures and remember the past.

Children are naturally curious about their origins; we make a grave mistake when we squelch that desire to know. A child's early experiences do affect the present; denying that fact will not undo the past. Why should we feel threatened with the truth?

Epilogue: A few months after I wrote Davy's story, his social worker decided to move him to another foster home in a nearby community, which was the same home where two of his biological brothers were living. I felt very comfortable with this decision, since Davy was quite attached to his brothers and did not seem to mind the move. Although this family never adopted him, they were willing to provide long-term foster care for Davy, and he is still in their home. I don't see him often, but his foster parents have always generously welcomed contact. I've had quite a few phone visits with Davy, have provided respite for him, and occasionally meet him in town or at foster family events. When we meet, I often share news of others in my family, and he still remembers them and seems interested in hearing about their lives. In spite of his turbulent early years, Davy appears to be doing very well as he enters adolescence. Sometime I would like to invite him and his family over for a meal, and then I can show them the many photos of Davy that I have in my albums. I want him to know we enjoyed the eighteen months he spent with us.

Thought for the Day

If you reject a child's past, you reject the child.
A child without a past will find it harder to bond
with the new people in his future.

Holes in Our Buckets

Marian Reinford

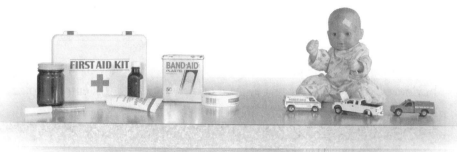

And be ye kind one to another, tenderhearted, forgiving one another,
even as God for Christ's sake hath forgiven you. —Ephesians 4:32
Read Ephesians 4

*E*ach baby comes into this world with a little bucket over his tiny arm. Every hug, every smile, every loving word puts in another drop of goodwill, filling the bucket. Every neglected cry, unkind look, harsh word, every feeling that nobody cares punches a little hole in the bucket.

As we grow older, many things have a bearing on how full our buckets become—sincere love from those who care for us, relationships with our friends and peers, and our own personalities. When we have lots of drops and very few holes in our buckets, we are happy. We feel worthwhile, protected, and loved. We reach out to fill others' buckets. Our buckets are comfortingly full and we want to share our happiness. We put drops into others' buckets freely and we receive many drops in return. Happiness begets happiness, and it makes us want to bring health and happiness to others' lives also.

If many holes are punched into our buckets, especially at a young age, they often take a long time to mend. Sometimes to protect ourselves we put a lid on our bucket; but then the drops others try to put in roll down the outside. In our frustration, anger, and pain over our empty bucket, we become obnoxious in our reactions and words. Often we find parents, siblings, schoolmates, teachers, and grandparents pulling away from us a little. Our negative feelings grow. We miss the drops they put into our bucket and the happiness we received. We may even become angry at our parents and God. (Shouldn't they be able to protect us from pain?) Sometimes it's hard for us to grasp that our own actions are causing our buckets to become dry, and we need others to show us how to change.

Some people struggle to fill their own buckets. They may try using food. They never feel full, so they eat and eat and eat, and still feel empty! Some people may try punching holes into other people's buckets by being selfish, harsh, and unkind. Somehow they feel that hurting others will diminish their own pain.

We all need help with our buckets, and we all know the feeling of pain in one way or another. A friend betrays our trust or laughs at our mistake. We lose a loved one. Our brethren misjudge our motives. Our finances just don't reach. When we have physical or emotional needs, we feel particularly vulnerable.

I need drops in my bucket, and you need drops in yours. God has a wonderful plan for our needs to be met. He designed the Christian home and church, where we can show love and appreciation for each other. In the home and in the church the strong can help the weak, and we all can put drops into each other's buckets.

How wonderful that we can find security in our Heavenly Father, who always understands and cares about our troubles and disappointments. As we bring our burdens to Him, He enables us to respond with quiet resignation rather than with resentment or self-pity. And we discover that ministering to others has a way of plugging holes instead of punching them.

Thought for the Day

Let's do our part to heal the holes in each other's
buckets and fill them with love.

Security

Name Withheld

When my father and my mother forsake me,
then the LORD will take me up. —Psalm 27:10
Read Psalm 27

Our adopted son was a very "together" sort of young man. In my opinion, he was the perfect son. Never once did I feel that he regretted that I was his mother. He was content to have me by his side at meetings, and while visiting or shopping. We talked about everyday things and spiritual things without faltering. So I was in for a major surprise one night nearly twelve years after he became our son.

He and I were sitting on the glider on the front porch, intermittently chatting and swinging in comfortable silence. Sensing that he had something to say, I simply waited.

"You know, Mom," he began, "the other fellows are going on that trip, and they asked me to go along." He paused. "I really would like to go if you and Dad say I may, but I can't."

I sensed his struggle to continue. "Lord," I prayed, "give him the words; give me the words."

In the darkness I heard him weeping. I reached for his hand and pressed it tightly.

"I'm afraid to be anywhere without you and Dad. I know I'm safe, but I'm just afraid," he cried.

"That's okay. Sometimes we have reasons to be afraid. Why don't you just tell me what you're thinking and feeling?"

"Well, remember the time we went to visit Aunt Victoria? We stopped to use the restroom and to eat. You and Dad walked around a corner where I couldn't see you. I was so scared. I was afraid you were going to leave me behind!" He shuddered as he cried.

"I don't like to be in big places where I can't see you or Dad. I hate to go places like Lowe's or Walmart." And my big, almost-grown son, so dear to my heart, wept.

After he had regained his composure, I said, "Why don't you tell me why you feel afraid."

The silence was punctuated with sniffs. Finally he whispered, "I remember one time when I was a little boy. I was playing along a river. I was with two women, but I don't know who they were. They were washing clothes in the river. I looked up, and they were leaving without me. The water was so wide I didn't know how I could get back across and get to them before they went too far. I was afraid I would be lost." Great sobs shook him.

I cried for the little boy who had been less than five years old at the time. His mother and grandmother had lived together, and I knew they were the two women. "What did you do?" I asked.

"I don't know. It is always black after that. I can't remember."

I patted his hand as he continued. "Then I guess it was my mother who took me to the orphanage. She took me to that big house and just left me, and I couldn't figure out how to get back to her."

Ah, my son! Now I understand your need to be close beside us.

That night I reassured him that his dad and I would never leave him without explaining our leaving. We would never insist that he go someplace without us. I reminded him that no matter who had abandoned him in the past, we would not, and he should remember most of all that God is with him *always.*

After this, my husband and I made a conscious effort to stay within his line of vision when we were in public. We also encouraged short ventures away from us, perhaps traveling to a neighboring church with other young men.

Finally, he was able to attend Bible Study Fellowship for a day at a time, coming home each night. He now enjoys spending time away from us with cell phone connection. We can go away for a week or two at a time, so long as some family member is with him.

I find it hard to fathom that I never realized my son's panic and fear until he was nearly eighteen years old, and then he had to tell me. My heart cries for the terror he hid within himself all those years. How lonely it must have been!

Thought for the Day

Lord, show us how best to respond to the
hidden needs of our children's hearts.

The Unknowns of Tomorrow

Crystal Van Pelt

an adoptee

The LORD shall preserve thee from all evil: he shall preserve thy soul.
The LORD shall preserve thy going out and thy coming in from this time forth,
and even for evermore. —Psalm 121:7, 8

Read Psalm 121

As a child I did not live with stability. I always felt insecure because things changed so drastically, so fast, so often. I had been in and out of foster care and the day care center. Then I was put in yet another foster home along with my two little brothers. I constantly asked this new foster mother, "What will happen to us?"

Her response was, "God will take care of you."

As a three-year-old, I could not rest in that. Because she, as a single foster mom, had been advised not to adopt boys, she felt she could not adopt my brothers and me. She made contact with Romania, hoping to adopt from there. As she sewed dresses for the two little girls she was planning to adopt, I sat and thought. The unknown of tomorrow looked overwhelmingly BIG. *Where WOULD we go? Where would WE go? Where would we GO?*

My foster mom's Romanian adoption plans fell through, and a widower asked for her friendship. After dating several months, they got married.

Now they could adopt me and my two brothers. They chose to! It took a while, but by the time I was seven, we were part of a new family. By then, that unknown was partially settled.

Now as a teenager I still find many unknowns in life, but I found a motto that helps me trust. It says:

God is too wise to be mistaken.
God is too good to be untrue.
So when you don't understand,
When you can't see His plan,
When you can't trace His hand,
Trust His heart![7]

Foster mothers, adoptive mothers—help your children to rest in your care—especially if your children are past the baby stage. You can't fathom the whirling thoughts that go through their small minds. Paint pictures of a loving God in their minds; pictures of judgment can wait until later. Show them that no matter what happens to them, you will care about them as long as you live. Assure them that if they do not stay in your care, your prayers will follow them.

Thought for the Day

Take heart. Face today, tomorrow, and the unknowns
with your hand in the Saviour's. He knows!

---

7 Words: Babbie Mason, Eddie Carswell © 1989 Dayspring Music, LLC/Causing Change Music (adm. by Dayspring Music, LLC/Word Music, LLC/May Sun Publishing/admin. by Word Music, LLC)

Adopting the Older Child

Carla Raley

Be not forgetful to entertain strangers:
for thereby some have entertained angels unawares. —Hebrews 13:2
Read Hebrews 13:1–6

When you think of adoption, do you visualize a sweet newborn baby handed to you in the hospital? Most people do. But in reality, with the costs of private adoptions soaring until they are out of reach for the average family, more people are looking toward foster care and adoption with the state.

It's the rare child, though, that is adoptable from birth through the state. The birth parents usually have their child removed from them for good cause, and then they have a year or more, depending on the state, to work out the plan the state lays out to have their child returned to them. Once the parental rights are terminated, there is an appeal period before the child is released for adoption. If you are a foster parent as well as an adoptive parent, then you have a good chance of receiving a child into your home from the very beginning, but there are many, many children who become wards of the state as older children. They are needy, hurting, and vulnerable. They need permanent homes just as much as a newborn infant, but many will never have them. A look at the state websites for children eligible for adoption will reveal thousands of children in need of homes. Most of these are harder-to-place children, because healthy young ones are usually adopted by their foster parents; or homes are already lined up to take them before they ever have a chance to be put on these sites.

Adopting an older child has a unique set of challenges. Most of the time these older children have lived at least part of their lives with their birth parents and no matter whether they were treated well or very, very badly, they have formed the bond that all children form with their parents, and they will carry the lifelong trauma of being parted from them. This can be hard for the new family to understand. They have sometimes waited many years to adopt, and they love the child and want nothing more than to give him a wonderful, happy life. They can't understand why the child does not respond to their love and desire—why he doesn't put the past behind him and be happy in the present and the future.

If an older adopted child is not allowed to release and verbalize his grief at losing his first family, he may internalize it, and become mentally disturbed. The new family needs to understand this before they take on the challenge. Remembering his biological parents is the child's birthright. If the new parents can meet the need of the child in allowing him to grieve, the bond between them and the newly-adopted child will grow stronger, and the adoptive parents will have contributed much to their child's emotional health.

Some will explain to adopted children that their birth parents loved them so much that they gave them up. That explanation can cause distress in the child, because how does he know that you will not someday love him enough to give him up too?

Raley children

Another explanation adoptive parents use is to tell the child that by being adopted he was chosen or specially picked out, and that other people who give birth have to just take whatever they get. That explanation is faulty also. Obviously, someone gave birth to this child, too, and either chose not to keep him, for whatever reason, or lost custody because of poor choices. Someday the child may well link those ideas. It may cause a playground battle when the adopted child tells another child that he was chosen while his parents had to take what they got. The other child may know something about adoption and may throw back at the chosen child that someone, somewhere, gave him up, while he was kept. A child should be raised to consider everyone of worth, whether the child is in the family by birth or adoption.

Carla Raley and children

Experienced adoptive parents generally agree that parents should tell their adopted child as much information in age-appropriate portions as they know. The older the child gets the more he should be told, until by the age of twelve he knows all the particulars. That way he does not have to digest new information during the unsettled teen years, while he may be trying to pull away from his parents and become independent. All information should be given truthfully. Problems in the child's birth family are certainly not his fault. Parents should avoid expressing negative opinions about the child's birth parents. They may be able to talk about unwise decisions the birth parents have made and consequences of those, as a starting point to teach the child how to make right choices as he grows up.

If your child expresses interest in meeting his birth parents someday, you will want to reassure him that you will be right there beside him, so that he will not feel as if he is disloyal to you in his desire. A reunion with the child's birth parents is unlikely to cause the child to love you any less. In fact, he may love you more, because this is yet another way you have expressed your love, supported him, and helped him grow. Your support will be invaluable to him, whether the reunion goes well or not.

Thought for the Day

Adoption of the older child is not for the faint of heart, but very few worthwhile endeavors in life are easy!

Must I Love Her Mother?

Janice Byler

He that saith he is in the light, and hateth his brother,
is in darkness even until now. —1 John 2:9
Read 1 John 2:1-12

always sort of knew it was there. But I never really faced it head-on until one Sunday morning when I was sitting in church. The minister was talking about God's love for all mankind, no matter their sins or their faults. All of a sudden it was so clear and plain. Just as if God had written it in bold letters behind the pulpit.

"You hate your daughter's birth mother!"

At first I tried to deny it, but God knew better. Then I tried to justify it. Who wouldn't hate a mother who drank while she carried her baby? It was all her fault that Jessica had so many physical problems to conquer. She really was the one who should have been barren!

Beneath all the shouting in my mind I heard God softly saying, "But, Jan, you know she didn't have the chance you had. She was an alcoholic by the age of thirteen. She didn't have parents to show love to her, so how could she know how to love her unborn baby?"

Oh, I was willing to accept that, but I still didn't have to love her as much as . . . let's say, my own sister. Why, I had never met her, never even seen a picture of her!

That didn't satisfy God. He wanted me to love her. Love her enough to forgive her for what she had done to Jessica. Love her enough to pray for her, to pray that she would learn to know God and His unconditional love.

The tears were falling thick and fast. I couldn't help it. I couldn't love her. I didn't even know her! But Jesus gently prodded, "Do you want Jessica growing up to hate her birth mother? You can talk all you want, but if you don't truly forgive and love her yourself, neither will your daughter. Do you want her growing up with bitterness in her little heart?"

No, no! A thousand times no!

I knelt with the rest of the congregation at the close of the message. But I have no clue what the minister's prayer was, because I had some heavy praying to do for myself. I prayed that the Lord would give me a true, caring, forgiving love for Jessica's birth mother and that she would somehow be shown the light and the way of salvation. You can imagine the amazement I felt as I considered my new love for her and the peace I had.

I have prayed for her many times since, even out loud in family devotions. I want my precious daughter to grow up hearing me pray for her birth mother. I hope when she's struggling with rejection and anger that hearing her mother's prayers will help her through to victory.

Thought for the Day

More is caught than taught.

When We Fail

Name Withheld

*Being confident of this very thing, that he which hath begun a good work
in you will perform it until the day of Jesus Christ. —Philippians 1:6*
Read Philippians 2:1-9

I was sitting in church and the sermon was penetrating my very soul.

"There is a way to stand for principle that is completely contrary to the truth we desire to get across. It is discipline without relationship. If our children feel that distance when we discipline them, that is abuse. The time will come when they realize they can get out of this. They will not need to stay and surrender to the abuse. Genuine warmth and love must prevail in order for discipline to succeed. And that warmth and true agape love comes only from God. Relationships must be established in our homes and churches before discipline can be effective."

Was that the missing link? Was I disciplining without my child feeling my love? Was she instead feeling and focusing on the distance in our relationship? *"You are always punishing me."* Does she feel my frustration over how impossible she is? *"Just leave me alone. I know you can't stand me."* And does she feel my exasperation at yet another uncompleted task or haphazard job? *"I don't know why you ask me to do it at all. I can't ever do it well enough for you!"* Was my discipline actually abuse? This distance that I felt between us . . . and yet I kept on disciplining her.

During the next several days, I mulled over the words of the sermon. *But she's not supposed to talk back. She shouldn't be allowed to do her work halfway. She can't get away with dishonesty. She can't be mean to her siblings. I am the mother. I am responsible to not let her act this way! She doesn't really want to be this way, either. So I must help her.*

The minister's words kept rolling through my mind, "If discipline without relationship is abuse, and we know abuse is wrong and unproductive, then either the discipline stops or else the relationship needs to become what it should be."

I know I love my daughter, my thoughts protested. *I always have . . . I always will. But apparently I am not doing a very good job of communicating my love to her. She was not born from my flesh (she seems to feel this is the reason for the distance), but she is mine just as much as if she had been.*

She was just a baby when she entered our home, the most darling little girl, with thick lashes, a rosebud mouth, and a delightfully spontaneous and interesting personality. She was smothered with kisses and hugs, as my other babies have been, and she was spanked a lot as well. It seemed she was always into things and so determined. Most times after a spanking she was sweet and sunshiny again—for a time, at least. We had experienced many happy times together.

Not to discipline her would be giving up on her, I argued inwardly. *It's like saying, "Go ahead and be that way then!" I can't do that.*

O Lord, tell me then, how I can build the relationship between us.

My husband and I decided to fast and pray together about this. Several fellow Christians joined us. We talked to others with similar experiences.

Each morning I open my hand to God and ask Him through the power of the blood of His Son to fill me with His love. I ask Him to allow me to be a vessel through which His love can flow to my children, particularly to my troubled daughter. I ask Him to help me to show this love through words of affirmation. I ask Him to help me be kind in my disciplining so that His love will shine through. I ask Him to remind me when I deviate and am in any way sarcastic, unkind, or hurtful. He is faithful. If I fail to heed the whisper of the Holy Spirit, I have no option but to backtrack and apologize.

It is helping. I sense our relationship improving.

Lord, we have only one chance to walk this path. You know my desire for a warm, loving relationship with our daughter. You also know how to bring it about. Please show us how.

Thought for the Day

God delights in helping us build relationships.

Haunting, Hurtful Memories

Name Withheld

And God shall wipe away all tears from their eyes; and there shall be no more death, neither sorrow, nor crying, neither shall there be any more pain: for the former things are passed away. —Revelation 21:4
Read Psalm 91

hree cute little girls were adopted into three different homes. All three girls were pretty and charming with normal desires for acceptance and love. Each has shared particular memories of when they were ten years old. Focus with me on their ten-year-old memories . . .

Delores was older when she was adopted. Her babyhood and younger years had left much to be desired, as her birth mother was not a Christian. Delores's experience with men had been mostly with relatives and the boyfriends who came and went in her mother's life. Fortunately, her purity was spared. At age ten, she was old enough to realize that she and each of her siblings had different fathers, but was innocent enough that she didn't comprehend the implications. When life changed drastically and Delores and several siblings were placed in a Christian home, she took the change in stride. Happily, she adjusted to her new environment with plenty of food, clean clothes, and a stable two-parent family. She especially enjoyed the privilege of having a dad.

Delores was happy, outgoing, and delighted in life as it was. She didn't waste a lot of time looking back. Often Mother had to remind her to tone down a bit, to keep to her work, or to redo a task. But there were so many fun things to do on the farm and a whole bunch of brothers and sisters to play and work with. And although she wasn't quite sure how this new mother viewed her, she was confident that Dad liked her. She could sense his goodwill and approval and smiled under it, eager to please.

Then the incident happened that changed her life.

Visitors were present, and a bunch of folks were gathered in a cluster in the family room. One of the boys had rescued an almost-expired fledgling hummingbird from the cat. He was showing it to Dad. "It doesn't look like it's going to make it," Dad commented. "Isn't it tiny though, and such a marvel of God's creation!"

Delores crowded in to see.

"Delores," Mother reprimanded, "come here by me." Delores detected disapproval in her voice as she went to stand by Mother. She wondered what she had done wrong. In a few minutes, Mother led her around the corner into the pantry where they could talk in privacy. Mother's voice was clipped and full of emotion. "Delores, I do not want you leaning over Dad like that. You need to be more careful. You know that your birth mother is a wicked, immoral woman, and we do not want to have anything like that in our home."

Delores was crushed. She had been totally innocent, and the insinuated accusation burned in her breast. It followed her all through her teenage years. *I would never . . . That Mother would even dare think that of me . . . One thing for sure, never again will Mother ever be able to accuse me of anything of that nature!*

Delores often found herself drawing inward, and she was very careful for the rest of her growing-up years to keep a healthy space between Dad and herself. One day he asked kindly, "Delores, have I done something that hurt you in any way or offended you? You act almost as if you are afraid of me." But she didn't answer him. What was there to say? She was sure Dad and Mother loved each other, and she would say or do nothing to come between them.

———————◦❖◦———————

Kristi was adopted as a baby. As a little girl, she remembers especially adoring her dad. Her mother tells her that as a tiny baby she slept best on Dad's chest. It seemed perhaps his heartbeat more closely resembled her birth mother's, and she was comforted there. She followed him around much of the time, chattering until he told her to hush a bit. At times she was stubborn and refused to obey Mom, but not Dad. He was to be reverenced, feared, admired, and loved.

Being the youngest of the family and a bit pampered and fussed over, Kristi felt much love and acceptance and security. Mom and Dad were quite affectionate in demonstrating their love to each other. Heading into their sunset years of life, they were together constantly, working and eating and going and coming together. Kristi always felt good about how much her parents loved each other.

Kristi clearly remembers one winter evening when she was ten years old. Dad would be home soon. She could hardly wait. She would give him a great big bear hug around his neck and tell him all about her day. Eagerly she watched out the window. His truck lights were coming up the drive. She heard the truck motor turn off, the door slam, and his footsteps coming up the walk. He opened the door. With a little cry of welcome, she reached up to hug him. He stopped, a bit startled. He unwrapped her fingers from about his neck and commanded abruptly, "You run along now!"

Never again has Kristi voluntarily touched her father. "Me, touch my dad? Never!" She recalls the incident of over a decade ago with evident wistfulness. Kristi has a warm, open relationship with her mother, sharing hugs and confidences freely. She respects both of her parents and clearly wants to please them.

————⚬•⚬————

The third little girl we will call Kelly. Her parents were not following God with pure hearts and their home was not a godly Christian home, although they attended church sometimes. The ten-year-old scene Kelly remembers clearly was at church. She remembers how uncomfortable she felt with the affection her dad displayed for her in front of her friends. One day she talked to her dad about it. "I wish you wouldn't put your hand around my shoulders and rub my back like that in front of my friends. It makes me feel ashamed or something."

"I wouldn't know why it should," he assured her. "They are probably jealous. They likely wish their dads would pat them a little more." But Kelly was unconvinced. The cuddling and the patting progressed to total violation at the age of fifteen. What a great victory Satan had won! As the bruised, crushed teenager was banished from her home, she was discarded and despised by father and mother, especially her mother. Years later, she continues to carry the scars of low self-worth and degradation.

"I was not entirely innocent," Kelly admits today, "but everything was so mixed that I didn't know where 'parental affection' started and stopped."

As a Christian mother now herself, Kelly desires to protect her children from pain such as she experienced. It has been a long, difficult road of heartache, frustration, and despair for her to find healing. This experience of sexual abuse has negatively affected her marriage, her relationships with church friends, and many other areas of her life. Satan meant to totally defeat her and take her down the road to ruin, but praise the Lord, it was through this terrible experience that she met true Christians who have helped her. She has a desire to do right and to press on.

As we work with Kelly and others like her, we are thankful for parents who set safe lines. What is the best way to set these lines? And if a child feels uncomfortable about displays of affection, is there someone safe with whom she can share?

————⚬•⚬————

As an adult and mother now herself, Delores at times wishes for a deeper, stronger bond between herself and her parents. Yes, she is sure they are happy with the wise choices she has made, and they share a pleasant relationship, but something is missing. Does the distance she senses between her and her mother stem back to a little conversation around a corner so many years ago? Did Delores sense that her new mother identified her with her birth mother and low morals? Would it have been better to share the concern for purity at a different time, with the adoptive mother identifying with her? Perhaps she could have said, "As you are getting bigger, I need to remind you that we as women need to be careful never to do anything that would make it hard for a man to keep pure thoughts, even Dad and your brothers." How much better to identify with our daughters instead of connecting them to some distant past over which they had no control.

Surely Delores's mother was trying to help her daughter. It also was her right and privilege to guard the relationship between her husband and their daughters. But it shouldn't be out of proportion. Sometimes in our zeal to avoid a catastrophe like Kelly's story, we overreact. Jealousy can become like a mountain in our minds and color our thinking and actions. Often it helps to be frank and honest with our husbands about our struggles. Maybe if Delores could realize that it wasn't anything personal against her, it could help bridge the gap between her and her mother.

———◆———

Now let us look at Kristi. Was her father actually rejecting her? Perhaps it had only then occurred to him how big his ten-year-old daughter was growing to be and that this kind of hugging was a bit inappropriate for her age. What is a good way for a father to help his daughter realize that touch, which was right and good as a little girl, changes as she grows older? How can Kristi be assured of her father's love in a pure, safe way as an adult? Is not ten years old a good time to show verbal approval and love? Affirmations like, "My little girl is growing up!" and "What a young lady you are!" help a girl feel treasured. First, help her to act like a princess; then treat her with the courteous respect a princess deserves. It is also good for a father to talk about it. "I treasure you and want to guard your purity." His teenage daughter needs to know that although growing up brings changes, changes are not necessarily bad. A daughter with a turbulent early life often needs extra reassurance and approval from her father. But it is usually best to limit his touch to a single arm around his daughter's shoulder, or less.

May we all be as wise as serpents and harmless as doves as we carefully monitor, guard, and protect these dear ones who have been entrusted to us.

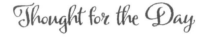

Thought for the Day

Let us give our children memories they can treasure.

A Cry for Help

Name Withheld

O give thanks unto the LORD, for he is good: for his mercy endureth for ever.
Let the redeemed of the LORD say so, whom he hath redeemed from the
hand of the enemy; and gathered them out of the lands, from the east,
and from the west, from the north, and from the south. —*Psalm 107:1-3*
Read Psalm 107:28-43

Several years ago while volunteering at a prison crusade, I came to a turning point in my life. A family of ten shared in song, followed by an evangelistic message. At the close of the sermon the father of the family stated, "My daughter Jane would like to share her testimony." As she shared, my heart constricted with fear, and yet a longing. A desire filled my bosom to have the freedom this girl was portraying. Jane was a victim of sexual abuse. My mind raced. *How can she have so much joy and freedom that she can stand in front of a crowd and share her story?*

When the altar call was given, a slip of a girl of about fifteen responded. As a volunteer, I went up to pray with her. Heart-wrenching sobs came from this young person. I asked her if there was something she wanted to share before we prayed. Before she had a chance to reply, I knew the answer, and my heart automatically closed to hearing her desperate need.

She kept her eyes on the button of her sweater as she twisted it in and out. Hesitantly she whispered, "I've been through the same thing that girl was talking about." A feeling of inadequacy enveloped me, and instead of praying with the girl, I asked Jane to pray with her.

I left that day with a sick feeling and a cry deep in my own heart. I had also been a victim of abuse similar to these two girls. So why couldn't I help this young girl? Simply for this reason: I had never dealt with my own abuse. From that day forward I knew I wanted help, not only for myself, but so that I would also be able to help others. Prior to this incident I had shared my story with a close friend, who gave a listening ear and shared how she found healing for her own abuse. That in itself was an eye-opener. When I realized other girls had gone through this very same thing and that my best friend had survived, I knew there was hope for me. But at that time, I wasn't ready to deal with it completely, or I would have been better equipped to help the young girl at the altar.

Sexual abuse is an awful thing for a child to deal with, but the scars are even harder to erase as you reach adulthood. It takes the healing ointment of Christ to deal with those memories, and also to resolve the feelings of self-loathing that accompany abuse. So how did I go about getting help? God saw fit to put different people in my life to help me find forgiveness and freedom in Christ. After many years of blocking any flashbacks, it takes time to break those walls of indifference to pain and to be open to confiding in a trustworthy friend. I have also read books with personal stories of other abuse victims. Still, I often struggled and wondered, *Is there any hope for someone so ruined? Is there really hope for me?*

Yes, there is! We will never be able to stop sexual abuse in our perverted society, but we can give a ray of hope to the hurting.

No, my struggles are not over. Neither is the anger or hate toward sexual abuse gone, but God's grace is sufficient for each day. Being willing to forgive has set me free from the bitterness and anger toward God and those who have hurt me. This has given me a sense of worth and purpose for living. I have also been able to think of my abuser as a victim of his/her own lust during my childhood. Was I easier prey because of being adopted? I don't need to know.

Most of all I praise God for allowing me to no longer think of myself as a victim, but as a victor in Christ.

If you've been through this kind of abuse, please find help. Find a trusted adult in whom you can confide—perhaps your mother, a minister's wife, or a good friend will be willing to listen and help you find peace and assurance in God's Word. A very dear friend and I have been keeping in contact, and it's helped both of us tremendously.

Thought for the Day

Yesterday you can't alter, but your reaction to yesterday you can.
The past you cannot change,
but your response to your past you can.

—Max Lucado

Always Trusts, Always Protects

Name Withheld

Blessed are the pure in heart: for they shall see God. —Matthew 5:8
Read 1 Corinthians 13

Our little child came to us with a story to tell, the kind no parent wants to hear. It was ugly. A family member had betrayed our trust, and consequently a young child was violated.

We had a motto on our family room wall at the time. On it was a portion of 1 Corinthians 13 from the NIV translation. It read, "Love does not delight in evil but rejoices with the truth. It always protects, always trusts, always hopes, always perseveres. Love never fails."

Always protects, always trusts, always hopes . . . I wept as the words chugged around in my weary brain. I wondered in despair how we could possibly trust and protect at the same time. In choosing to trust one individual, did it not put innocent little ones in danger? Where was our place? What did God expect of us as parents? *Always hopes, always perseveres . . .* Did that mean never giving up on individuals? *God, You know I love them both, and You have said, "Love never fails." What do You want of us? What shall we do?*

When we trust someone, we are bestowing on them the highest honor we can. "The heart of her husband doth safely trust in her." What delightful, restful joy when our loved ones deem us trustworthy! Our God, who knows the past, present, and future, can see into our very hearts and souls. He knows whether we are worthy of someone's trust. But how can other people know the integrity of our hearts? How can we know the integrity of someone else?

Is it possible to rebuild the relationship when we or someone else has failed and betrayed trust? Will it ever be the same again? Is it worth trying? Are there some sins that are just unforgivable?

When we were at this very low spot of rebuilding broken trust, I received a letter from a friend. A note at the bottom read, "As a way of encouragement, I will tell you that Roger and his wife are completely able to trust their children now. They really can!" I remembered some of the family's earlier struggles, and I marveled. It gave me a ray of hope and courage to try. *Lord, please show us how! How did they get from where they were to where they are?*

It may take years to build back trust to where the relationship was before. Sometimes the same level of trust is never attained again. Suspicion always hovers. Sometimes trust is broken again and again. There appears to be little or no foundation to build on. Other times the relationship is richer, better than before trust was broken. Wherein lies the difference?

If there is sincere penitence, brokenness, and openness to advice, there is much hope for the situation. Is the one who has failed willing to be accountable to trusted adults? How much easier it is to trust someone when there are no secrets! Temptations are faced, failures acknowledged, and victories delighted in together. And strength is found through prayer and fasting and sharing together, if the desire to do right is there.

People often say, "But it will never be the same again!" That is true, but we can testify that it can be better than it was before. Satan would have these children. He has introduced his wickedness to some through no fault of their own at a tender age. His desire is to turn these victims into perpetrators so that he can watch with fiendish glee as more innocent ones are tainted and scarred. But God has a much better plan. He saves, restores, forgives, and heals broken and damaged hearts. He is enlarging

His kingdom with these precious souls. Who do we really believe to be the strongest, to have the most power—God or the wicked one?

"And the Lord said, Simon, Simon, behold, Satan hath desired to have you, that he may sift you as wheat: But I have prayed for thee, that thy faith fail not: and when thou art converted, strengthen thy brethren" (Luke 22:31, 32).

God delights in taking the very things the devil planned for our ruin and defeat and turning them into good. Perhaps the child who has experienced pain and betrayal will be the first to sense when another is hurting. If he has found healing and victory, he could be the very best worker as an adult to walk beside another who may be struggling in a similar experience. God has great plans for these children in His kingdom. Like Jesus said to Simon, "And when thou art converted, strengthen thy brethren."

Thought for the Day

If God be for us, who can be against us?

Father-Daughter Relationships

Dallas and Rhoda Witmer

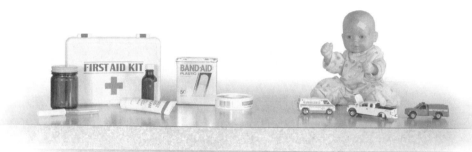

But whoso shall offend one of these little ones which believe in me,
it were better for him that a millstone were hanged about his neck,
and that he were drowned in the depth of the sea. —Matthew 18:6

Read Esther 2

It is a not-so-well-kept nasty secret of the public welfare systems that many men abuse their adoptive, foster, or step-daughters. The adolescent orphaned girl is especially vulnerable to sexual abuse. Coming into a new home with a father, after having had none, she now senses security. Happy is the daughter who is granted a father worthy of that trust, with whom she may develop a wholesome father-daughter relationship like that of Mordecai and Esther.

Adoptive fathers, beware of the temptation that a new, dependent adolescent girl coming into your home presents to you. The chemistry between you is not the same as with those daughters raised on your knee from babyhood. A greater reserve is necessary than that which you may practice with your birth daughters. If equality is an issue, you must transition all daughters away from your hugs and good-night kisses at adolescence. Real love and security do not depend upon physical touching between father and daughter, and have too often been violated by it. Real love and security instead depend upon the confidence that Father is a man who would never take unwarranted liberties with his daughter.

Your new daughter badly needs you, Father. But to betray the trust and dependency of youth is to offend a little one. Jesus said that such an offender would be better drowned in the depths of the sea.

Thought for the Day

He that troubleth his own house shall inherit the wind.
—Proverbs 11:29

The Result Of Bitterness

Name Withheld

an adoptee

Follow peace with all men, and holiness, without which no man shall see the Lord: looking diligently lest any man fail of the grace of God; lest any root of bitterness springing up trouble you, and thereby many be defiled. —Hebrews 12:14, 15

Read Matthew 6:9-15

As a toddler, I knew the pure love of my papa. His ill health required him to do light work, so he cared for me while Mama and the older ones did the outside chores. But Papa died when I was four. How I missed him! Mama's family from many miles away came for my penniless mama and us five children. We were put into the homes of strange relatives.

From age five until age eight I was here and there among strangers who knew how to feed and clothe me, but alas, did not know how to comfort and love me. How I longed for my own dear papa's love and security! Where did I belong?

At the age of eight I entered as a foster child into the home of a childless Mennonite couple. "You took me from my mama," I accused this couple, who were trying to do their best. When I was twelve, two little ones came into the home through adoption, and now I was to call my foster parents Daddy and Mother.

Daddy was usually distant with me, but as I developed physically, inappropriate touch began when we were alone. I tried to avoid him. When Mother was busy with her heart's delight, caring for the little ones, Daddy seemed to find more time to be alone with me. In my longing for attention and love, I began to respond to his wishes and to the desires he had illicitly awakened in me.

Several years passed. The day came when I refused him. That evening I sassed him about something. Before this, Mother had always been the one to punish me by slapping my mouth or spanking me. But this time, Daddy slapped me over and over until I nearly passed out. My brother, who was six at the time, also remembers that day. Daddy must have been very angry at being rejected. But he left me alone after that. Several years later another attempt was made. Again I refused.

I had given my heart to the Lord when I was ten, and in my early teens I repeatedly responded at revival meetings, but the real issue never surfaced. At tent meetings when I was twenty years old, I finally yielded to the Holy Spirit's pleading and again responded to the invitation. I was determined to clean up my life. I told the counselor that I had to make things right at home, although I didn't tell her what it was. I called Mother upstairs that evening and told her that Daddy and I had been impure. She asked Daddy to come into the room and asked him if this was true. He said, "It could have been a lot worse." Those were the only words I ever heard from him about it. At the time, I was just so grateful for forgiveness from God and that Mother treated me kindly and that I wasn't sent away.

In all my twenty years there, I struggled with the feeling of not belonging. The adopted children shared my parents' name, while I did not. And although my parents weren't unkind to me, I was treated differently, with little affection shown.

Daddy's nephew's wedding took place some distance away. I had just moved to my own apartment, but was invited to the wedding, so I traveled with others. A lady came to a group of us and asked if Oliver Witmer[8] was here at the wedding. "He's my Dad," I informed her, and I took her to him. As they talked, she asked about his family. "We have two children," he

---

8   Not his real name.

said as he pointed them out to her. There I stood, claiming him as Dad, and I wasn't counted as one of his. How crushed I felt! Where *did* I belong?

At the age of thirty-one, I married a godly man who was a bit older than I and lived in another state. For the first time since I was four, I felt I truly belonged to someone. My kind husband blessed me over and over. I gave birth to two precious children. Our home centered on Christ, and love flowed freely.

But I was troubled with episodes of deep depression, often being hospitalized and even receiving electric convulsive treatments. My faithful husband held me lovingly, even when I'd say, "I'm so bad, too bad to be loved."

At Daddy's funeral many things were said about this "upright" man. I sat there screaming inside, "But you don't know him!" For some years after that, I battled the desire to smash his tombstone and smear his good name in the community.

Five years after his death, I heard a message on bitterness. Through this, I recognized my sin of great bitterness toward the man who had robbed me of so much. This bitterness had caused my depression.

Thus began my journey of recognizing that I had a choice—a choice to forgive totally, asking God to forgive *my sin* of bitterness. At first, I looked at Daddy as an enemy, and Jesus required me to love my enemies. But as God worked in my heart, He led me on to want to show some honor to him as my father by sending Mother flowers on his birthday and on the anniversaries of his death. This helped me greatly in my healing. It also helped me see how precious Mother had become to me.

In spite of the episodes of depression, all through the years I have had much to praise my Lord for. He loved me and kept me, giving me a loving husband and children. Now my healing feels complete. I find opportunities to minister to other troubled souls. I have real peace.

Thought for the Day

Make stumbling blocks into stepping-stones to higher ground.

A Real Brother

Janice Byler

To have respect of persons is not good. —Proverbs 28:21
Read James 2:1-10

We had company for dinner, and they had a girl my age. We were virtually strangers, so to take up the slack I suggested we take a walk to the river. By the time we made our way back, we had both loosened up and talk was flowing freely. I was beginning to think of her as a possibility for a new friend, maybe a pen pal, until the conversation took a jagged turn.

She said, "How could you possibly feel like a Negro was your brother? I'd be embarrassed to have him in my family picture!"

I was shocked and appalled. How dare she talk about my brother like that? The nerve, to say it right to my face!

"I don't even think of the color of Bobby's skin," I declared. "It absolutely doesn't make any difference. He's as much my brother as my biological brother, Dale. I'd never want a family picture *without* Bobby. It wouldn't be complete."

She tossed her head and said, "I don't care what you say; he can't seem like a *real* brother. I'm sure glad I don't have a mixed-up family like you do!"

We walked the rest of the way in icy silence, and when we arrived home I didn't ask for her address. I was glad when they left. I was twelve or thirteen years old, and I don't even remember her name.

Afterward I shared her remarks with my mom.

"Janice," she said, "some people just don't understand.

The author with her parents and siblings

To us the color of the skin makes no difference. In fact, we like different-colored skin. And think about how much fun it is to pat Bobby's curly hair. Because he is Indian and African-American, his hair is curly, yet soft. God made everybody special, just the way He wanted us. Regardless of comments people make, we can respond in love, and we can always be kind."

Two lessons were etched firmly in my young mind. One was that God loves us no matter what our nationality, and He's pleased to have us be a part of His family. The second was that I need to be forgiving of others. Not everyone has had the privilege of having a real brother with a different color of skin.

Thought for the Day

And be ye kind one to another, tenderhearted, forgiving one another, even as God for Christ's sake has forgiven you. —Ephesians 4:32

Created for
A Purpose

Rhoda Bontrager

Thus saith the LORD that made thee, and formed thee from the womb,
which will help thee. —Isaiah 44:2
For we are his workmanship. —Ephesians 2:10
Read Isaiah 44:1-8

It is imperative that we help our children grasp the truth that, yes, God created them. He didn't have to; they weren't accidents. God had a special plan in mind and a unique purpose for their lives when they were formed in their birth mother's womb. One of our birth mothers told me, "What I did was wrong, but I know God is going to make something good come out of it." She recognized that God had a plan for her unborn baby.

Can our children feel God's love and compassion through us? Their first impression of an Almighty God is the impression their earthly father (and mother) make on them. Do they sense our loving compassion in the struggles they face, unique to their particular situation? Are they free to come and talk to us about their burdens, feelings of rejection, and frustrations with learning disabilities? Do we hold their hands as they seek to find purpose in life? Or do we do all the talking, telling them how they should feel and act? It is a challenge for me, as a mother, to listen quietly to their lurking fears and struggles. That is often more important than spewing off pat answers and giving them the feeling that their problems are trivial and easily solved.

Do they truly feel that we have accepted them into our hearts as our children—that we are convinced they were created for a purpose and that it is our sincere desire for them to fulfill that purpose to the honor and glory of God? Are they assured that our adopting them is not for any selfish reason?

Our daughter once came to me with a struggle she was facing. "Mama, almost every time we are together, Beverly[9] asks me, 'Who were your first parents, and where do they live?' I don't mean to be unkind and just walk away, but when I say you and Daddy are my parents, she says, 'No, I mean your first parents.' I don't know what to say next."

I was thankful she opened her heart to me. We discussed some possible responses that would be appropriate. Grandma came up with a gem and our children loved it. Now when they are asked that question, with a grin they reply, "Adam and Eve, just like yours!" That's usually the end of the conversation!

Poem for the Day

You Are Who You Are

You are who you are for a reason.
You're part of an intricate plan.
You're a precious and perfect unique design,
Called God's special woman or man.

---

9 Not her real name

You look like you look for a reason.
Our God made no mistake.
He knit you together within the womb,
You're just what He wanted to make.

The parents you had were the ones He chose,
And no matter how you may feel,
They were custom-designed with God's plan in mind,
And they bear the Master's seal.

No, that trauma you faced was not easy.
And God wept that it hurt you so;
But it was allowed to shape your heart
So that into His likeness you'd grow.

You are who you are for a reason,
You've been formed by the Master's rod.
You are who you are, beloved,
Because there is a God![10]

—Russell Kelfer

Whom Will She Marry?

Anita King

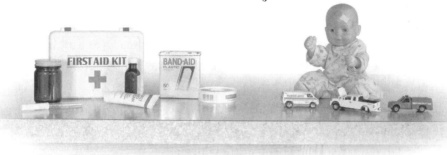

Draw me, we will run after thee: the king hath brought me into his chambers . . . I am black, but comely. —Song of Solomon 1:4, 5

Read Numbers 12

I must admit that who my beautiful eight-month-old daughter was going to marry was not high on my list of concerns. I would soon learn it would be a question we would hear repeated many times with regards to her, as well as the other four children we were eventually to adopt.

At first it just angered me. Then it grieved me. Then it frustrated me. How do you answer such a question?

My husband answered it perfectly as he snuggled his precious little daughter close. Another father bouncing his child on his knee had asked the by-now-annoying question. My husband replied, "Well, I don't know. Has God told you yet whom your little boy is going to marry?"

We have come to simply respond with, "We have searched the Scriptures and find that God has one command for marriage, and that is that it be 'in the Lord.' So long as our children marry in the Lord, we don't care if their companions are lime green."

Should the basis for whether or not to adopt a child be whether we know whom he will marry? We didn't adopt our children so that we could plan their weddings and receptions far ahead of time!

What if our parents wouldn't have kept us because they couldn't give a satisfactory answer as to whom we would marry? When we are tiny, all bundled up in pink or blue, red-faced and squalling, our future companion is seldom what comes to our parents' minds.

I have been facilitating adoptions for at least fifteen years now, and I still hear, "Whom will he/she marry?" Empty arms are still empty because the answer isn't clear enough to a couple. God doesn't plan for all of His children to be married. He is also very able to take care of who the marriage partner will be.

I understand that many people still believe that interracial marriage is a sin. However, it seems they believe it is more of a sin for a white person to marry someone of another race than for any other combination to marry. What does that tell us?

We didn't ask who our oldest birth daughter was going to marry (it never occurred to us). When her future husband came to us, prior to asking her to court him, he asked this question: "Does my being black cause a problem?" (At least that is what was translated to us, because not only was he black, but he couldn't speak English either).

Long ago we had decided the answer to that question. "To marry only in the Lord is what is important to us and what we want for each of our children."

We have been incredibly blessed with our son-in-law. He has a reputation of godliness among black and white people alike. He treats our daughter like a queen and raises our beautiful biracial granddaughter for the Lord. What more can we ask?

As to the rest of our children—we still don't know who they are going to marry, but I am pretty sure their spouses won't be lime green.

Thought for the Day

All nations of the earth are of one blood.

Bad Blood

Christine Diller

What mean ye, that ye use this proverb concerning the land of Israel, saying,
The fathers have eaten sour grapes, and the children's teeth are set on edge?
As I live, saith the Lord GOD, ye shall not have occasion any more to use this
proverb in Israel. Behold, all souls are mine. —Ezekiel 18:2-4
Read Ezekiel 18:1-23

God commands parents to teach and train their children in His ways. This gives us the assurance that environment is important in raising God-fearing children. Other verses talk about fathers' sins being passed down to their children. Some argue that this means genes are the deciding factor in how children will turn out, and that bad blood produces bad blood.

When I look at my heritage, I see bad blood. I see humans who've made mistakes. I see men and women who have sinned. I also see the power of the new birth and the power of the Holy Spirit living in them. I see repentant hearts, and despite the original bad blood, I see men and women after God's own heart.

I know my parents' failings perhaps better than anyone else, and I am determined not to repeat their mistakes. Yet, in spite of this, I often find myself reacting the same way they did. Is this genes or environment? Those of us with adopted children know they act very much like we do too. Probably both genes and environment shape our lives. And maybe this debate isn't so important.

What is important, however, is that like my parents, I can claim the power of Jesus' blood and the power of the Holy Spirit living in my life right now. I can serve Him even though I have sinned and will struggle with sinful tendencies as long as I am in the flesh.

Am I of a special lineage that I receive forgiveness for my bad blood? Are there those in the world who can't receive the power of new life in Jesus because of bad blood? No, of course not! We know Christ died for all. These Old Testament verses assure us that Christ will break any generational sin.

One adoptive mother was asked, "Aren't you worried about what traits your adopted child might have inherited from his birth parents?"

She replied, "No, I'm just glad this child won't inherit my weaknesses."

This is the spirit of Christ, when we can humble ourselves and realize we didn't inherit any special merit with God because we may have had godly birth parents.

Thought for the Day

For God so loved the world, that he gave his only begotten Son, that whosoever believeth in him should not perish, but have everlasting life. —John 3:16

Not Too Dark

Becky Wenger

Did not he that made me in the womb make him? —*Job 31:15*
Read Job 31:15-35

The young woman before me gently stroked the honey-brown skin of my biracial baby. "Will he get any darker?" she queried.

"Probably not," I answered, wondering if I should explain that usually by six months old, the skin tones have reached their peak, except for what a normal suntan would add to it.

But before I had a chance to decide, she was talking again. "That's nice," she said, smiling. She must have seen the shocked look on my face, for quickly she went on, "I mean, we love the dark ones too, but it's nice when they don't get *too* dark."

Her comments set my mind reeling. Not *too* dark? How dark is too dark? When we had applied for adoption, we had stated that we would welcome children of any race. Would she accept our children of the future if we adopted ones that were "too dark"?

What stung the most was who this woman was. Not an ungodly neighbor. Not a nosey stranger. Not even someone unfamiliar with adoption. She was a friend of mine in one of our churches, herself a sister of adopted biracial siblings.

Lest we perpetuate prejudice, we may need to rethink our attitudes and take an honest look at what God says about the people He created.

"Did not he that made me in the womb make him?" (Job 31:15). "The LORD is the maker of them all" (Proverbs 22:2). "Seeing he giveth to all life, and breath, and all things; And hath made of one blood all nations of men for to dwell on all the face of the earth" (Acts 17:25, 26).

Austin Wenger

I have often pondered the verses in Acts that talk about the struggle the apostles had to accept that God was allowing the Gentiles to be included with God's people. I wonder if part of their struggle was not only in accepting the diversity of language and culture, but also of accepting people of different skin color. In the end, they rejoiced that God was making a way for people of all nations to be joined together in His name.

What can we do to help our children through the maze of varying attitudes about race? One thing we stress with our children is that it is okay for others to talk about what they look like. Just as we say, "Give this to the boy with the blond hair," we should have no problem with, "I think it belongs to the black girl." What you look like is a part of who you are and is nothing to be ashamed of.

We need to help our children understand that if they are in a setting where others don't often see people of their race, some have a simple curiosity and need to be given the opportunity to become familiar with someone who looks different.

I still chuckle to myself when I recall one incident that took place at church. My daughter was surrounded by curious little friends. They were touching her hair, holding her hands, and stroking her skin, examining her as if she were some exotic petting zoo specimen. "Your skin is black . . . and your hair is black . . . and look, even your lips are black!" After various exclamations were shared all around, one of the children asked, "Is your tongue black too?"

My daughter shrugged. "I don't know!" she laughed good-naturedly.

"We wanna see, we wanna see!" came the cry. Obediently, she stuck out her tongue for all to see. Lo and behold, it was pink like all the rest!

Rosalie Wenger

As I later discussed this with my daughter, I did not sense that she was bothered by it. I realized then that a lot of the prejudice children pick up comes from the adults' responses to situations like this. I would not have wanted the parents of any of those children to scold them for what took place. My daughter said she liked that they wanted to talk to her and find out what she was like. Now that they know, they accept her, and it has not been an ongoing issue.

It is inevitable, however, that sooner or later our children will face cutting remarks. The most important thing we can do for them is to be there for them and help them through their pain. The anger and frustration they may feel should not be a taboo subject.

Have you considered the importance of learning how to properly care for your child's skin and hair type? Knowing there is a way to manage their hair can go a long way in helping your children to know they are normal. I well remember the discouraged look on the face of a twelve-year-old girl who was admiring my daughter's neatly braided hair. "It looks so nice combed this way," she said wistfully. I didn't understand why she looked sad about it until she sighed, "My mom says my hair is such a mess." Mothers, what are we telling our girls if we let them know we are frustrated with caring for their hair?

When I saw how the mothers in Africa braided their girls' hair into neat rows, I decided if their fingers can do it, mine can too. I was blessed to have had a Haitian woman living across the street from us at one time, and she delighted in teaching me how to care for my girls' hair. Instead of struggling every day to comb their hair into the traditional one or two braids their friends have, I spend about an hour every Friday or Saturday with my two girls' hair, and then it is done for the week. No, their hair is not a mess. I enjoy working with it! Some have asked me if I will keep on combing their hair this way when they get older. "Won't they mind being so different?" I can't predict what their hair will be like then. Maybe

Bethany Wenger

as it gets longer it will be more possible to comb it "like everyone else's." On the other hand, I have seen how their friends get used to seeing them that way and accept it as a part of who they are. Though I have experimented some with other styles, I keep coming back to the braided rows or the multiple braids because it is the healthiest for their hair type. This I learned from the Haitian neighbor and from experience. They don't have nearly as much trouble with dandruff and fungus this way. Braiding their hair into many sections exposes the scalp to sunlight and air.

Helping children accept their race becomes easier if they can learn to know other children and adults as role models in Christian families who look like them. If the only time they see people of their own race is at the grocery store or across the street, they may wonder if it is possible to be a Chinese Christian, or an African Christian, or whatever race they are.

Perhaps you adoptive parents have experienced what I call reverse prejudice: comments from people who go out of their way to assure you they have no problem with your dark children. "You have beautiful children!" "I love your daughter's hair!" "You have such sweet little darkies, and we love them all the same as the others, don't we?" Comments such as these can be just as confusing and painful for children to deal with as the negative ones. They still make the child feel, "I'm different; I don't fit in." It is just as important to discuss these comments with your child and help him work through his feelings regarding them.

We need to be constantly alert for comments people make in front of our children's listening ears and help them learn how to deal with them. Instead of strangers asking my children's names and ages, the first question is usually along this line: "Who is this?" "Are they foster, adopted, or what?" "Is he a prison baby?" "Where did they come from?" and even, "What are you doing with those children!" Sadly, these are all real comments from real people. Sometimes I long to simply be accepted as a mother of all my children.

For a refreshing change from all of this, ponder with me the question one dear lady asked when we met as strangers after church. After we greeted and exchanged names, she playfully tugged at my son's chubby baby fist and said, "Is this your son?" Words like these are music to my ears! Let's join this woman in spreading encouraging words, showing to others that God's love in our hearts reaches out to all and is not based on skin color!

Alex Wenger

Thought for the Day

If we teach our children the song "Jesus loves the little children . . . red, brown, yellow, black, and white, they are precious in his sight," we should also teach them how to make it a real part of our lives.

Surprise Package

Christine Diller

Are not five sparrows sold for two farthings, and not one of them is
forgotten before God? But even the very hairs of your head are all numbered.
Fear not therefore: ye are of more value than many sparrows. —Luke 12:6, 7
Read Jeremiah 1:4-10

*E*ach adoptive family has a beautiful story to tell of the time a new child joined their family. For most, that glad day came after years of searching for a child, or years of wondering if this child was going to stay.

Each child is a surprise package. Many a father has looked at his newborn son and dreamed of the day Sonny would follow his footsteps into the family business, only to find out years later that God had mapped out a different plan for this baby's life.

All parents, when they hope for a family, dream of healthy children. Again some parents are surprised. One young couple we know has an autistic child. Another couple has a child who is extremely difficult to teach and train, though there's been no definite diagnosis. A third couple has a child who grows too slowly, though tests show nothing is wrong.

One parent of a mentally handicapped child wrote, "It was like preparing for and taking a trip, and upon arrival, finding out I was in a different country than what I had planned."

An adopted child can be even more of a surprise package, because we do not know what genes he or she has inherited. Outside factors such as poor prenatal care or child abuse may adversely affect this child. We can and should ask about our child's history, but often little is known.

We do know that God knows exactly what is in each of these surprise packages. He created each one especially for a purpose, and He has been watching over each "sparrow" since birth.

All our children, biological or adopted, are unique individuals. Some of them will serve God wholeheartedly. Some may make wrong choices and bring sorrow to their parents and others who love them.

Perhaps you and I will need to stretch farther and give more to some children than to others. One thing we can be assured of is that God created each child. He has a plan for your child and our child. He wants to use everything in these children's lives, even unfortunate beginnings and hurtful pasts, in His glorious plan.

Thought for the Day

With God's help we can face all the unknowns.

Diller Family

School Days

(Part 1)

Name Withheld

Seek, and ye shall find. —Matthew 7:7
Teach me thy way, O LORD. —Psalm 86:11
Read Psalm 86

So many reasons for learning problems exist that I hesitate to write about what I've learned. The one most important thing I've learned is that God will help. As we grappled with learning problems in our family, I earnestly prayed and God led us to people who could support us. Learning difficulties do not go away overnight, but we and our children did receive help.

Academic problems can plague any child, but the troubles are often more pronounced when an older child has been institutionalized or moved from foster home to foster home and from school to school.

Emotional struggles can also interfere with school relationships and with learning. Maybe you and your child need to discuss some facts and feelings related to adoption. Books such as *Twenty Things Adoptive Children Wish Their Parents Knew* by Sherrie Eldridge can be helpful.

A birth mother's drug abuse can cause learning problems. Another common problem is the birth mother's use of alcohol. Adoptive parents are usually informed if a child has full-blown fetal alcohol syndrome. But many children aren't diagnosed because they don't have all the symptoms, though they may still be affected to some degree.

The effects of fetal alcohol syndrome can especially cause difficulties with math, and these children may have difficulties sticking with a task and using time wisely. They may be impulsive and easily influenced. These children do well in protected, structured environments. They need lots of love, patience, coaching, and supervision.

One of our sons was developmentally delayed. We spent years going over the basics. A special education teacher told me the goal for children like this is the fourth grade level, because adults can function passably at this level. Not all children will reach this goal in every subject. Where they don't, they will need extra help all their lives.

Some children appear intelligent until they start school, then they just can't make sense of all those squiggles on the paper. Sometimes learning difficulties are caused by mixed dominance problems with the right and left sides of the brain. Such cases are often helped with vision therapy, but not necessarily with glasses.

Children with learning problems may seem lazy and disobedient. They may not be able to hear directions and follow through properly. It is important to have them repeat directions back to you to help keep their full attention.

Whatever the problems your child is having at school, ask God to help, and then actively seek and knock. Read. Ask questions. Hunt for answers for your child.

Thought for the Day

God loves each child, and He knows the need of each child.
When we make the effort to seek and to knock for
answers for our child's learning difficulties,
He will be faithful in guiding us to the right answers.

School Days

(Part 2)

Name Withheld

I therefore, the prisoner of the Lord, beseech you that ye walk worthy of the vocation wherewith ye are called. —Ephesians 4:1

Read Ephesians 4

Our child is having difficulties in school. What should we do? With today's option of homeschooling, a good plan might be to bring him or her home for a while. But, homeschooling isn't an option for all. What can we do when our struggling child has to stay in school?

We need to work with our child's teacher and find ways at home to support what he or she is learning in school. Here are some ideas.

1. Look over homework every day. One mother of a poor math student made sure her daughter's math homework was correct each day.
2. Drill math facts or letter sounds for the beginning reader. One mother says, "Her teacher tells me that every fifteen minutes I spend drilling at home really helps."
3. Each phonics program and math program is different. Try to get a copy of what your teacher is using so you can teach the same way at home.
4. Get your child to bed early every night.
5. When your student is assigned reading in a subject like social studies, read it aloud with him.

6. Have your child read five to ten minutes a day throughout the summer if he's not reading independently so that he doesn't lose reading skills over the summer.

7. Volunteer to help the teacher at school so she has more time to help her special needs students, or ask to tutor them yourself.

8. Read aloud to your family. This helps the child who struggles to read on his own.

9. Don't overdo schoolwork at home. Give your child plenty of time to relax from schoolwork. He works harder in school than other children do.

10. Look for something extracurricular your child enjoys doing and provide lessons so there is something he or she can excel in. Maybe this could be painting, drawing, woodworking, or sewing.

11. Keep a good relationship with the teacher. Find out exactly what she wants your child to learn.

12. Pray with your child about school. Also pray for your child while he is in school. Surround him with the awareness of God's presence. Reassure him daily that God cares . . . and that you care.

Ephesians 4 speaks of our calling. Sometimes our calling is to raise a child with learning difficulties. This chapter also speaks of different gifts. Each person has something to offer others, even if he doesn't read well or if math doesn't click for him. We can help our child find ways to be a help to others. Study Ephesians 4 with your child and discuss ways he can contribute to producing unity at school.

Thought for the Day

Attitudes are so very important, and my child knows how
I feel about his schooling. Lord, help me to keep my
attitudes toward learning positive. Help me be loving and kind,
and keep me from becoming fretful or discouraged.

We Needed Help!

Name Withheld

For whom the LORD loveth he correcteth;
even as a father the son in whom he delighteth. —Proverbs 3:12
Read Proverbs 3:1-12

The Lord always knows what He is doing. When He blesses our lives with special little people who need help, I like to picture our heavenly Father scanning the earth.

"We have this child who is going to need special care, and we will need just the right set of parents who will be able to care for him. I know just the family . . ."

And then we are chosen! But some days it is hard to pull this mental picture together because of the stress and trials we are coping with, perhaps particularly brought on by our child with special needs.

We have a cherished son God has given to us. I will call him Tony. Early on we realized we would need more knowledge than we had at that point to be able to raise him in the fear of the Lord. At one year of age he already showed stress when interacting with people, especially little people with aggressive personalities. At first it was easy to subconsciously blame the little companions, because around more calm-natured children he could play fine all day. But realistically, Tony needed to learn to relate to any personality and not fight.

Tony is our fifth child, but the training methods that we thought were tried and true were not working. We tried stronger discipline. That pushed our problems totally out of hand. We backed off that route and made the playroom a "think room" or "time out."

By the time Tony was four years old, our hearts were seriously crying out to God for help beyond our experience and the local counsel we were receiving. Any type of correction or just a word of guidance brought an avalanche of emotion—usually anger, kicking, screaming, thrashing, and hateful disrespect and untrue accusations. It seemed extremely important to him to feel totally in control.

Tony's level of frustration made normal living a trial. It seemed like everything we did or wanted him to do was a fight. To a given command, either he did nothing or became very upset if we tried to enforce obedience. Even holding a pencil or crayon was frustrating to him.

We needed help! A friend suggested a place where other children with similar problems had been helped. She explained how the brain works and how it needs help sometimes to work properly. Often when different parts of the brain don't work properly, the cause is a lack of oxygen to the brain at some point. Maybe it was before or after birth or during a sickness. Sometimes a genetic disorder can affect the brain.

As with other adopted children, there are unknowns in Tony's history, things we were not informed about. *Was there a time when he didn't get the oxygen he needed? Is there hope for Tony? For our family?*

We went to the seminar and took Tony to be evaluated. A program was mapped out for us to help develop the parts of his brain that were struggling. They said the reason he was so frustrated was because his brain was disorganized. He was smart, but the lack of organization caused immense frustration and irritability. He was overly sensitive to noise, touch, and stimulation. That helped explain why people with aggressive personalities were too much for him and why pencils and crayons were too much. Even to obey a simple command seemed too much.

Tony is a very strong-willed child. The combination is very difficult. None of us can change the strong will. And really, we wouldn't want to. That part God may still need. But the people at the seminar did give us hope that with the right type of program, we could help reduce the frustration he faced constantly in his brain. Tony was a healthy, bright child, but unless we could help that confused brain, we wouldn't know how to train him for the Lord. That was our driving goal!

We were told to change Tony's diet drastically. At first he was to have only vegetables and meat. A food supplement was added to help his brain take in more oxygen. Gradually we were able to add other foods back into his diet. Often after an especially difficult time, we could trace his behavior back to change in diet. Also, Tony needed massive amounts (so it seemed to us) of creeping and crawling, along with extra stimulation from smells and textures, and word flash cards.

A month ago we went back for our first reevaluation. Tony had progressed fourteen and a half months in six months time. We were jubilant! Although buttons still frustrated him sometimes, he mostly dressed himself. He now enjoyed coloring. At the reevaluation he drew a picture for them. His frustration level was much diminished. The progress was amazing. At this point, he was enjoying life and was mostly cooperative. We limited how much company we had and learned to keep things scheduled . . . everything the same, day after day. As we worked diligently, he continued to improve.

Tony began to respond to discipline also, although it still doesn't work to spank until he gives up, as we would have done with our other children. Along with spanking, we have learned to give choices with consequences, such as withdrawing privileges or assigning extra jobs to help Mom. In some situations we have found that time alone does wonders. After each situation is taken care of, we determine not to withhold affection from him. All is forgiven and we are ready to begin again.

We think of the despair we felt four years ago and our heart-wrenching prayers for help. It looked impossible that our son would ever grow up to be a godly man. But we remembered that God has promised, "If any of you lack wisdom, let him ask of God, that giveth to all men liberally, and upbraideth not; and it shall be given him" (James 1: 5). We are confident that with much prayer and with doing all we now know to do, God will continue to heal Tony's brain. Our prayer is that God will use Tony's life and his story for His honor and glory.

Thought for the Day

Every child born into the world is a new thought of God,
an ever-fresh and radiant possibility.

—Kate Douglas Wiggen

What Can We Learn?

Elizabeth Yoder

*He that hath the Son hath life; and he that hath
not the Son of God hath not life. —I John 5:12*
Read Matthew 11:28, 30

Cathy was one of God's special people. She was not able to feed herself. She could not walk. She was not toilet trained. She required one-on-one care.

We were fortunate to be given the blessing of caring for her for eighteen years. Cathy came to us through Child and Family Services with the consent of her mother when she was one and a half years old. We welcomed her, and as years passed, she lost the title of foster daughter; she was "our Cathy."

Cathy taught our family many things. She taught us the beauty of being handicapped. She taught us that a handicapped person is not someone to fear or feel repulsed by. She taught us acceptance and patience through suffering. She taught us rejoicing, even if the accomplishment was small and insignificant to the world around her. Most of all, she taught us to love God's special people.

Yes, Cathy was different, but we knew that someday she would be released and she would go to Heaven. It made caring for her earthly needs so burden-free.

When Cathy needed major surgery, I stayed with her. Through all the sleepless nights away from the rest of the family, the question came to me, "What am I doing here? This is some other woman's child." That thought made me realize how much I loved Cathy. Very willingly I stood by her bedside trying to give her some comfort.

During one of the worst illnesses she had, she suffered intensely. As I was preparing her for bed, my heart ached for her. I asked her, "Cathy, would you like to go see Jesus?" I was not prepared for her response. Her eyes brightened with excitement. She flashed a bright smile and answered with an enthusiastic "Yes!"

Two years later she really did go to see Jesus.

The greatest thing Cathy has taught us is to bear the cross daily and willingly. This gives us a greater longing to see Jesus and live with Him . . . forever, burden-free. One glimpse of His dear face will erase all sorrow.

Thought for the Day

God sends us children for another purpose than merely
to keep up the race—to enlarge our hearts.

—Mary Howitt

Love Is a Choice

Rebecca Brubaker

Every one that loveth is born of God, and knoweth God.
He that loveth not knoweth not God; for God is love. Beloved, if God so loved us,
we ought also to love one another. —1 John 4:7, 8, 11

Read 1 John 4

It is natural for a mother to love a child to whom she has given birth. It is natural to care more for one's own flesh and blood child than for any other child. But to love a child that was born to someone we have never known, and to love him with the same love as one born to us, is a choice we make.

It is easy to love a sweet, darling baby who is placed in our arms. Our love seems to flow without effort. But sweet baby days pass so swiftly. Does love flow naturally when baby throws a temper tantrum and we realize his temperament is different from our biological children? Love is a choice.

He brings papers home from school with failing grades, even after we have drilled and drilled and spent much time helping him with homework. Then love is a choice.

One day he gets upset and says, "You're not my mother. I don't belong in this family. I wasn't born in this family." Then love is a choice. (On one such occasion when a daughter told her mother this, the mother replied,

"Neither was I born into this family." That was a new thought to the child. This mother explained that there are three ways to become part of a family—by birth, by adoption, and by marriage. Whatever the way, we belong.)

Our teenager goes through difficult stages of growing up and is rebellious. Then love is a choice. This does not come naturally for either biological or adopted children.

Love is a choice. God chose to love us while we were unlovely. In marriage we choose to love our spouses. As parents we choose to love our children.

Love endures. Love never fails. It will carry us through the difficult times of parenting. When loving is difficult—CHOOSE TO LOVE!

Thought for the Day

We love our children because of who they are,
not because of what they are. Every child deserves love.

By God's grace
We embrace the virtues
Of love.
Divine love is not automatic.
We CHOOSE to love.
Then God energizes our capacities
And makes it possible
For us to live our choice,
TO LOVE.

—An Adoptive Mother

Perfect Babies

Janice Byler

And whosoever shall give to drink unto one of these little ones a
cup of cold water only in the name of a disciple, verily I say unto you,
he shall in no wise lose his reward. —Matthew 10:42
Read 1 John 4:7-11

We prayed for a tiny newborn baby in perfect health. But God had other plans. He gave us a precious two-year-old girl with lots of physical problems and delayed development. But He also gave us the ability to look past all that and see a lovable, charming personality.

I can't say we didn't have doubts or struggles at first, but watching God work out the impossible gave us a strong faith that this was the child He wanted us to have. She is Native American, and her tribe asked to choose her family. The caseworker thought we were foolish to even try, because they had especially requested that she be placed with another Native American family. So when the phone call came that they had chosen us, we were shocked, excited, and scared. Could we really meet all her needs? In answer, we felt God clearly saying, "Trust Me; I have chosen you."

We've truly never regretted going through with it. I strongly believe that when one area of life is lacking, God makes up for it somewhere else. In Jessica's case, He gave her lots and lots of love to pour on everyone her little life touches. He added smiles and charms to turn all our sadness into joy.

To Wes and me, Jessica is perfect just as she is, because that's the way God made her, and we love her dearly. I remember clearly my best friend's response when she found out we were adopting Jessica. She said, "But why would you want a child who isn't normal?" I was hurt and shocked. When I relayed this to my mom, she replied, "Well, who of us is normal? We are all abnormal in one way or another." That has always stuck with me and given me comfort many times when people make unkind remarks.

Jessica

Still at times it hits me, such as when I see other three-year-olds running to play while my daughter has to be carried in a body cast—or when I hear other children chattering on all sides as she tries desperately to talk. Then I wish I could take a key and unlock all the potential within her. Those keys, I think, will be her determination, along with our love and patience.

But when I see the tender side shine forth in others who chance to meet her, I know I wouldn't trade her for a thousand perfect babies.

Thought for the Day

The will of God will never lead you where
the love of God can't keep you.

Reaching Our Child

Janice Byler

And, ye fathers, provoke not your children to wrath: but bring them up in the nurture and admonition of the Lord. —Ephesians 6:4

Read Luke 11:1-11

When Jessica came to our house, she was a quiet two-year-old. She didn't chatter or hum. Because she was tube-fed as a baby, her speech was very delayed. Her tongue lay dormant in her mouth. I wanted to find out what was inside my little girl . . . to really know how she felt and what she was thinking about. It was easy to see she understood quite well, but she seemed unable to give us any response.

Since I have a deaf brother, I know sign language. I started teaching Jessica words in sign language, which she picked up quite fast.

You can imagine my delight when one day as I set her in her high chair for lunch and she looked at me and signed, "Play finished." I smiled and nodded. Then she signed, "Eat." Then with a funny grin on her face she signed, "Bed."

I called my husband Wes on his cell phone and exclaimed, "Jessica just said a sentence!" His response was pure disbelief. I continued, "Yes, she said she's all done playing and now she's eating lunch and soon she's going to take a nap." Then I went on to explain how it really happened.

That day was a breakthrough into Jessica's own little world.

Before long, when she saw me getting ready to go somewhere, she'd sign, "Church?" "Shopping?" wondering which we were doing. After we came home from a trip on an airplane, she asked, "Drive?" "Fly?"

When she didn't like something, she would throw herself backward to show us how she felt. We didn't like that, so I taught her the sign "angry." She soon caught on and used it for everything, even when she was just frustrated because she couldn't open a bag. We decided she needed to be able to show degrees of dislike. It took a while, but now she just slaps her leg and shakes her head when she spills her water, and I add, "Too bad." Now she can save the angry sign for when she is really upset!

We still have frustrating moments when we hardly know what she wants or when we don't understand why she's upset. With her speech getting better all the time and her use of signs, those times aren't nearly as frequent as they once were. The more we are around Jessica, the easier it is to understand her and to supply her needs. I had to think how similar this is to our relationship with our heavenly Father. If we don't stay close to God and share our needs and desires with Him, we miss a great blessing of understanding and friendship. Only if we commune with Him do we truly feel His love and compassion in our lives. And then I'm sure if we ask Him for bread, we won't receive a stone!

Thought for the Day

You must *reach* your child so you can *teach* him.

Stretch!

Brenda Weaver

But grow in grace, and in the knowledge of our Lord and Saviour Jesus Christ.
To him be glory both now and for ever. Amen. —2 Peter 3:18
Read 1 Peter 1:2-8

ecoming Eddie's foster mother was a stretching experience. His first foster mother was gravely ill, and the agency needed someone to care for him—someone who was not intimidated by his need for continuous oxygen, careful monitoring, and multiple medications. As a nurse, I was selected to provide respite care for him until a more permanent foster family could be found.

The day we carried Eddie and all his equipment into our home, life changed. Suddenly our spare room was a clutter of things waiting to be organized. Flashing lights and beeping monitors became familiar. The hum of the nebulizer four times each day was accompanied by motherly humming, sisterly singing, or fatherly story-telling. All of us learned to step over and around the forty feet of oxygen hose that enabled Eddie to crawl throughout the house.

Months later when Eddie learned to walk, his circles around the table or a chair would bring calls of, "Stuck, stuck!" Then one of us would hurry to rescue him as he tugged on his tangled oxygen hose. I soon learned that this child's care would challenge more than my nursing skills.

"Str-e-t-c-h," God seemed to say as we encountered behavioral storms, limitations on discipline, and uncertainties about the future. Stretch we did, all of us. Our biological children stretched to share their parents with their needy brother. They shared their home, their toys, and their time. They stretched their imaginations to capture Eddie's less-than-five-minute attention span. My husband stretched his fatherly skills to include this child who so desperately needed to feel included. He stretched long, strong arms to reach encouragingly to this teetering toddler, swing him squealing into the air, or lift another eager story-listener into his lap.

A mother stretches for every child, but this child stretched me at times till I snapped like a taut rubberband. Often I sought forgiveness from my family and my Lord. I prayed for strength, wisdom, and grace. Lovingly God answered. Gently He called me to stretch farther.

Eddie

When the day arrived that we were asked to consider being Eddie's forever family, we had been stretched long and hard enough that we could carefully and prayerfully answer "yes" and know that God's grace was available for future stretching.

Thought for the Day

Gently He calls us to stretch farther.

Advocate
As Needed

Name Withheld

My little children, these things write I unto you, that ye sin not. And if any man sin, we have an advocate with the Father, Jesus Christ the righteous. —1 John 2:1

Read Romans 8:16-18, 26, 27

hree of our children followed me into the room. My teenage son took his place in the examination chair. Settling into chairs along the wall, his siblings displayed interest in the coming exam.

I considered my options. *Will I have a chance to speak alone to the optometrist? Should I have spoken to someone at the front desk?* The door opened. A lab-coated older man stepped into the room and picked up the chart. Quickly he glanced over the information before him. He smiled at my son and cracked a joke—one that would have made most teenagers laugh. My son smiled; he had missed the meaning. I glanced at the eye doctor, wishing I could convey a message about my son's limitations, but his eyes were accustomed to reading lenses, not thoughts. Undaunted by the first attempt, the doctor tried a few more witty comments as he highlighted a row of letters on the eye chart.

"Read this line of letters to me," he said as he covered Earl's right eye. Slowly Earl read the letters. At least half of them were wrong. More lines. The other eye. More mistakes. Other tests. The eye doctor peered over his spectacles and looked quizzically at my son.

Should I say something? Is Earl faking in hopes of being able to experience the novelty of wearing glasses? Is he confusing his letters? I did not know.

"Hmmm, let's try this," the doctor said. He inserted new slides into his projector. Pictures, rather than letters, appeared on the wall. Earl named every one correctly. The doctor's eyes pierced the dimly lit room. Turning, he snapped on the bright lights and hurled his words toward me: "This boy doesn't need glasses, he doesn't know his letters!" He paused as if the announcement would surprise me; then he surveyed our family through accusing eyes. "Is anyone helping him?" he demanded.

A flush crept up my neck and inflamed my cheeks. I scraped for words to explain that many had tried to help, but still letters and words confused Earl. I wished so desperately to appear competent and deliver an intelligent answer, but the words tangled inside and only a mumble squeezed past my hurting heart. How could I begin to explain to this less-than-considerate man that it was hard for all of us to know what Earl knew and what he did not know? Sometimes he just was not able to find the right answers among the damaged synapses of his brain.

Numbly I paid the bill and we stepped outside. Earl was unusually quiet. I pretended the bright sunlight had caused my eyes to water as I dabbed away the tears that insisted on spilling from my trembling eyelids. It was not the first time we had experienced such treatment. To the casual observer, Earl's appearance gave no clue of his limited abilities.

That afternoon, I determined to do two things: I would continue to prepare Earl for the world, and when I had opportunity I would prepare the world for Earl. I would be his advocate. It meant doing some groundwork.

I spoke to teachers, doctors, and new neighbors. I found a new eye doctor and a new dentist. Whenever I could, I prepared people for what to expect and how to relate to Earl. My efforts were rewarded. New neighbors understood his curious ways. The new dentist treated him with kindness and respect. Records at the doctor's office alerted new physicians to his limitations. Teachers accepted suggestions for including him in lesson plans. Someday prospective employers will learn what to expect.

As the parents of a mentally handicapped child, we have learned to be advocates for our son. Protecting him from every embarrassing or uncomfortable encounter is not possible, but we can cushion the falls and bind up the wounds. We can help others be accepting and adjust their expectations.

Playing the role of advocate helps me appreciate Jesus, my advocate. How thankful I am that He speaks words to the heavenly Father on my behalf!

Thought for the Day

Be an advocate when an advocate is needed.

Lessons From Odd Socks

Brenda Weaver

For I say, through the grace given unto me, to every man that is among you,
not to think of himself more highly than he ought to think;
but to think soberly, according as God hath dealt to
every man the measure of faith. —Romans 12:3
Read Romans 12

Yesterday I prayed that the Lord would help me match some odd socks. I suppose it seems like a silly prayer, but I tell the Lord about my big troubles and my small ones. My son was low on socks, and I knew a few more sets would help him have clean socks until I needed to wash whites again.

While I rummaged through the odd sock box in the laundry room, I pondered something he had said to me several weeks ago.

"I like to wear odd socks, Mom." I must have looked incredulous or exasperated, because he added, "Really, I do."

I paused in my rummaging. *Why am I here looking for matching socks when he likes to wear odd ones? And why does he like to wear odd socks anyway? Is it another thing to exasperate his mother? If he wants to wear odd socks, should I try so hard to provide piles of carefully matched ones?*

I thought about my son's odd sock proclamation for weeks. Finally, today, I decided to put those thoughts in black and white so I can order them. I have a feeling there are lessons for me to learn from odd socks.

Does Eddie see himself as an odd sock?

Born to African-American parents, he is being raised in our Caucasian home. Born with disabilities, he is often surrounded by people who can do things he cannot. Although he belongs to us and we love him dearly, he seems dissatisfied. The grass looks greener to him elsewhere. *Does he ever think he's been mismatched? Does he wonder what it would have been like to grow up with his birth parents? or another adoptive family? On a hot day like today, an adoptive family with a swimming pool probably suits his imagination very well. How can we as his family help him feel included, appreciated, and needed?*

I quickly reviewed the past sixteen years. We had tried to give Eddie a secure home. We poured love into his frail little body when he first joined our home. We included him in everything. I know he felt a part of our home. He was ours. But as he grew, so did his discontentment. It was as if he were asking, "Who else might I belong to? Who else's might I have been?"

I think I see the connection. Eddie knows he belongs here. He knows we love him, and most days this teenager loves us. But sometimes he is an odd sock in a basket, waiting and wondering about being matched. *I know they chose to adopt me, but do I want to adopt them? Are these my people? Is their God my God? Is their church my church? What might be out there that feels like a more comfortable match? Who am I?*

"I like odd socks, Mom." Maybe there are hidden messages in his declaration. Is he asking to try his wings? To look through a basket of people and churches to see if he can find out who he wants to become?

As adulthood claims this questioning teen, will we as his parents be committed to loving him, but letting him go? Will our prayers follow him wherever he goes? He wants to move far away. Will I send him chocolate chip cookies and let him feel his mother's care?

What about wearing odd socks? Sure, it's hard on a mother's pride, but doesn't God want to weed out the sin of pride? I can provide clean, matched socks and encourage my son to wear them. Can I humble myself and let Eddie learn some lessons about life and odd socks on his own?

Can I love and let go? Can I pray while my child seeks answers for himself?

Eddie and his family

More than a year has passed since I deliberated about odd socks. Eddie has now reached the age of adulthood. He has moved far away. I send him chocolate chip cookies and speak encouragement to him on the phone.

More important, Eddie has found our God to be his God. And he has made connections with many people from several churches. Struggles aren't over, and he is washing and matching (I wonder if he does?) his own socks now. Our prayers follow him, and our hearts leap when we answer the phone to hear him say, "Hi, Mom! Hi, Dad! What's up?"

Thought for the Day

While it might not be wise in your laundry room,
in life we may say, "Never throw away an odd sock!"

Proof of
Purchase

Name Withheld

I am the LORD that healeth thee. —Exodus 15:26
I can do all things through Christ which strengtheneth me. —Philippians 4:13
Read Philippians 4:4-13

I am different! I am different because I'm adopted.

"No," you may say, "you're just like any other child inside."

But I will say, "No, I am different."

When you want to return an item for warranty or refund, you usually need proof of purchase. I know I am different because I have proof.

I can't do schoolwork like the others in my grade. Other girls my age make their own dresses. Even girls younger than I can do lots of things better than I can. Boys my age drive tractors, even on highways. Dad doesn't trust me. It must be because I'm adopted. And I can't play ball well or run as fast as my younger brother who isn't adopted. So you see . . . it must be because I am adopted.

Mom doesn't understand me. I try so hard to make her understand, until I finally realize she just doesn't. She can't . . . probably never will . . . because, you see, I am adopted. So I quit trying and she says I'm clamming up. I'm not! You see, there again she doesn't understand! What more proof do I need?

It's not fair! My little brothers and sisters have life so easy. They have a real mom and dad. I feel so angry with them. Why can't I have blood relatives too?

———————•❖•———————

Dear child, you are hurting deeply. My feelings for you are so deep that I will not try to argue away your proofs. Your feelings are important to us. I pray that you will come to feel as much a part of our family as our other children do.

When I try to imagine how life would be without you in our family, I can't. You are a part of us. Sometimes I wonder why God didn't just give us to each other right away since He planned for us to be together. Not because it matters to me, but it hurts to see you hurting and struggling with all these feelings. I want you to know I care about you. You are my own because God gave you to me. When I prayed for a child, I was so happy that God sent you. I wanted to share your life with you and show you how to walk with my heavenly Friend. When I see the areas that are hard for you, I do not think of your adoption; instead I long to help you.

My friends have talents that are different than mine. Is it because I am adopted? God just gives each of us different gifts. I also see places in which you excel. I will not tell you that you are like everyone around you. There are no two people exactly alike in this world. God made each of us different from anyone else, because He has a place in life for us to fill that no one else can fill. God has already begun carrying out His plan, by placing you in our family. You belong here and we would miss you awfully if you were not here. Your smile, your laughter, and your helpfulness prove that you are distinctly you.

As you give yourself to your heavenly Father, He will mold you and use you to bless those around you. You have much to give, maybe even more because of being adopted. You will be able to understand and care about children who are sad or lonely. As you yield to Him, His proof of purchase will be evident in you . . . in your thoughts, your words, your kind acts to others, and your outlook in life.

Now that is a proof of purchase worth having!

Thought for the Day

We need to let God take the hard things that have
happened to us and, rather than nurse our hurts to ourselves,
turn them into a blessing for others.

Do You Really Love Me?

Marta Wagler

An Adoptee

For I know the thoughts that I think toward you, saith the LORD, thoughts of peace,
and not of evil, to give you an expected end. —Jeremiah 29:11

Read Psalm 139:13-18

"Do you really love me as your biological child?"

As an adopted child, I struggled with this question. I always had this fear that my wonderful parents couldn't love me as their own flesh and blood. I was adopted at the age of two from El Salvador, Central America, and don't remember living at the AMA orphanage. My parents were very kind to me and showered me with lots of love, to the point that the rest of the children thought I was spoiled. I felt accepted by the family for the most part, and that acceptance I attribute to my dad. I guess maybe you could say I was Daddy's little girl. Whenever my parents were asked how many children they had, he would always say five. He never sequestered me from the rest of the children, and he'll never know how much that meant to me.

When I was about twelve, I had a very rebellious streak. One afternoon my parents and I had a confrontation, and I threw out the comment that they don't love me like the rest of their children. I'll never forget the look of hurt and love in Dad's eyes when I said that. He calmly replied, "Marta, I'll always love you, and your name is on our will just like the rest of the children." He also said, "If anything ever happens to me, don't let anyone try to deceive you into doubting my love for you." Dad was always so reassuring, even when I lashed out in anger. When I think of those times, it makes me sad to think that I actually questioned my parents' love.

As adopted children, we struggle with identity issues and wonder exactly why we were born and where our roots came from. It can be even more of a struggle depending on the circumstances of our adoption. Sometimes there's that desire to look like a family member. You never hear anyone saying, "Oh, yes, I can tell what family you come from. You look just like your mom." We're noticed, but not for some genealogy people are putting together in their mind. Often our skin color raises questions. So parents, do your children a favor by taking time to sit down with them and explain what adoption is about and why there are different races in this world. Please let them know that adopted children are just as much a part of the family as any other child, and there really isn't a reason to make a big deal out of where we come from or why our skin might look different from theirs. Children deserve to know, and it could save some embarrassing moments.

Since I'm older, I realize that God created people with three basic emotional needs: to belong, to feel loved, and to feel needed. I no longer think that only adopted children struggle. When I finally came to that realization, my adoption was a lot easier to accept, and it was easier to accept myself for who God created me to be. My identity is found in Christ. If it hadn't been for parents who cared enough for me to show me the way of salvation, I wouldn't know Christ as my personal Saviour.

After being in Mexico for nine days working in an orphanage and viewing the poverty of the homeless and unloved children, I came back more thankful for having the privilege of being placed in a Christian home and grateful that God spared me from all that pain and hurt of growing up as an orphan. I want to be an instrument that God uses to bring help, hope, and love to hurting people with whom I come in contact.

Thought for the Day

Our true identity is found only in Christ.

Canticles

Joshua Bechtel
an adoptee

O my dove, that art in the clefts of the rock, in the secret places of the stairs,
let me see thy countenance, let me hear thy voice; for sweet is thy voice,
and thy countenance is comely. —Song of Solomon 2:14
Read Song of Solomon 2:1-14

After reading the above verse, I think, *Abba, is this really your desire for me?*

I seem to hear Him say, *You think you are small and ugly . . . that you have a plain, unmelodious voice . . . and that you have an unsightly, ugly face. You believe you have no song. If you had a song, you seem to fear that your voice would mar it.*

My heart replies, *Aren't all of these so? What about ME do You want to see? What about my voice makes You so desperately long and demand to hear it? Are You so tone deaf that You don't realize how bad and ugly and raspy my voice (if you can call it a voice) is? Are You mocking when You claim I have a comely face? Are You so blind that You cannot see all that makes me want to hide?*

The answer surprises me.

I am not tone deaf, My child—you are. I am not blind—you are. I have given you a song and a voice. You have deafened yourself to it. You have closed your eyes to the beauty I have put in you.

233

You have heard and believed what men and fallen angels have spoken to you, calling you all these things. You have believed their unfounded words. What will convince you to believe My words regarding the truth about you?

It is true that you have weakness. It is true that you are small and worth less than nothing . . . of yourself. Have you forgotten that without Me you can do nothing? Have you never known that I give voice to the mute? Has it never occurred to you that I give beauty for ashes? Have you never caught on that My strength is made perfect in your weakness?

You are weak. Embrace that fact, but also step from your weakness into My strength. When you feel pain, come to Me for healing. Stop clinging to yourself and all the reasons you must hide within yourself. Come out of your shadows and experience what you are in Me. I bought you as a wreck and am redeeming and restoring you to Myself. Come out and let Me see you, and let Me be glorified in you.

Thought for the Day

My Beloved is mine, and I am His. I am secure in His love.

Antique Shop Pondering

Joshua Bechtel
an adoptee

Ponder the path of thy feet, and let all thy ways be established. —Proverbs 4:26
Read Proverbs 4

I don't know what it is with antiques and me. As much as I like looking around, it leaves me feeling sort of . . . depressed? . . . pensive? . . . wistful? All of those things and then some, maybe. Some time ago as a friend and I were browsing some antique shops, I spotted a set of those bland-faced plastic Fisher Price people—the ones with round, flat bottoms that fit in those circles in the toy airplanes, the Fisher Price dollhouses, and so on. Well, I spotted a whole "family" of those old toys. The one I would have called the mom had long yellow hair.

I could not believe the wistful longings that rose up in me. I longed for a childhood where my main concern was the next Dr. Seuss book. I wished for a reality like the feeling evoked by that musty antique store. It awoke memories of a childhood I have tried to forget. But God will not allow me to forget. Why is such longing, such sadness, such pain evoked by the memory of a *toy?*

I feel like a bundle of confusion. I find myself wishing my childhood had ended at three years old. A moment later I know I could not bear to have had life end that way. I give thanks for the life that is now—or

I think I do. But I wonder what the "other" life would have been like. I wonder about the life I left when I was put into foster care as a toddler. What would have happened had I not been adopted at ten? Where would my life have gone if God had not directed it the way He has?

As I stood in that room full of old items with obvious stories, I wondered if I had a coherent story. I found a hunger welling up for . . . for what? Maybe my hunger for I know not what, my longing for what I cannot explain, my thirst for what I cannot taste in this life is intended to drive me . . . to find God?

What else did Augustine mean by, "We bring to Thee the thirst we cannot quench at any other spring, and the hunger that can be satisfied only by Thyself"?

If this is a signboard, perhaps I am on my way home.

Thought for the Day

It is sweet to know as I onward go,
the way of the cross leads home.

—Jessie B. Pounds

Our Special Spot

Brenda Weaver

*For, lo, the winter is past, the rain is over and gone; the flowers appear
on the earth; the time of the singing of birds is come, and the voice
of the turtle [dove] is heard in our land. —Song of Solomon 2:11, 12*
Read Psalm 91:1-4

Today I drove to a special spot about forty minutes from our home. Signs of spring are creeping across the meadow and into the tree-lined dell where I am parked along a quiet country road. Birds chatter merrily above the sound of the babbling brook. A cardinal gathers twigs for a nest. A squirrel leaps from a branch to a telephone wire. But the distant, wistful lament of a mourning dove reminds me that parking at this special spot has not always been peaceful and pleasant. Tears were shed here. Battles fought. Outbursts calmed. Lessons taught. Although I have visited in each season of the year, I suppose this spot always held signs of spring for me—even in the dead of winter. This is a special spot of new beginnings.

I recall my son's words to the family one evening after he and I spent two study halls in this dell. "Mom and I found a really neat place today. Nobody knows about it but us." I knew that he, too, saw signs of spring, even though autumn's splendor was falling to the ground. In desperation had driven him to this spot to escape the distractions at school and stop his worried glances (Who will see that Mom is at school tutoring me?). Besides, we both needed to air out our attitudes, and the tiny schoolroom was stuffy. Thus began a weekly trip to this special spot—special because my adopted son and I connected here. This was a safe place to practice primer reading and addition, to learn to count money, and to talk about being a teenager. It was a place where one could stalk off to the stream, stamp one's foot against a fallen log, and angrily ask, "Why me?" Answers did not fall from the sky, nor did we demand them. But here we could speak honestly, listen for each other's heart cries, and look for signs of spring.

I tutored. We both learned. And we prayed. Yes . . . this *is* a special spot.

Thought for the Day

Recognize signs of spring in relationships
that have long weathered winter.

Revisiting Our Special Spot

Brenda Weaver

And the servant of the Lord must not strive; but be gentle unto all men,
apt to teach, patient, in meekness instructing those that oppose themselves;
if God peradventure will give them repentance to the acknowledging of
the truth; and that they may recover themselves out of the snare of the devil,
who are taken captive by him at his will. —2 Timothy 2:24-26
Read Psalm 96:9-13

ighteen months have passed since my son and I began driving to this special spot. Today I am here alone. Only rarely do I come to this spot now, but never without a flood of memories. I should not say I am alone, for I have always found it easy to meet God here. He heard our desperate cries for help in raising our troubled teenage son. He gave grace and wisdom beyond our own. He planted seeds of springtime in this dell—and in our relationship. He gave us hope.

A year ago I drove to this spot alone for the first time, tears coursing down my cheeks. "I miss him so much," I whispered to God, even while I felt a sense of relief in the help we were receiving.

Last week I got a call from Wilderness Boy's Camp, where our son has been residing and learning for the past year. Today I know that some-where in the woods, many miles from here, our son hikes trails with other

239

ιoubled boys and committed Christian men. From the reports and his letters, I know that even as spring has returned to our special spot, signs of new life are springing up in the son who shared this spot with me. I have returned to thank God and celebrate spring: the green grass, warm breeze, and bird calls of earthly spring . . . and the hope, deepened love, and renewed commitment of a relational spring.

Are you struggling to raise a troubled or handicapped child? Find a special spot and pour effort into reaching his soul. The results are in God's hands, but your efforts are not wasted. Think of them as loving sacrifices for another's soul.

Do not consider yourself, or an adoption, a failure when you have to ask for help. Although it may feel like a humbling experience, it takes parents of strong character to ask for help. Read 2 Timothy 2:24-26 again. The snare of the devil is strong. Ask for the help of the believers around you in releasing those that are held captive.

Thought for the Day

Make loving sacrifices for another's soul.

Love Woven True

Love knows no borders and harbors no ill;
Love in a crisis will keep loving still.
Love counts the flowers, never a thorn,
Never stops growing when once it is born.
Love is forgiving and will not rehearse
The wrongs of another by chapter and verse.
Love remains loyal in spite of the wind,
Does not disappear when another has sinned.
Love doesn't demand, and love doesn't quiz.
Love, being Love, like the truth . . . simply IS.[11]
Taken from 1 Corinthians 13:4-8

—*Margaret Penner Toews*

God can do more in a moment of total surrender,
than we can with a lifetime of struggle . . .
Allow God to heal the pain.

PART 4

Our Unprotected Hearts

When Love Brings Pain

"Open arms leave the heart unprotected,
leave it open for the better or the worse." [15]
—*Paul Steven Chapman*

Open Arms

When you meet someone who needs your love,
And he carries you away with his charms,
When you reach out to let him into your life,
There's something you should know about your open arms.

Open arms leave the heart unprotected,
Leave it open for the better or the worse.
Open arms make the good times sweeter,
So let the Healer touch your heart when it hurts.

Now you might be the one who's been wounded;
And you may wonder if your heart can stand the hurt.
Call on Jesus; He knows just how you feel,
'Cause on the cross He loved us all
With open arms.[12]

—Paul Steven Chapman

12 © 1984 Shepherd's Fold Music (BMI) (adm. at EMICMGPublishing.com) International copyright secured. All rights reserved. Used by permission.

Open Arms Leave the Heart Unprotected

(Part 1)

Emily Martin

Be ye therefore followers of God, as dear children; and walk in love,
as Christ also hath loved us, and hath given himself for us an offering
and a sacrifice to God for a sweetsmelling savour. —Ephesians 5:1, 2

Read Ephesians 5:8-21

"Sweetheart, wake up!" I felt my husband shaking me gently. "I went upstairs to wake the boys and found both David's and Joe's beds empty! A bunch of their clothes and prize possessions are gone as well."

I sat up in bed. The alarm clock said 6:20.

"We didn't go to bed until midnight. That was six hours ago. Did they run away or did something happen to them?"

Worried, betrayed, and numb, we called family and friends. Then as soon as our lawyer's office opened, we called him. He was the one who had drawn up the legal guardianship papers for the boys, giving us equal rights with the birth mother. He advised us to call the police, which we did.

"Two boys, ages thirteen and fourteen, with a bicycle, a rifle, bullets, and a great deal of luggage are missing," we informed them.

The deputy who came out to investigate was very kind. After writing down information about the boys, he took along with him photos of our family, the boys, and their birth mother.

Malvern and Emily Martin Family, 1992

Joe and David had been two and three when they first came to us as little foster boys. Three little girls had just left our home at noon the day before, and we were wondering if foster care was worth the heartaches, when we received an emergency call at 2:30 a.m. Adrenalin kicked in, and I found it impossible to sleep. *This is the exciting part of foster care. Oh, what will the new children be like?*

The boys arrived around 5 a.m. After the social worker left, Malvern and I each held a brand-new son in our arms. Malvern was rocking Joe, a pitiful little waif with tattered shoes and mismatched clothes and hair cut so short it was hard to tell what color it was. As the rocking continued, the little two-year-old's

Dari, Kenton, Joey, David

eyes slipped closed and a look of acceptance rested on his innocent face.

"How is it," Malvern asked me, new love shining in his eyes, "that we always get such perfect ones?"

A week later David and Joe's two-month-old half sister joined the boys in our home. The next several years were very busy for us with five and then six preschoolers. I felt so overwhelmed at first. When another foster family from our church offered to take David and Joe, I thought, *Maybe we should let them go before we get too attached.* That evening at the supper table, Malvern looked lovingly around our little brood and asked me quietly, "How could we possibly give any of our children away?"

David

I agreed. We were committed to making it work. And it did. We were busy, but enjoyed each one.

Three years later another adjustment was in store for us when the court ruled that the boys be returned to their birth mother in a distant state, but that we could adopt Brookie.

David was happy to go. He seemed to have a perpetual view that the future would be better than the present. He was sure there would be definite advantages in switching. When I expressed concern about the teaching of evolution in the public school, he said calmly, "But I just won't believe them. I already know God made everything!"

Joe begged to stay with us, but we were helpless to do anything about the court order. We promised to write, to call, and to visit when we could. During the five years they lived with their mother, we did that, including summer vacations when they came to our home in North Carolina for extended visits. Their mother was friendly and open.

When we stopped at their house en route to Wisconsin from North Carolina, she served a

Joey

delicious meal and even offered us her own bed, compelling us to stay for the night. She seemed pleasantly amazed when my husband accepted the offer.

That night, city noises drifted in the windows. Horns beeped. Thumpety, thump, thump, thump! Hard rock music vibrated as cars slowed down in front of the house. A distant siren wailed. From the illumination of the streetlight, I could see our children slumbering safely on the floor around us. Pungent cigarette odor clung to the blankets and furniture. The door was cracked to the adjoining room where David and Joe slept.

"This is the other side," I whispered to Malvern in the darkness. "I feel like I've been stretched out of my comfort zone considerably . . . like I'm visiting Mars!"

"Really?"

I could sense a hint of amusement in my husband's response. It wasn't the first time he had led me tentatively down an uncharted path. And almost always I was glad later. "I'm glad they haven't smoked in the house since we came. Even so, I can't believe that Jill hasn't had an asthma attack and I don't have a headache. God must have wanted us to stay." I was grateful when they had turned the television off. I certainly didn't want our children to watch it.

"David and Joe seem happy," I added. My thoughts skipped on. "I'm glad we could visit their school. Joe has a caring teacher. It's just all so . . . ungodly. The language, the attire, the subjects of conversation . . . our values are worlds apart! Oh, what will the future be for our dear little boys?"

"I know. That's why I felt we should stay," Malvern said simply. "Keeping a good relationship between their mother and us is important, I think. We can be kind and quietly remind them that God is. We can try to show them Christianity in real life. Who knows how it might affect David and Joe's future?"

Thought for the Day

When we open our arms to sweet, innocent children,
cords of love bind them to us.

Open Arms Leave the Heart Unprotected

(Part 2)

Emily Martin

Cast thy bread upon the waters:
for thou shalt find it after many days. —Ecclesiastes 11:1
Read Ecclesiastes 11:1-6

The good relationship we established with David and Joe's mother resulted in phone calls and even the boys traveling the seven hundred miles to our house for several weeks or several months each summer.

During this time, Joe, especially, was showing the effects of his biological family's lifestyle, with increased hyperactivity, learning disabilities, and low self-esteem. Their mother was now a long-distance truck driver, leaving the children—two boys and two girls ages eight through twelve—largely on their own for extended periods of time.

At the end of the summer when the boys were ten and eleven, the opportunity came for David and Joe to continue staying with us. We felt overwhelmed with the decision and truly sought God's will. Malvern said, "David and Joe both want to do what's right. I don't feel I could live with myself turning them back out into that godless society if we have a chance to do something about it." So they stayed. God helped us, and His people helped too.

The boys wanted to stay, especially Joe. David weighed the situation in his eleven-year-old mind. One morning he came downstairs and said, "I didn't sleep much last night. I've thought it all through, and I want to stay. If we stay we can attend the Christian school here and go to church. I know everyone here and I feel good about it."

Their mother signed an agreement, making us legal guardians over the boys, equal to her in authority. Our lawyer said that was the best we could do. He said a paper stating anything more would do little good, for if the mother really wanted the boys, she could likely get them no matter what our paper said.

The boys' progress in the three-cord Christian environment of church, school, and family was beautiful to watch.

During the next three-and-a-half years the boys did not see their mother, but they had contact with her a couple of times a year by telephone or letter.

Joey, age 11

Joe often begged us to adopt him. When hard times came, he'd say, "You aren't really my parents. You don't really love me or you would adopt me!"

"Oh, Joe," we assured him, "we would gladly adopt you, but we need your mother's permission. How can we get that when we don't even know where she is?"

When his mother finally called, Joe told her right off that he would like to change his name to Martin and stay with us.

"If that's what you want, it's up to you," she said simply. David wasn't as sure about it, but both boys freely used our last name.

We started legal steps for adoption. When we explained this to the boys' mother, she was clearly upset. She talked to the boys, asking them if they really understood what this meant—that she would no longer be their mother and that she couldn't call them anymore or send them gifts. Joe helplessly handed the phone over to Malvern. Malvern kindly explained that she would still be able to contact the boys sometimes, but that we felt the boys, especially Joe, needed the security of knowing they were adopted.

Several months later their mother called again, saying she had moved. She was now only five hours away. This made us uneasy. She had lived in the western states many miles away for the previous three years. Phone calls continued to come, and with them promises and declarations of her love. With trepidation, we monitored the phone calls. She asked for the boys to come to her house for Christmas. We said no. Their relatives had called and warned us not to let the boys go anywhere with her. That past summer she had picked up her daughters from their uncle's home to do some shopping for a few hours. None of them had returned.

The uncle pleaded with the boys to go nowhere with their mother. He talked to the boys at length, telling them how much happier they were here with us. They were skeptical. They thought if they went to their mom, they were big enough now to help take care of her and help fix her life.

The next several months were difficult. The boys became dissatisfied and hard to please. Anger surfaced often. They threatened to run away. Our long conversations alone with them stretched into the wee hours. At times we were sure we were seeing progress. In so many ways the boys loved it here and wanted to stay. They made long-term plans for next year . . . two years from now . . . and five years from now. They often made reference to always staying here and being a part of our family, the school, and the church. We felt they were accepted by our church community, their friends, and our extended family.

They also wanted to do what was right. One time after I had apologized for being impatient with the children, in particular with Joe, he came for a hug before he went to bed. "Mom," he confided, "I'm never getting married. I'm going to stay here with you always." He watched me expectantly. "Don't you want to know why? I do want to be good, and it seems staying near you is the only way I can be. I am planning to go to Heaven. I want no part with that other place!"

We had many happy times mixed in with the challenges, and in numerous ways the boys were both very promising. We still carry a dull ache inside and wonder why. Why did their birth mother have so much pull, and why wasn't our love enough? Faith teaches us that we don't need to know.

But now, apparently their mother had picked them up right from our house. Many times when they were little, I had checked on them several times a night. We had been warned that some foster children have been abducted by their birth parents. But I had long since ceased to worry about that.

Our other children accepted the change in our family remarkably well. It was a bit tough at first, especially on Kenton and Dari. David had been Dari's roommate, and Joe had been Kenton's for several years. Often we could hear their voices droning above us at night. But both Dari and Kenton stated that we shouldn't ask the boys to come back. "If they don't want to be here, we sure don't want them here," they said.

This experience helped us better understand why God doesn't force us to be His children. How it must hurt Him when the vast multitudes walk away from the relationship He longs to have with each one.

Later, I had a very nice talk with Joe on the phone. He said he had taken his pitch pipe with him, but he would love to have a *Zion's Praises*. I knew right away what we would send for his upcoming birthday. I missed his cheerful, contagious singing as he worked around the house. He also said he couldn't find his Bible when he was packing his stuff, and he sure would read it if we would send it to him. He had always loved to pass out tracts. He said he'd pass them out if I sent him some. "The people around here sure need it!" he said.

In the midst of open arms and hurting hearts, I found comfort in Ecclesiastics 11:1-6. "Cast thy bread upon the waters: for thou shalt find it after many days . . . In the morning sow thy seed, and in the evening withhold not thine hand: for thou knowest not whether shall prosper, either this or that, or whether they both shall be alike good."

Thought for the Day

It is our responsibility to sow the seed; the harvest is up to Him.
It is His seed, His children, and His harvest.

An Agonizing Choice

Name Withheld

*Give ear, O Lord, unto my prayer; and attend to the voice of
my supplications. In the day of my trouble I will call upon thee:
for thou wilt answer me. —Psalm 86:6, 7*
Read Psalms 75; 82

It was a cold, gray sort of day when Anne swept away the curtain
and looked out toward the barn. Tears flooded her eyes again as she
saw her husband Josiah come out the door and round the corner
toward the calf hutches. A small figure followed him. There should have
been two. It was only a week ago that Levi had gone back to his other
foster family.

She blew her nose. It had been a hard week. Her throat was raw from
crying, her nose sore from blowing. Sitting down in a nearby chair, her
mind went back to when Levi had first come as a five-year-old.

They were so excited about another little boy joining the family . . . two
little boys to grow up together, to be brothers and best friends. Levi had
brought along many dreams to their home. But he wasn't there long
before little things started creeping in. "Oh, well," they had decided,
"he's just adjusting. With a lot of love and prayers, he'll come out of
this."

Jordan, at two, welcomed his new playmate excitedly, but Levi seemed to resent Jordan and was extremely jealous of him.

What could I have done differently? The question had been going through her mind for the last week. *Are we bad parents? Why couldn't he bond with us?* They had tried so many things. They had planned special times alone with just Levi and Dad or Levi and Mom. They had spent hours rocking him and singing to him. They had made a cassette tape for him, telling him of their love. *All of that, and he only got worse. Why?* He seemed scared of getting close. And the harder they had tried, the more he had pulled away.

In desperation one day, Anne had finally pulled out the file of papers from the caseworker. She was amazed at what she found. "Levi has been diagnosed with Reactive Attachment Disorder," it read. *What? I am doing everything I can to help us bond! What more can we possibly do?* In her bewilderment, she called the caseworker and started asking questions. The caseworker explained how children with this disorder have difficulty attaching to anyone for fear of separation.

Why hadn't someone explained this to them earlier?

"We thought he was doing so much better," the caseworker had told her. "We expected him to just keep going from where he left off at the last home. All I can say is, watch him closely and keep trying."

Watch him closely! Anne thought wearily of the many hours she had lain awake in bed sensing something was wrong, but not quite able to put her finger on it . . . especially after Jordan started running from his room into theirs at night, screaming. He had never acted like this before. Something was wrong. Did it have something to do with Levi? Every time they would go into Levi's room to check on him, he appeared to be sleeping.

Then there had been the acting out. She didn't want to dwell on that.

She thought of the time Jordan had come running to his dad carrying a puppy in his hands. Through his tears, he managed to sob out, "Puppy hurt, Daddy." She remembered Josiah's disbelief as he tried to describe to her the scene of the three mangled pups he had found behind the barn. Surely a five-year-old wasn't capable of such destruction.

And then there was the little tractor, Jordan's gift from Grandpa and Grandma. Levi had gotten a toy skidder, but a couple of times Anne had seen Levi looking at the tractor with a contemplating, calculating glint in his eyes. She wasn't surprised to overhear Levi one day offering to trade with Jordan. Jordan just clutched his tractor closely and said, "Mine!" One day the tractor disappeared. Levi had just glared at her through half-closed eyes when she had gently approached him about it.

Gradually, Josiah and Anne started noticing more changes in Jordan. He walked around with a troubled look on his face and often cringed when Levi came close. There was definitely something wrong. *Is something going on that we are missing? Where can we go for help? We are desperate!*

They found and read the book *Children Who Shock and Surprise* by Elizabeth Randolph. It answered many of their questions. This was not an isolated situation. Rather, these were typical responses for some children with attachment disorder. But where should they go from here? Could they continue to expose Jordan to these dangers? Would things keep getting worse until something irreparable happened?

Their constant prayer had been, *"Lord, give us a fervent love for Levi, and help him feel that love. Lead us through each hour of every day. We don't have the strength on our own. And if You want us to do something more, please direct us. Make Thy will plain."*

Gradually it became more apparent that something would have to change. With much agony and many tears, they had finally made the heart-wrenching decision to send Levi back. Anne felt that a part of her heart was torn away the day she watched the car disappear with Levi inside.

It seems that God's will has been made plain, Anne mused. *Doors opened. We acted. Peace again reigns in our home, and Jordan is safe. But I think of our darling little Levi and the good that is in him. I reflect on our hopes and dreams for him. I contemplate the future, and still I wonder, did we really do the right thing?*

Thought for the Day

Sometimes it takes a great love,
and a greater humility,
to release one we love to another
who may be better able to help him.
Are we really serving the child
when we deny failure
and doggedly hang on
to a seemingly futile assignment?

Not My Will

Name Withheld

He that dwelleth in the secret place of the most High shall abide under the shadow of the Almighty. I will say of the LORD, He is my refuge and my fortress: my God; in him will I trust.   Psalm 91:1, 2
Read Psalm 91

"There, now, you may get down," Anne remarked to Jordan as she finished wiping his hands and lifted him down from the chair. "You play nicely now," she cautioned as he looked around for some other little people to play with. She smiled to herself as he sauntered off. Her little boy was gaining back the personality he'd had before Levi had come. (See "An Agonizing Choice.") She settled back in her seat to enjoy watching the rest of the wedding guests. She used to enjoy these kinds of days. But she felt too vulnerable since Levi had left their home only two weeks before. Her husband Josiah was engrossed in a conversation with some old friends, so Anne was free to sit and watch and think. Her thoughts were rudely interrupted, however, when Mary Mast moved in her direction, double chin quivering with suppressed emotion.

Seating herself gingerly on the squeaking chair, Mary burst out, "I just heard the news!"

"Oh?" Anne lifted an eyebrow, wondering if the news had something to do with her or her family.

"Is it true?" Mary asked accusingly.

"What are you referring to?" Anne asked.

"Did you really send that precious Levi away, like someone disgraced?" Mary's voice cracked with emotional fervor.

Anne took a deep breath. *Give me wisdom, Lord,* she breathed silently. Aloud she said, "Mary, it was the hardest decision we have ever made in our married life. We did not send him away in disgrace. We let him go because we felt there was someone else who better understood his needs and could help him in ways we couldn't."

"There was nothing wrong with that child that a lot of love and hard work wouldn't have taken care of!" Mary argued.

Anne flinched. *Love and hard work? What else had filled their days?* Taking a deep breath, she replied calmly, "There are many things in Levi's past that he must work through, and Josiah and I felt like we did not have the knowledge we needed to—"

Mary interrupted with a sniff. "Past! That's just what it is, past! In no way does it relate to the present." Rising from her chair, she continued, "I think it's pretty pathetic when we blame our shortcomings and failures on a little boy's past. How does he feel about all this, anyhow? But I suppose you didn't stop to consider his feelings, did you?" She hurled this last sentence over her shoulder as she swept into the crowd.

Anne groped around her chair for her handbag. Pulling a tissue from it, she blew her nose. *Oh, I just want to leave. Maybe a visit to the ladies' room will give me a chance to get my emotions under control. What does Mary Mast know about the situation, anyway?*

Rounding the corner toward the restroom, she brushed shoulders with her friend Amy.

"Oh, hi!" Amy exclaimed. "I was just coming to find you!" Then she noticed Anne's tear-filled eyes. Reaching up, she gave her a hug. "Do you want to talk about it?"

That was all it took. The tears that had been threatening before came spilling out. Amy quickly looked for a protected little nook where they could talk in private. After directing Anne to a chair, she offered a fresh tissue.

"Thanks." Anne blew her nose and took several deep, quavering breaths. Looking up at Amy, she asked tremulously, "Did we really do the right thing?"

Amy leaned against the wall. "Because of your love for Levi, you can't share with just anyone the things that took place while he lived with you. You are going to face a lot more criticism as you shield Levi. We prayed for months about what to do with Levi, and it seemed like this was how the Lord answered those prayers. You need to find comfort and rest in that, even when someone looking on makes you doubt your decision."

"Thank you, Amy." Anne's eyes were shiny with unshed tears. "I think the Lord knew I needed you right now." The two friends soon moved back to mingle with the crowd. Anne sent a quick look around for Jordan. She was relieved to see him playing quietly with Amy's two-year-old daughter. Anne and Amy visited for a while before Leah Weaver came up with a smile.

"Hello, Amy and Anne," she said. Then she asked Anne, "Where's Levi today? I didn't see him with you."

"No," Anne said. "He has gone to live with another family. We felt like it was getting to be too much for us to handle."

Leah's smile faded. "Oh, I see," she answered coldly, and then turned and walked off.

Anne met Amy's eyes. "So, how should I respond to something like that?"

Amy gave her a compassionate smile. Slowly she said, "Respond with a Christ-like attitude. He was oppressed and He was afflicted, yet He opened not His mouth. How would Jesus respond to all this?"

In the days to come Anne had plenty of chances to think of Amy's words, "How would Jesus respond?"

One day Josiah's sister called. "Anne, why didn't you tell us it was getting so bad with Levi? We would have been glad to take him into our home."

Anne pictured her sister-in-law's four preschoolers and knew she didn't know what she was talking about. But she answered, "Thank you, but Levi is doing well in his new home."

Another day Josiah was on the phone with a concerned brother, who asked, "What about the commitment you broke to Levi?"

Josiah flinched. Anne watched him take a deep breath, then answer slowly. "The way I see this, our commitment went two ways. And while I can't go into detail about what we were facing, we felt that for Jordan's physical and possibly someday his spiritual safety, we needed to look into something else for Levi. Because we have already adopted Jordan, our first commitment is to him. So in that sense our commitment went two ways, and we had to make a decision."

That night after the lights were out, Anne could sense Josiah's restlessness. She knew something was on his mind. Josiah didn't usually act like this. Finally she patted his arm and asked him gently, "What's wrong? Can you talk about it?"

"Oh, Anne," he burst out, "don't you just miss that dear little fellow sometimes? It just goes through me so often during the day. I see something I want to show Levi, or think of something that would be fun to do with the boys . . ." His voice trailed off.

"Yes," Anne replied, "I know what you mean. It is hard to adjust to only Jordan again. But then I remind myself that it seemed so plain that God opened the door for Levi to move back to his former foster home. And Jordan has become such a happy child again that . . ."

"That you feel assured again we did the right thing," Josiah finished for her.

"Right!" Anne lay thinking for a few moments before continuing. "God knows how we yearn for more children, and I pray in time He will give us more. But we also need to be ready to accept whatever His will is for us."

"True, but there are so many things I don't understand." Josiah contemplated for a while, and then added, "I think that is why Levi's leaving was so hard for me. I struggled to give up all the hopes and dreams I had for my two little boys. After we had accepted Levi as our son, why would God want us to break that bond? Why couldn't we meet Levi's needs? What was I doing wrong? The greatest lesson I had to learn through this all was to be able to say without hesitation, 'Not my will, but Thine be done.' We have learned so many things from Levi that will help us go on to be better parents."

"But isn't that how all of life is?" Anne mused. "When we look back we can see how beautiful God's plan always is for us."

"Well said," Josiah commented. "Good night, dear wife!"

Thought for the Day

Never judge another man until you have
walked a mile in his moccasins.

To Shine as Lights

Fannie Miller

Let your light so shine before men, that they may see your good works,
and glorify your Father which is in heaven. —Matthew 5:16
Read John 1:1-18

My heart's desire is to shine for Christ in this dark world, but I am perplexed as to what kind of witness I am, for two of our sons have gone astray. Oh, how my heart aches for them!

We tried hard to protect them from the cold, dark world, but they did not fear the dangers about them. Rather, danger seemed to challenge them, to beckon them, and they found it hard to understand why we'd tell them to watch out. They struggled to find their places in life, trying to understand our cautious approach to what they considered harmless.

After all, other youth out there are doing these things. They have it nice. Free from unreasonable rules, they can do as they want. We can make friends with them and share their lifestyle. It can't be like Dad and Mom say.

Groping along and longingly thinking that life *out there* would be better, they fell into sin. Their sin caused them to feel trapped, thinking that returning was not an option.

But I am grateful to God for the relationship we still have with our sons. Being dependent on their friends for transportation has at times brought other young people to our home. When they leave, I like to stand by the door and wave. They honk and wave in return.

I had never thought about it being a witness to the community. It is not a way I would choose to be a light, but through these experiences, perhaps they can see our love for our sons.

One evening one of our sons asked to come for a meal. He had his friend bring him, and the friend joined us as well, a boy who otherwise probably would never have entered our home. What did he see when he was here? Did he wonder why our son left? He seemed to be observing our conversation and conduct, particularly as we concluded the meal with a song. Afterward our son wanted to talk, even after his friend went on out to the car.

I need wisdom for these times when he lingers and shares happenings at work and other things that are important to him. I see that he is learning from life's daily experiences. What hurts me the deepest are the scars he will carry for life as he lives *out there.*

What can we do for our wayward sons? We can love them. We can forgive them for the heartache and pain they have brought to us. We can continue to stand true to Bible principles. We can pray for them. And we can be lights to them and their friends, that our Father in Heaven may be glorified.

Thought for the Day

No matter what happens in life,
there is always a right way to respond.

Can We Trust God?

(Part 1)

Emily Martin

Though he slay me, yet will I trust in him. —Job 13:15
Read Job 1

*A*lex and Ricky leaving? After living with us for more than four and one half years! How could that be possible? They are totally a part of our family! I can't imagine life without them!

In 1990 we found our faith severely tested as we faced once again the possibility of our two little foster boys, Alex and Ricky, leaving us. We had a happy Christian home. We sang together and memorized Bible verses. We told them Bible stories, sharing about God and Creation and how God answers prayer. They had prayed with us as Dari's adoption was finalized. And when God answered that prayer with a baby brother who grew up to love balls and bats and trucks and tractors as much as they, what fun they had together!

Most of all we had tried to fill their hearts with a love for God. One night as I tucked the boys into bed, they were talking about saving money to buy their very own fishing poles. "You just go to sleep and dream about fishing poles," I said as I left the room.

"Not me," Alex called after me. "I'm going to think about God and Jesus and Heaven."

"Me, too," Ricky added.

Another time when Alex was about six or seven, he ran into the house all excited. "Guess what! God just answered my prayer! I lost my pocketknife and never told anybody. I just prayed about it. Right now, when I was swinging, I looked down and saw my knife." About two minutes later he added quietly, "You know, that's the first time I remember God answering my very own prayer like that!"

When Kenton was born, our hyperactive six-year-old Ricky sat calmly for long periods of time, holding and hugging and loving the baby. He coaxed smiles from Kenton, and when he started to crawl, Ricky was right beside him directing the way. Often the two of them were up early, playing together quietly until the rest of the family began to stir.

Both boys were a very real part of our family, and we were the only family Ricky remembered. Their birth mother showed little interest in them. When her rights were terminated, the boys showed no sign of grief. The occasional card signed *Daddy Rex* reminded them that somewhere they had another dad, but mostly they didn't even think of him.

Now their father had been released from prison. It was evident that he loved his boys very much, but he also saw the hopelessness of raising them by himself. He said he knew he had nothing to give them. When he saw how happy they were with us, he admitted it would probably be best if he signed them over to us for good. Our hopes soared.

Then the picture changed again. Their dad met a woman named Catherine and in a very short time had a job, a home, and a mother for his boys—everything Social Services required. Overnight visits began with the goal of Alex and Ricky returning to their dad.

We couldn't believe what was happening. In our private and family prayers we begged God to work another miracle. I honestly did not expect them to leave. I knew we served a God who easily performed miracles. We remembered how He had marvelously intervened before (See "In Answer to Our Prayer"), and we fully expected Him to do so again.

We knew well that God sometimes says no and that we need to accept what we can't change. Our family had experienced death. I had lost my dad and our treasured premature baby within three weeks of each other. But I couldn't apply that to this situation. I was confident that my father and baby Bradlyn were safe in Heaven. We knew death was something we needed to trust God about and rest in that. But this felt different.

Surely it could not possibly be God's will to allow two little boys to be taken from a sheltered Christian home and exposed to the filth of the world again. I felt a peace in my logic and sat back and waited to see what miracle God would work for us this time.

The social worker kindly explained that though they would much prefer the boys staying with us, because of the improvement the father had made, they would need to suggest to the judge that the time was right to reunite the birth family. But I continued to pray and wait and believe that God would intervene.

In the meantime we tried to make our summer an extra special one. Malvern quit work early in the evenings to have more time with the boys. He helped them build a tree house for a sleep-out. We took a special trip, stopping to camp along the way and letting them help with outdoor cooking. With the night sounds surrounding us, we sat in the lamp-lit tent and told stories.

October came, and with it the dreaded court day. As our case advanced in court, I knew it sounded hopeless, but I still clung to the fact that we serve a miracle-working God.

Finally the judge looked across the courtroom to where Malvern and I sat with our two little boys sandwiched between us and said reluctantly, "I hate to do this, but I see I really have no choice."

He paused, "Since there is no one representing the foster parents, and all other parties are petitioning that the children be returned to the birth father," he paused again, "I hereby do declare the two minors, Alex and Ricky Spring, be returned to the birth father, Rex Spring, as of Monday evening, October 28."

He went on to say that the Spring home would continue to be under the supervision of the Hyde County Department of Social Services. "Due to the long-term foster care situation and the attachment that is evident between the said minors and their foster parents, I am adding an unusual clause. The Martins will have the right to monthly visitation with these boys. Clerk, is that clear?"

Alex and Ricky were actually leaving! I shook with sobs as the full impact of this realization struck me. *Where was the miracle?* I felt like God had let us down big time, and I didn't understand why. The boys hugged us and cried with us. Their tear-drenched, stricken eyes searched ours. We felt we had let them down as well—Mom and Dad, who in their minds should be able to fix anything.

Helplessly we packed their things. The social worker said it would be better for the boys if the transfer took place at another house other than ours. So, when the dreaded evening arrived, we met Rex and Catherine at Dan and Jane Hershey's home for a last meal together. Then we bravely gave Alex and Ricky last kisses and hugs through our tears. I remember the little animal cry of pain Alex gave as they turned and climbed into their father's pickup. Our last view of Alex and Ricky were two little heads buried in their arms.

We felt like part of our hearts had been torn out. Heartache. Grief. Pain. It was different from death in that we knew Alex and Ricky were still alive. Though we had the promise of talking to them occasionally and monthly visits allotted to us, we knew they would be moving into the middle of much corruption.

Malvern and I asked Jane to watch our two remaining children so we could go on a walk. As we walked the half mile to the end of Main Stem Road and back, the cool October evening dried our tears as we cried and talked and walked and cried. Finally we were ready to face people again. We didn't understand, but we had no choice but to trust God.

Where is our faith when we feel God is allowing a mistake? Isn't that when faith surfaces, when what is happening really doesn't make any sense to us? We have a choice to make. Will we choose faith or unbelief? Will this experience make us better? Or will it make us bitter?

Trusting God is a way of life. It is a giving up of self and saying, *God, You know best.* It is something we do over and over again. He is worthy! He gets glory from our absolute trust in Him. *God, I trust You, especially when I don't understand.*

Thought for the Day

Sometimes it is when God says "no" that we truly learn to trust Him.

Can We Trust God?

(Part 2)

Emily Martin

O LORD, thou hast searched me, and known me. Thou knowest my downsitting and mine uprising, thou understandest my thought afar off. Thou compassest my path and my lying down, and art acquainted with all my ways. —Psalm 139:1-3

Read Psalm 139:1-10

*I*t was healing to me to spend hours working on scrapbooks for Alex and Ricky, packing them full of love and memories. Quilts were lovingly stitched by aunts, cousins, and grandmothers who wanted them to know they were loved.

We tried to cultivate a relationship with their parents by being friendly and nonjudgmental. We admired their dad's garden, took them firewood, and shared homemade treats with them. Carefully we chose character-building books and Bibles to send for the boys' birthdays. We made sure they had a cassette player that worked and kept them supplied with singing and story tapes so that good seed could be planted in their minds.

And many times a day we cried out to God to protect them. There was much comfort in knowing that each time we prayed, God heard. Each time, through the Holy Spirit, or a still small voice, or some other means, He reminded them of His love and care. We knew that when we couldn't be there, God was with them, watching lovingly over them. *He knew their downsitting and their uprising and understood their thoughts afar off. He was acquainted with all their ways.*

For the first three or four months, Alex and Ricky came home for weekend visits. Gradually that stopped. At times we went to their house. Several times in the summer they came for a week or longer. We limited our visits

Ricky, age 7   Alex, age 8

during the school months since their parents claimed the boys were naughtier and struggled more with their schoolwork after they had been with us.

Then the summer Alex was ten and Ricky was nine, Rex and Catherine surprised us by allowing them to spend the summer with us. I was extremely busy as God had blessed us with three more foster children. Although I wanted the boys at home, I often didn't feel well and was overwhelmed with the responsibilities of seven young children.

Alex was very responsible for his age, and I depended heavily on him to help me with the work. While Ricky was kept occupied whenever possible with Malvern, Alex had the humdrum job of babysitting the five little ones between the ages of one and six. He helped peace reign in our busy household, along with sweeping floors and gathering up toys. Looking back, I am amazed at how much I expected from a ten-year-old. But during our working together, the bond between us grew.

Over that time our family went on a camping trip. One day, Alex chose to stay and help me as I tidied the tent. It was a special time to me as he opened up and shared how things were going at home. Some of it was really ugly. I never had a father who drank. I could only listen and cry with him.

Then he looked up with tear-filled eyes and asked a searching question. "There is something I just don't understand," he said. "Why did God ever let that judge say we could go back to our dad?"

"I have struggled with that question too," I told him honestly. "Then I think of all the children who have never heard about God at all. God looks down and sees everybody at once. God saw two little boys that He loved very much. 'I want Alex and Ricky to know about Me,' He must have decided. 'I will send them to a Christian home, even if it is for only a few years.'

"We had the privilege of having you in our home for four and a half years. We were able to love you and teach you about God. It is something you will always know. You know that God is real. You know what a Christian home is like, and nobody will ever be able to take that knowledge away from you. God is good. Because you were with us, we will always love you and pray for you no matter where you are."

I reached over and squeezed his shoulders. "Does that make sense to you? Does it help?" He nodded, and I was relieved to see a measure of acceptance written on his face.

Thought for the Day

Wherever we are, we have a Father's hand to
lead us and lovingly embrace us.

Ricky, age 15   Alex, age 16

Can We Trust God?

(Part 3)

Emily Martin

Whither shall I go from thy spirit? or whither shall I flee from thy presence?
If I ascend up into heaven, thou art there: if I make my bed in hell,
behold, thou art there. If I take the wings of the morning,
and dwell in the uttermost parts of the sea; even there shall thy
hand lead me, and thy right hand shall hold me. —Psalm 139:7-10
Read Psalm 139:1-24

"I'm afraid our marriage is breaking up," Alex and Ricky's stepmother told me during one of her calls that summer while the boys were staying with us. "If that happens, would you consider keeping the boys?"

We assured her we would and began planning a life with the boys beyond the summer.

How shocked we were when several weeks later, she called again and asked us to have the boys ready to leave the next day. When she arrived to get them, Ricky hid in the blueberry patch, and Alex locked himself in the bathroom, refusing to come out. While Malvern went to find Ricky, I could hear Alex sobbing his heart out. I had to command him to open the door and go with his stepmother.

Forcing the boys to leave with their stepmother was tremendously hard on all of us. When we tried next to contact them, the family had disappeared. We heard nothing from them for ten long months. In the meantime we continued to pray, taking comfort in knowing that God was where we could not be.

When we did find them, the parents were quite angry, especially the stepmother. She told us she wanted us to leave them alone . . . to get out of their lives. But a soft answer turns away wrath. Malvern quietly reminded them of the monthly visits that the judge had allotted us. An agreement was reached. The boys were not to call us Mom and Dad. We were to be friends, not parents to them. And since they said visits to our home upset the boys too much, future visits were to take place in their home—not ours. We agreed to their terms. We told the boys that being friends was better than not seeing them at all.

By working peaceably with the boys' parents, through the next years they relaxed on the terms they had earlier demanded. At times the boys visited in our little Mennonite community, meeting friends and family.

One evening we received a phone call. "Malvern," Rex's southern drawl came clearly through the phone. "Do you remember that promise I made to you eight years back? I told you if anything happened to me or my marriage, that I want y'all to have my boys. I was wondering if you would take them, at least for the summer. Our marriage has gone to the rocks, and I'm gonna need to move on out of this house. I don't have nowhere to go, and I can't keep the boys with nothin' but a car to live in."

We were stunned at the thought. *Alex and Ricky come back after being gone for so long? Really, Lord? Why now, instead of when they were young and still moldable? Is this how You are answering our prayers?*

We knew that during this time the devil had taken the opportunity to sow many tares in their hearts. Television with its engrossing pictures, along with songs and wrong thinking patterns had become engraved too deeply to be easily rubbed away. Ricky was also struggling with rebellion and dishonesty. It was a very low time for us. After loving and praying for the boys for so many years, we implored our God who loved them even more than we did, to show us how we could best help them. We worried about their influence on our younger children. We sought advice. It became clear Ricky needed more than we were equipped to give him. And although we did not agree with his stepmother that the best place for him was military training, we needed somewhere for him to go. We were informed of a Christian wilderness boys' camp that had an opening for him.

When we asked Rex if he felt that was a workable option, he answered, "Do whatever you can. Without help, that boy is headed straight for prison, and what a filthy, rotten place that is! Ask me. I know. It's not anything I want for my boys."

As we gathered the boys' clothes and personal things together, Rex watched in a detached manner, hiding the obvious ache in his heart. When it came time for us to leave, he gave each boy a big bear hug and gruffly told them he loved them. Tears were streaming down his cheeks as he sat down on the step at the end of the walk and watched his boys climb into our van. This time it was the boys' father saying the good-byes, and my heart ached for him. Voluntarily he was giving up his right to be their parent because he loved them and knew they would be better off with us.

"Sometimes the greatest love is to let go," I told him. "That is what you are doing for your boys." He nodded, and we left him, a forlorn figure sitting alone.

So, at the ages of fifteen and sixteen, Alex and Ricky were back in our care.

Some time after Alex's return to our home, he made a commitment to Christ. In time he was baptized and became a member of our church. Alex says that in spite of those turbulent years back with his father, he always felt God was with

Malvern Martin family 2001

him, walking beside him. He has continued to know Christ as his constant companion.

The twenty months Ricky spent at Bald Eagle Wilderness Camp taught him much about working with others, responsibility, and accountability for his actions. As he battled the great outdoors, cooking his food and blazing and sweeping trails, he was learning important tools for life. But choosing to trust God is a personal choice for each of us. Even after Ricky graduated from camp, there appeared to be a certain holding back. More than once he responded in revival meetings. Over and over he was encouraged to get back up and try again. Many loving Christians reached out to try to help him and show him love. Some opened their homes to him when he was no longer able to live with us.

Although Ricky hasn't always taken the advice that was given him, we are grateful for the relationship between us. We are truly Dad and Mom to him.

After Alex and Danette were married, Ricky moved in with them. Several years before that, he had lived a distance away. We enjoyed having him close again. Often Ricky would stop in for supper and family devotions or for Sunday lunch.

"Ricky's here!" his little sisters would call as they ran to welcome him and give him a big hug. A bit later I might see him reading to them or sitting patiently as they combed his hair, adding barrettes and little ponytails. We never outgrow our need for family.

Another of the joys for Ricky over this time was three little foster children who lived next door. They wormed their way into his heart as almost daily he found a reason to stop in at their house. He delighted in them, and they loved him. It was as if he were reliving his own early years as he related to them.

Once he confided to me, "Oh, Mom, I don't think I could bear it if these children had to leave. They can't go back into the setting they came out of!"

He told them Bible stories and stories from his own life as a foster child. As they confided in him about their fears, he encouraged them to turn to God. He explained to them about adoption and how it's okay to love both our first and our second parents. They trusted him and admired him. To them Ricky could do anything. Being there for these little ones gave Ricky a new reason to live and to be a good example to them.

Then suddenly they were ripped away without even a chance for Ricky to say good-bye except over the phone. He could hear them sobbing, but knew he was totally helpless to do anything. Big, strong, with bulging muscles . . . he was powerless!

It was all too familiar to him.

In anger he cried out to God to do something. God, who with just a snap of His fingers could change everything. He felt like he had betrayed the children's trust . . . and that somehow God had betrayed his too.

We assured Ricky that God can take the ugly situation those children are in and somehow turn it

Ricky, 21

to good for them. He can keep the memory of Himself alive to them and walk beside them always. We reminded him that God delights in taking impossible situations and turning them into good to those who love Him. We encouraged him to pray for them just as many have done for him and Alex. God hears and answers if we are righteous. *The effectual fervent prayer of a righteous man availeth much.*

We realize that trusting God is a way of life. It is a giving up of self and our own ideas and saying, "God, You know best."

When Alex and Ricky were taken from us at seven and eight years old, Malvern told me with tears streaming down his cheeks, "If I could only know that they will grow up to be Christians . . . I think I could bear it."

We had no promise of that then and realize that even now, after we have done all we can, the choice is still theirs. It is a very individual thing. God wants each of us to desire and yearn for Him ourselves. Then with the eternal end in view, we accept the path God has chosen for us.

Thought for the Day

A foolish man chooses his own way and accepts his destiny;
a wise man chooses his destiny and accepts or trusts God as to the way.

What Shall We Do?

(Part 1)

Name Withheld

Trust in the LORD with all thine heart;
and lean not unto thine own understanding.
In all thy ways acknowledge him,
and he shall direct thy paths. —Proverbs 3:5, 6
Read Proverbs 3:7-27

J eremy's mother was in the valley of despair when she called me. She was clearly frustrated and at the end of what she could handle. "My husband agreed that I could call you," she said. "Do you know of someone who would take our son Jeremy? If we can't reach him, maybe someone else can. We have the other children to think about as well. I never wanted to be a part of a failed adoption, but perhaps it would actually be better for Jeremy . . . for all of us. Things can't keep going on as they are."

Jeremy was a very cute little Hispanic boy, barely six, and small for his age. He had been in an orphanage until his third birthday, and his lack of bonding had caused a great deal of frustration. When he first arrived in his adoptive home, he allowed his parents to rock him to sleep every day. He sat on their laps if they asked him to, but it seemed like he was enduring it rather than enjoying it. That is . . . until company came. When someone else was around, he often asked to sit on his parents' laps or would lean up against them and appear affectionate and lovable. When company was there, he also put on the air of the perfect little gentleman, offering the nicest toys to his brothers. Visitors would say, "Oh, isn't he darling? I would love to take Jeremy home with me!" Little did they know about the other side of Jeremy.

Although a quiet child, Jeremy was very controlling. The biggest challenge the family faced was his reactions when angry or upset. If someone crossed his path, he would deliberately urinate in the most ridiculous places—in his pillowcase . . . under the bed . . . in his closet . . . behind the refrigerator . . . in the coat closet . . . outside on the deck. Then he'd deny it, whether he had been caught in the act or not.

This had gone on for almost a year. His parents had used many methods of punishment. They had tried firmness, hard spankings, and withholding privileges. It was as if he was saying, "This is the one thing I will do! In this part of my life you will not control me!"

A social worker told his mother that acting out by urinating in inappropriate places can be a sign of sexual abuse. No one knows what may have happened, nor can anyone change what happened to Jeremy during the first three years of his life, but this helped shed a little light on the problem.

His adopted brother Danny, who was very near Jeremy's age, had been killed a little over a year before. Jeremy was the only witness, and although it was apparently an accident, he blamed himself. His parents assured him over and over that it wasn't his fault, but whenever his behavior became obnoxious, he would blame the way he was acting on the time his brother was killed, saying he was feeling bad about it again. This happened so many times that his parents felt it was unproductive. They recognized the hurt Jeremy had felt at the time and the pain he was still feeling. After all, Danny had likely been the closest person to him in the world. They had slept together, eaten together, and played together. Surely his loss and grief was extremely deep. And it would have been unquestionably awful to watch Danny die.

Although Jeremy's behavior had not been perfect before, everyone recognized that he was considerably worse since Danny's death. He had become defiant and disrespectful. When punished, he had his own quiet way of getting even. He knew just how upsetting his urinating trick made everybody, and he reveled in the power it gave him. He also knew that his parents could not abide a sneak or a liar.

With their seven adopted and two biological children, Jeremy's parents had had many joys in parenting. But they had an older son who also had a very hard time bonding. He had caused his parents twenty years of untold grief and heartache. They could not bear the thought of walking down the same painful path again.

Now they were beginning to wonder if Jeremy would ever really bond with them. If not, would it be better for him to leave? Would there be another family with whom he could bond better? But what would changing families do to Jeremy—or to his siblings?

Jeremy's parents had reached a crisis. They were open for advice and asked for prayer that God would show them what would be the best for him and everybody else involved. They knew that their future and Jeremy's hinged on how they answered these troubling questions.

I could hear the anguish and tears in her voice as Jeremy's mother shared their recent struggles, and my heart went out to her. I also understood why she hadn't felt free to share her situation with her church friends. Too often she had been given quick answers and tips on parenting that she had already tried without success.

The Holy Spirit gave me some words of comfort and encouragement to share with her. Just a listening ear seemed to help somewhat, but I was truly at a loss to really know how to advise her. With her permission, I shared Jeremy's story with some trusted friends who agreed to join us in prayer about the situation.

We all agreed to pray that God would make it very clear to the parents if Jeremy was to leave their home, maybe even to the point of someone else offering Jeremy a home. Or else God would fill their hearts with abounding love for their little son and he would respond in kind. In this way they could be assured of it being God's will for Jeremy to stay in their home and family. This assurance would also help them the next time when things got rough.

Thought for the Day

God made our children.
He knows their frames and what they need.
If we felt His leading in the initial adoption or placement,
we need to reach back to that assurance
as a source of comfort and courage.
He will continue directing us,
sometimes just a day at a time.

What Shall We Do?

(Part 2)

Name Withheld

*If there be therefore any consolation in Christ, if any comfort of love,
if any fellowship of the Spirit, if any bowels and mercies, fulfill ye my joy,
that ye be likeminded, having the same love, being of one accord,
of one mind. For it is God which worketh in you both to will and to do
of his good pleasure. —Philippians 2:1, 2, 13*

Read Philippians 2:1-18

A week after Jeremy's mother had called me, I spoke to her again by telephone. "I don't know if this will last or not," she said, "but Jeremy is much better. The acting out has stopped. He is even trying to please me by doing special little things like picking up the toys when I haven't asked him to. Even if it doesn't last, we are certainly enjoying a pleasant break from his earlier behavior."

About a month later his mother called again. "I just wanted to tell you that things are continuing to go well with Jeremy. He is also much happier and blends in with the other children. He especially loves the baby."

What an answer to prayer! Some of us as parents face rougher spots than others. But I had seen again that when we care enough to share and pray, how much lighter the load becomes for those who are crumbling under the weight of their particular burdens.

Some months went by. I felt such relief about Jeremy that praying about him was no longer a priority to me. It wasn't until I heard that Jeremy had been moved to another home that I contacted his family again by telephone.

"Is it true that Jeremy is no longer with you?" I asked her. "Do you mind sharing what happened? The last time we spoke together, he was doing so well!"

"Yes, it is true. Jeremy went to another adoptive home two months ago. Perhaps it was because of the threat of leaving that he improved for a while. But he regressed again. Until you actually experience something like this, you can't know the strain that living under it brings." She seemed almost afraid to try to explain for fear that I would be critical of their decision. I assured her we were not, and she continued.

"At the time of Danny's death we felt sure that it was an accident and assured Jeremy of that. But later, doubts lingered in our minds. Jeremy carried so much guilt about the death, and I remembered that he was highly upset at Danny before they ran out to play together that last time. Some of his behavior was so strange. He had a calculating, distant look in his eye as he watched family members at times . . . as if he had little or no feeling. Other times it seemed he had intense hatred. He reminded me of a seven-year-old foster son we had years ago who killed three of our animals in the three weeks he was in our home.

"Oh, the doubts and fears we lived with! I felt like I didn't dare leave him alone with the little ones, especially the baby, for fear someone might be harmed. My husband agreed with me. At night we kept all four of our younger children in our bedroom just to make sure they were safe.

"And the bond was not there. When Danny died, we all cried our hearts out, but when Jeremy left, it was with a sense of relief. He walked out of our home without shedding a tear and entered his new home without looking back. He doesn't ask about us or seem to care. Of the other children, only one of our daughters seemed to even mind him leaving. The rest were glad. It was like a neighbor child leaving after a visit. The bond was just not there.

"We send pictures of everybody to Jeremy, and we call him. He is polite, but obviously unattached to us. His new mother says he doesn't ask about us or look at the pictures. I hope he can attach to his new family. He is the youngest there, so at least little children will not be in danger.

"We feel very vulnerable about the decision we made to move Jeremy to another home. Many of our friends do not understand. At an especially low time, when I was questioning if we had actually done the best thing, I met a woman from the ambulance crew who had been along when they came to get Danny.

" 'I heard that Jeremy has been moved to another home,' the EMT stated. I affirmed it to be true. 'I am so glad,' she told me. 'His eyes have haunted me ever since that day we picked up Danny. I never saw anything like it in a child so young, and I feared for your other small children. You did the right thing by having him moved to another home.'

"What a confirmation! What comfort!

"At the time of Danny's death, all I could think about was Danny and what we could do to revive him. I was overwhelmed with grief when I realized he was actually gone. I can't recall Jeremy's expression that day.

"We continue to pray for Jeremy. We ask about him, and we love him and miss him. We especially miss what he could have been and the relationship we could have had."

My heart went out to these parents. "I have not walked a mile in your moccasins," I told her. "I will certainly not judge you and say you have made a wrong decision. Sometimes someone else can bond with a child where one set of parents could not. You have lost not one child, but two! My heart goes out to you, and my prayers will follow you."

After I hung up the phone, my thoughts churned on. I thought of commitment and promises made to both Jeremy and to the other children in the home. I knew the other children's safety and welfare was imperative. They couldn't sacrifice four for one. I thought of Danny safe in Heaven and wondered where Jeremy and other children like him would spend eternity.

No, I did not blame Jeremy's parents for the choice they made. I have small children as well. I understand. But who will help the Jeremys in this world? No child is all bad. Is it their fault they missed that vital love and cuddling that is so necessary to bonding? Is it possible for them to learn to trust adults? Can they ever learn to trust God? Can they become trustworthy? When they are adults, will they be able to bond with their children? How can we keep these troubled children from turning into the incarcerated serial killers of tomorrow? Perhaps there are untried methods that could be used to help break these negative cycles. Are there safe ways to help without putting other innocent children at too great a risk? As Christians, do we have hope and help to offer?

Six years have now passed. Several more adopted children have been added to the Christian home that Jeremy had shared with Danny. Their home rings with childish laughter and good cheer. And we can see a bit more of the picture that God saw all along.

Where is Jeremy now? Because of his behavior, it became imperative for Jeremy to be moved again, this time to a more controlled environment where both he and those near him could be safe. He is still loved and remembered in prayer by the family who cared for him during those rough years.

Thought for the Day

As parents, our lives are wrapped up in our children.
And in actuality, there are so very few of the vast multitudes of children that we personally can reach. We need to be totally open so that God can choose exactly which children are best for us.

The Bungee Cord Ride

Philip and Louise Hoover

For my thoughts are not your thoughts, neither are your ways my ways,
saith the LORD. For as the heavens are higher than the earth, so are my ways higher
than your ways, and my thoughts than your thoughts. —Isaiah 55:8, 9
But now mine eye seeth thee. —Job 42:5
Read Job 40:1-14 and Job 42:1-6

"She told me that if you pray for patience, you are in essence asking God for trials," the new mother shared with a group of us. "Do you think this is why our baby has Down syndrome?"

With heart racing, I stole a glance at the mother holding her new baby. I knew just what she meant, but to vulnerably share my struggles . . . wouldn't that only expose spiritual immaturity compared to these women's unshaken, childlike faith?

"I could never get through a day without praying for patience!" another friend exclaimed.

A third woman nodded in agreement.

I cleared my throat. "I've wondered, too, about . . . " I stammered, "all my prayers for a—a—more Christlike character. Then we got Sammy."

In September 1999 it appeared as though God was finally giving us the desire of our hearts. The call from Children and Youth Services was as exciting as being told that we were expecting a baby! When the caseworker appointed a meeting time, I felt as though I had been given a due date. When I walked into the room and picked up nine-month-old Sammy, I was ecstatic! Our eyes met and I was smitten. I basked in the pleasure of feeling God's hand on my shoulder saying, "Take him home. You have My blessing." Or at least that is what I thought I heard that day.

Sammy quickly became a joyful addition in our home. His pleasant character labeled him a "good baby." To walk into his room in the morning and hear his baby voice lisp "Goo' morning!" was delightful. His contentedness was all we could idealistically ask for in our family.

The only threat to our dreams was his birth parents. Weekly we took him for visits, alternating between his mom and dad. In spite of the fact that we were secretly hoping neither parent would get him back, we found ourselves favoring one of the parents if it was God's will that he should return. But surely it wouldn't be God's will! Of course the caseworker favored reunification because that is the primary goal for each foster child as long as the home is safe—physically safe, that is. But wasn't God more interested in spiritual safety? Though these birth parents professed Christianity, there was hardly the godliness present which the soul of our precious baby should be exposed to! Surely reunification with his biological parents was not God's intentions for "our" baby!

But supervised visits soon became unsupervised. Visits of a few hours were extended to visits for most of the day. Each time Sammy's parents did not meet expectations, we were jerked high into the region of hope. But with each advancement toward reunification, we would feel the stretch of elasticity to its limit, crushing any hope we had built.

Would this never end? Did God enjoy teasing us by unmercifully jouncing us up and down on this awful bungee cord ride? Plenty of times the bungee cord became stuck in a miry pit of depression. Why should God grant us this dream come true, when I was such an inadequate and failing human being?

Despite these low times, deep within my heart I held on to a faint hope that perchance God would intervene at the eleventh hour. I hoped for something of a miracle, such as Abraham's sacrificing Isaac when God took him the entire way to the altar, yet spared his son.

"Mama! Mama!"

I immediately paused in my work to see what was terrifying twenty-month-old Sammy. "En dere! En dere!" he screamed, pointing toward the living room.

"Come now," I comforted. "Let's go see."

Clinging frantically to me, he warily watched as we entered the room. Upon hearing the fluttering racket inside the fireplace, I promptly identified a trapped bird. To me the situation was minor. I was in control and could easily solve the problem. To Sammy, however, it was traumatic. How well this incident paralleled our own struggles just then! We couldn't see the big picture. God did. We weren't in control. God was. Could I cling to Him as my baby was clinging to me? Could I relax and be reassured when handing the problem over to God in the same way my baby had relaxed his grip and was no longer screaming?

This small trial of Sammy's would only prepare him for more major ones in his future. Was the trial of our giving Sammy back only preparing us for more major ones in our future? At that point, losing Sammy was as severe a trial as we felt capable of handling, and even then we could hardly fathom coming out on the opposite side and surviving. This was not a comforting thought. The realization nearly made me refrain from praying my prayer for spiritual growth. Truly I could identify with the caution the mother of the Down syndrome baby felt when praying for patience.

"What's happening by now with Sammy?" a good friend questioned.

I weighed my answer. Once when she had asked, I had shared of our soaring hopes. Immediately afterward we found ourselves near the bottom. Friends coming to support us at the bottom would find us suddenly whirring past them on our way to the top again. So the bungee cord ride continued.

We didn't underestimate our friends' care, but realized the difficulty they must have had in relating to us. There was one Friend always available, but to accept His help, we had to look beyond the image of Him standing at the top purposely giving or allowing hard knocks. We had to recognize that He was also at our end taking those bounces with us.

Overnight visits began. There were times we were ready to wash our hands of the entire case. If Sammy was going to leave us, then we might as well get it over with. It was difficult enough to see our darling son go through the transitional period, without even considering our own pain. Sometimes after visits, our normally calm son would be literally bouncing off walls. Other evenings he just wanted to be rocked. He solemnly watched our faces as if in search for some revelation of what was happening in his life. Those were heartbreaking moments.

It was in those moments that our trust in God was challenged the most. Where was God's goodness? It seemed to us that God's plan consisted of throwing our son into the very streets of Hell. Was this the kind of Friend we wanted to have with us on this bungee cord ride? Did God care so little about our baby's soul?

We felt like traitors. When Sammy's innocent, trusting eyes searched ours, how could we remain composed? Although we referred to his birth parents as Mommy and Daddy, we still felt guilty. We were going to betray our baby's trust by abandoning him, to his uncomprehending mind. There was no doubt that he recognized us as Momma and Daddy. How can a momma and daddy do what we must in Sammy's case? God, how could we do this to our baby?

We eventually received the official letter stating a going-home date of April 14, 2001. Reality slapped me as I marked that dreadful date on the calendar. I cried. God's time to perform a miracle was running out.

Did He or did He not care about Sammy? By faith, we knew what the Bible told us about God. He is kind, loving, merciful, and just. We understood His ways to be much higher than ours. We read that we were worth more than the sparrows which God deems important. We could believe that the creature needs to trust the Creator. But it was so hard when it required releasing our son to a godless world.

Oh, God, why? How we cried from our heart's depths as we numbly lived through our dream's slow, agonizing death!

Sammy did not go home on April 14, nor did he go the next given date. Each time the date was postponed, we would bounce back up with hope. But June 3 came, and this time it was not postponed again.

In tears I packed the last of Sammy's things, while watching him interact with our new foster baby. In tears I rocked him, wondering if I'd ever again hear him say "I wov you, Momma" or sing "Goin' down valley, goin' down valley."

As we handed Sammy to his father in the courthouse parking lot, he reached to give me one last hug. It was a special parting gift, but I could no longer retain my composure. I escaped to our van while my husband Philip spoke yet a few parting words to both Sammy and his father.

It was in that parking lot that we understood the finality of Sammy's case. God had chosen not to perform a last-minute miracle. The bungee cord went down, down, down.

No one was there for us except God, and He seemed distant.

Would we ever be able to go on? Would we ever reflect and thank God for this?

Yes. We have. We do. We recognize that God sees a much larger picture than we do. Our bite-sized, jagged pieces of trust grew and became strengthened.

God offered us one significant thought—He was not doing this to punish us. Granted, we had the blessing of learning from it, and we had prayed for spiritual growth, but we were told to never think a trial is a result of not measuring up to God's expectations. This is especially true if we have sincerely been trying to walk a Christian life. *God does not punish us with trials, but rather polishes us with them.*

Another thought explained to us was that Sammy came into foster care not because we needed a lesson, but because of the curse of sin on the world. Foster parents stand on call as God's ambassadors to give these little ones a glimpse of Jesus.

God is love. God hurts with us at the bottom of the bungee cord while in control at the top. We don't understand why He allows certain situations, but we do understand He loves us and our children. All that He does is good and deserving of praise and glory. Life isn't about us and what makes us happy. It's about our ability to glorify God through our trials . . . to praise His works even when we can't understand.

When we place our complete trust in Him, we need not question "Why?" We trust that God has a special plan for Sammy exactly where He has chosen to place him, and we can rest reassured with that thought. We also can fearlessly pray for patience and other Christlike traits. "When he hath tried me, I shall come forth as gold," Job said. Apostle Paul agrees, saying, "For I reckon that the sufferings of this present time are not worthy to be compared with the glory which shall be revealed in us" (Romans 8:18).

Thought for the Day

Just as a diamond seems to sparkle more brilliantly
when displayed in a black velvet case,
so the radiant beauty of Christlike character
seems to shine more splendidly
against the backdrop of suffering.

—Anne Graham Lotz

The Eternal God Is My Refuge

Chris Reinford

The eternal God is thy refuge, and underneath are the everlasting arms. And the LORD, he it is that doth go before thee; he will be with thee, he will not fail thee, neither forsake thee: fear not, neither be dismayed. —Deuteronomy 33:27; 31:8
Read John 14:1-16

Oh, God, it's so late and I want to go to sleep. But my mind just keeps going around and around. I miss my precious children! Why, Lord, why? Why did they need to leave? What is going to happen to them? They are so sweet and vulnerable, so dear to my heart. I knew one of the hardest parts of being a foster mom would be saying good-bye if ever they had to leave. But God, this is so hard! I feel so alone.

Being a single foster mother was big and overwhelming sometimes, but I had felt affirmed. I felt that I was making a positive difference in their tumultuous lives. I was busy with four little ones, and I felt loved and needed. I had a purpose for living. *Without them I am so lonely, and so scared about the future. Lord, what do You have planned for me?*

My mind drifted back to one night not long before. My little foster daughter could not sleep. I was holding her close as she shared with me that she was afraid . . . afraid of what her future was, that she might have to leave our home, and that she was feeling temporarily left out in her circle of friends.

I was glad she was talking and sharing with me. I knew she would feel better when she was finished. As she opened up many painful memories from her heart, I felt tears welling up in my own eyes. My teardrops got bigger and fell down on her head as my heart ached for what this small child had already been through in her young life. I didn't want her to see me crying, but before I could do anything about it, she turned and looked at me. With surprise and tears in her own voice, she said, "Mama, why are you crying?"

"Because, darling, I love you and care about you so much, and when you are hurting, I hurt with you. I know how you feel, because I have been through some of the same things you have been. I don't want you to have to feel this way. I want to protect you and be here for you."

"Mama, I wish you had someone to care about you like you care about me. I would hold you, but I just can't. But I can hug you!" she said.

"Oh, thank you so much, sweetie. I love you and I love your hugs."

I prayed with her and explained God's protection over her. I could tell she felt better. I kissed her good night and with the usual, "Good night, sleep tight, don't let the bedbugs bite!" I tucked her into bed.

The next morning when she got up, she gave me a special little smile, as if we had a secret between us. Then she wrapped her arms around me and hugged me tight. She didn't say anything, but it meant more than a thousand words.

Chris and children 2005

I lay in the darkness remembering.

Then my thoughts rambled on. *I just wish I could hold her again now. She was so sweet and open. She believed me and soaked up everything I told her like a sponge. If only I could be as accepting as she was!*

Does God weep with us? I wondered. *Does He hurt with me like I do with my little girl? Does He long to comfort me?*

And then it was as if I could see my Father with His arms stretched toward me. In my mind I could hear Him saying, "I want to hold you and hug you!"

"But I am not a child! I shouldn't need to be held or hugged. If I could just hold and love someone else, it would help so much. Please, Lord," my heart cried out, "I do want Your will for my life . . . but can I please have my children back?"

I lay there in the darkness of the midnight, my arms aching to hold my little girl. Then I heard God's whisper among my thoughts, *I'll hold you, if you'll let Me.*

"Is that You, God? My little girl said she wished I had someone to hold me! Could I actually find comfort in You? Are You saying You don't like when I feel alone, scared, and rejected? You want to be here for me?"

A verse in Deuteronomy came to my mind. It was as though God was telling me personally, "I will *always* be here for you. I am the eternal God who is thy refuge and I hold you with everlasting arms. I love you more than you know."

"God, sometimes I forget that. Help me to feel your presence and to trust in You—to let go of my desires and to see myself through Your eyes. I do want Your will for my life and for my children."

As I lay there, I felt His presence envelop me. The feeling was a little frightening at first. Then it started to comfort me.

Immediately I thought, "This can't be me!"

In my mind God said, "Why not?"

I was about to request Him to "put me down" when I pictured my little girl. *How would I have felt if when she had so much pain in her tender little heart, she wouldn't have let me hold her? What if she had rejected my help and my love for her?*

I let myself slowly relax in God's presence. I felt so safe and secure, I wished it could last forever.

Then another thought came to me. *You don't deserve this—you have doubted God too much.*

Gently the Spirit reminded me, *Did you hold your child because she deserved it?*

Of course not! I thought. *I held her because I loved her with all my heart and wanted her to feel safe and secure in my love.*

The Spirit continued, *That's why I'm holding you in My everlasting arms. I understand. I've been through the same things you have.*

I realized I felt just like a little girl. I loved the comfort of His acceptance and His presence. I whispered into the darkness, "Thank you, Jesus. I want to hold You in my heart forever."

The next morning I felt God everywhere. He was in the sunshine and the breezes, and I marveled at the vastness of His presence. I smiled a special little smile of thanksgiving for all the valuable lessons He had taught me through that sleepless night. And the confirmation I felt back from my Father meant more than a thousand words.

I know it meant:

- *When I feel alone, He will never leave me (Hebrews 13:5).*

- *When I am afraid, I can trust Him; He doesn't give the spirit of fear (2 Timothy 1:7).*

- *When I can't figure things out, He will direct my steps (Proverbs 3:6).*

- *When I am worried or upset, I can cast my cares on Him (1 Peter 5:7).*

- *When I feel nobody loves me, I know He loves me (John 3:16).*

- *When I feel I am not strong enough, He will give me strength (Psalm 27:14).*

- *When I've failed, He offers forgiveness (1 John 1:9).*

- *When I feel I just can't do it, I can do all things through Christ (Philippians 4:13).*

- *When I feel worried about my children, I know God sees the little sparrow fall (Matthew 10:29).*

- *And I know that when I need comfort, I can go to Jesus, the author and finisher of my faith (Matthew 11:28; Hebrews 12:2).*

Thought for the Day

God strengthens our faith in Him through difficult times.
Don't be afraid to ask Him for help and comfort.
He will never leave you nor forsake you.

Mended Hearts

Connie Bear

He healeth the broken in heart, and bindeth up their wounds. —Psalm 147:3
Read Psalm 77

Our hearts pounded with excitement as we bounced along the Belizean road in our pickup. Our family was serving in Belize and we were on our way to meet with a mother who wanted to find an adoptive family for her baby. Upon arriving at the house, we talked with the mother, cuddled the precious little baby, and then went home to wait anxiously for her decision. A few days later, when a freshly-powdered, chubby five-week-old baby boy was placed in our arms, we were ecstatic!

What joy little Jared brought to our home! Jeremy adored his little brother and toted him all around. For Janelle, he was a real live doll to mother. And Bobby was going to have a playmate. We spent hours holding and playing with Jared, delighting in having a baby again. Even hanging out his diapers elated me with the feeling that I was hanging out a line full of white flags, announcing triumphantly to all that I was a mother to a baby once again!

At times during the next month our hearts were stabbed with a pang of fear, especially when the birth mother came for a visit. Would she change her mind? When we voiced these fears to the birth mother's family, they always assured us we had no cause for worry, because the birth mother considered the baby ours.

Jared

What a relief it was to us when we met at the end of the month to sign the preliminary adoption papers. Now Jared would soon really be ours!

The next morning our family was together in the bedroom enjoying Jared's early morning playfulness when we heard the unmistakable squeal of the bus braking in front of our house. Who could be coming so early? Someone ran to check and in worried tones announced that it was the birth mother.

With each step she took toward the house, our dread grew. I couldn't go to the door and face what I knew in my heart was coming. From the bedroom the children and I caught snatches of her conversation with my husband Phil. She had decided she couldn't go through with the adoption. Would we be willing to give Jared back even though she had signed the papers? In the bedroom we clung to Jared. How could we give him up? But what else could we do? We had come to Belize to show the love of Christ to these people, and that love makes sacrifices. So Phil took Jared out to his waiting mother and returned with a breaking heart to comfort his devastated family. As I picked up tiny socks, pacifiers, and toys that were lying around, I felt like I was picking up and putting away shattered pieces of our dreams. I determined to never allow us to be hurt like this again.

Several months later the other couple with whom we were serving at the mission

Phil and Connie with Jared as an adult.
See *Biographical Sketches* section.

had to leave due to sickness. They had been caring for a baby until the adoption paperwork was completed for her family in the States to come get her. Now who would take care of this baby? My heart was dead . . . we couldn't do it. But there was no other choice. And a heart can't stay dead long with a baby around. Gradually we felt the warmth of love for this little one stealing into our hearts. This time we knew she wouldn't be ours, but delighted in giving her the care we knew her adoptive parents would shower on her. We also anticipated their joy in receiving her. Our loving Father had used this little one to bring healing to our hearts!

Poem for the Day

The Heart

This heart of mine is such a fragile thing.
Like fine porcelain, I could set it on a shelf,
But I tend to put it rather in the midst of life.
Thus it has been broken a million times.
Perhaps the glue with which God mends it
Is stronger than the stuff of which it is made.
Knowing that His blood was shed to make me whole,
Encourages me to pick up the pieces, go on and love again.
My heart is not a very pretty thing,
With all these cracks and mars and flaws.
But I feel. And it is certainly much more loving
Than a heart that is never touched at all.

—Author unknown

Be a Hummer

Brenda Weaver

Sing unto the LORD, bless his name; shew forth his salvation from day to day.
Declare his glory among the heathen, his wonders among all people. —Psalm 96:2, 3
Read Psalm 96

"There goes a Hummer!" calls either our biological son or our adopted son. A few years ago an argument may have ensued after such a find.

"I saw it first."

"Well, I called it first, so it's mine."

"That's not fair; you got the last one." (I have always wondered how they could argue over having things they did not actually own.)

In recent years their eyes have scouted for the boxlike vehicles called Hummers. I am thankful they have outgrown accumulating vehicles in their imaginations. Nor would I encourage them to pursue such an expensive one.

As one Hummer (in vehicle form) appears on the scene of time, I fear another hummer (in human form) is becoming nearly extinct. I am making efforts to revive one in our home. The hummer I refer to is the humming or singing mother. Before technology littered our homes with noise, I suppose humming mothers were more common; at least I hear a number of older people talk about their singing mothers.

As a young mother, I hummed or sang often when I rocked babies to sleep or tucked children in bed. I even developed the habit of singing softly or humming happily while shopping in the grocery store. I found it quieted my ever-active foster child (who would later become our adopted son). It also soothed my spirits as I surveyed the rising prices and struggled to keep the wiggling child upright and obedient in the seat of the shopping cart.

Our children are older now and would be embarrassed if I sang while we shopped. Life has changed to include older children and more complex cares. In the midst of it all, I want to display a happy, contented heart. On the way to the wash line, while weeding in the garden, or with hands plunged in the kitchen sink, I want my children to see and hear—and claim—a hummer!

Thought for the Day

If your spirit does not feel like singing,
hum your way there.

*"God needs
friends and a church family
to hold up the hands
of the father and mother in the battle . . .
not because it is so hard to lift up
one's own hands,
but because he has to keep doing it—
on, and on, and on."*
—An Adoptive Father

PART 5

Understanding Hearts

Lift Up Their Hands

Two are better than one; because they have a good reward for their labour.
For if they fall, the one will lift up his fellow: but woe to him that is alone
when he falleth; for he hath not another to help him up. —Ecclesiastes 4:9, 10

Hidden Wounds

Name Withheld

For I am poor and needy, and my heart is wounded within me. —Psalm 109:22
Read Psalm 38

*I*t was Saturday evening. Sandra and her husband were enjoying tea together at the kitchen table, the children all in their beds.

"So are you looking forward to tomorrow?" Wesley asked.

Sandra stirred her tea aimlessly, staring at the flickering candle on the table. She sighed. "I almost never look forward to going to church anymore," she admitted. "How can I face people going about their happy lives when I feel like crying all morning? How can I stand the stares, the meaningful looks . . . I can just feel their eyes on me, now that we've taken Anthony out of Sunday school. Justina told me she thinks we made the wrong decision, that we aren't letting Anthony enjoy his childhood. She said I ought to let go of him, let him be a normal boy, instead of pulling him in tight with all these restrictions. Sometimes I don't know if I can take it any longer. All the misunderstandings and criticism, besides what I'm facing every day at home . . ."

Wesley patted his wife's arm and said tenderly, "I know it's hard, dear. I'll be thinking of you and praying for you tomorrow."

They sat in silence for a while. Sandra wiped tears from her eyes and took another sip of tea. Then she looked at Wesley. "You know," she said hesitantly, "sometimes I wonder . . ." Wesley waited patiently until she went on. "Sometimes I wonder how much my own past may still be affecting me. I mean, when I see what Anthony is going through . . . how difficult it is for him to learn to trust because of that trust being broken as a small child and because of all the rejection and neglect he experienced, it makes me think of my own life. And I wonder if . . ." Sandra sat pondering, not knowing how to explain the feelings she was wrestling with.

Wesley nodded understandingly. "I think I know what you mean, Sandra. You wonder if you have things in your own life that were never resolved. Like the rough childhood you had, the neglect and abuse you suffered, and what your own mother was like."

Sandra nodded. "And then I think too of my first courtship. I thought, *Here is someone who finally sees something good in me.* Then how devastated I was when my boyfriend dropped me and turned to another girl so quickly! That was all in addition to the things I faced at home. One thing after another made me feel rejected. Sometimes I think I never got over it. The rejection, I mean. And I think maybe that's why I take it so personally when Anthony rejects my love and nurturing over and over again. And now I feel as though most of my friends are rejecting me too, by criticizing and condemning instead of taking time to listen to how it really is for me and showing their support . . ." Sandra's voice broke, and she could not go on.

"You've gone through a lot in your life, Sandra," Wesley said sympathetically. "Tell me more about how you see yourself in Anthony."

Sandra thought for a while, then said falteringly, "It's just so hard to take the way Anthony is treating me. As a child, my fondest dream was to have a happy Christian home. I often struggled with wondering what was wrong with me that my mom didn't like me. And now I struggle with wondering what's wrong with me that Anthony doesn't like me. It brings back strong memories of how I related to my mom . . . I didn't like her, either. I even hated when she hugged and kissed me—just like Anthony hates it when I try to show affection to him. I remember my mom saying she wished I'd never been born, and Mom and Dad fighting in front of us—you know what all I've faced . . ." her voice trailed off.

"I wonder if this is part of what's making it so hard for you to accept Anthony," Wesley suggested. "All the rejection he is throwing at you is bringing your own pain right up into your face again. Then you struggle with anger and resentment toward him for the pain he is causing you."

"You're very discerning," Sandra smiled through her tears. "That says it well." She was quiet for a while, then went on slowly. "You know, sometimes my own feelings scare me. How strong they can be! I used to wonder how a mother could ever abuse her child. I don't wonder anymore." She shuddered at the awful truth she was revealing.

"God has been carrying you, dear," Wesley told her. "This child has been doing everything possible to drive you crazy, but you have endured."

"I don't know if I have—the story is not all told," Sandra confessed, hanging her head and resting it in her hands. "I've never been under such extreme pressure before. I keep thinking, something has to give, somewhere. I can't just keep going on and on . . ."

Suddenly a shrill cry sounded from Kendall's bedroom. "Da-a-a-addy!" he shrieked. Wesley got up and stepped quickly back the hall to his three-year-old son's bed. Sandra could hear his gentle voice trying to soothe whatever had been troubling the little boy. Kendall had been waking up and crying in the night so often lately. A fresh stab of pain went through Sandra's heart at the thought. And eighteen-month-old Susie, though she slept through the night, was very restless and stirred at the slightest noise, sometimes crying out in her sleep. *Does this have anything to do with Anthony's problems?* Sandra wondered. In her heart she knew the answer.

Then there were the older children—twelve-year-old Judith and ten-year-old Jordan. Jordan had drawn a picture of their family one day and given it to them, with Anthony's place in the family conspicuously vacant. In his boyish scrawl he had written, "No Anthony. This is the way I want it." Judith, too, in her silent way, was showing signs of the stress their family was under. All because of a little five-year-old boy. Sandra sighed.

While at his job on Monday morning, Wesley felt a heavy load pressing down upon him, more than just the normal burden of a day's work. "Oh God, help us!" he cried out from his heart. "Help me know how to help!"

It's not just about helping Anthony's wounded heart to heal, he pondered. *Sandra needs help too. Help with her housework so she can focus more on Anthony and on giving the other children what they need. Help with her emotions, and help with her own pain. Then there's Kendall and Susie. They're hurting, in their own little way, by witnessing all the anger and bizarre behavior of their big brother, someone they should be able to look up to for an example. And I know Judith and Jordan suffer too, from being pushed aside because so much of the focus is on helping Anthony.*

A phone call from a customer forced Wesley's mind back to the reality of his job. But all day Wesley's heart was heavy with the responsibility of guiding his family through the chaos that had erupted in their home. And it had all begun with trying to help a wounded lamb.

Yes, there are hidden wounds. In the heart of the mother, who is the primary target of the child's anger and rejection. In the hearts of the siblings, whose lives are disrupted by the turmoil, and who resent the disturbed child getting all the attention. And, perhaps most hidden of all, in the heart of the father, as he shoulders the heavy load and tries to keep it all from falling apart.

How can we bring cleansing and healing to these hidden wounds? If you are the mother, find help. For your own emotional, mental, and spiritual well-being, you need someone with whom to counsel who can help you find rest in the torrent of emotions and the tremendous pressure you are under each day. Find someone who is willing to listen and learn rather than judge, someone who helps you see the big picture, someone who can help you see that all the terrible things your child is doing are because of his wounded heart, not because you have failed him as a mother. You need someone who can help you find cleansing and healing for any unresolved issues of your own so that you can reach out to your child with a calm confidence and help him find the same.

Make an effort to show kindness to those who are criticizing and do not understand, for really, they don't, and they mean well by trying to help. Forgive them. Release them of any obligation to you, of any demand upon them to see it from your side.

If you are a sibling, my heart goes out to you. It doesn't seem fair. The "bad" child is getting all the attention, just by acting so crazy. It makes you feel like doing bad things to get attention too. So sometimes you do. You resent all the focus being on this child, and you may also resent his very presence in the family and hope Dad and Mom decide he can't stay. You have wounds too, and they are real. Go to your parents or write them a letter if they don't have the time or energy to talk with you. Tell them how this makes you feel. Tell them you wish you had somebody to talk to who knows what it's like. Tell them you admire them for crying out to God in the storm, for trying to find help, and for doing what is best for the family even when it's hard.

If you are the father, God bless you for braving this desolate journey with all its confusion and misunderstandings. Yours is a lonely lot, for not even your wife will always have the emotional strength to listen to your problems and minister to your needs. But know that, even if she doesn't tell you so, she does admire you tremendously for your endurance, your faith in her, your strong arm to lean on, your tender support in this extremely difficult time. And sometime, when she is at a different place in the journey, she will tell you so.

If you are a friend, be kind. Gossip inflicts terrible wounds. If you think that the stories you've heard demand attention, go directly to the hurting family and gently ask if they are true. If they are, listen to their explanation and believe them, or respect them if they do not care to share. If it still does not make sense, trust that there is something more to it than you can see, and commit to keeping the story to yourself. Support the parents, especially the mother. The pain they face as they help a wounded child is a pain like no other, bringing grievous anguish of heart. Don't add to their pain by trying to tell them how to help their child, unless you have lived with a child like this yourself and really do know how to help.

It is not always wise to ask regularly about the child and how he is unless you are intimately involved in the progress for a good reason. It can be very tiring emotionally for the mother to have to explain over and over to friend after friend about all the bad days and the good days and how it fits into the progress.

Nor is it wise to try to make friends with the child, thinking that if you can get him to respond to your love, it will make it easier for the mother. This is counterproductive. The child can easily use you as a tool to push Mom away if you initiate lively, cheerful conversations with him on Sunday morning after he's been throwing hateful words or hostile silence at Mom all week. And friends, the worst thing you can do to the mother of one of these wounded lambs is to imply that she is not loving the child enough. Consider how much love it takes to make up for what the wounded heart is not absorbing!

There are ways to help one of these exhausted mothers. Send her a card of encouragement with a meaningful Scripture passage or poem. One friend sent me a pack of poems with a note to open one a day. Friends called and offered to bring us a meal. Sometimes we found a plate of cookies or a box of food in our van after church. Sometimes what meant the most was a simple, "I'm praying for you," or an arm around my shoulder when I could only answer the question "How are you?" with tears.

If the mother is taking her child to therapy, think what an added stress it would be for an already overworked mom to be gone for several hours once or twice a week. Offer to stay with her other children while she is gone so that they do not always need to go to a babysitter. Then surprise her by doing her laundry or cleaning.

It also goes a long way if you learn how to relate properly to a troubled child. Since the child is looking to others to fulfill needs that only the mother can truly meet, it is best to keep your distance until the child has demonstrated a secure bond with his family. Usually a simple, "Hello, how are you this morning?" is all you should try to do. Ask the parents if you are not sure how to relate.

One of the most important, supportive things you can do for the family is to learn how to take care of the child so that you can give them a break. They need time to focus on their other children and their marriage relationship without the emotionally unstable child there to interfere. This is not regular babysitting—it is respite care that takes intense structure and routine with which you should become familiar. The child must be cared for away from home in a way that will make him appreciate his mother more, not in a way that makes him look forward to running away from Mom to your house where you let him do all the fun stuff. This is a whole subject in itself. Ask if you may read some of the family's books, or do your own research so that you can understand why the child needs what the parent is telling you he needs.

Another thing to remember if you want to support the family, is that surprise visits are usually not pleasant surprises. When you ring the doorbell and nobody answers, though you are sure someone is at home, go away praying rather than judging. The mother may be too exhausted to face anyone. The child may be in the middle of some bizarre behavior. Maybe the mother is taking a nap. Or she might be deep into an emotionally intense discussion with her child which must not be interrupted, because it could be an important part of healing.

Healing—what a precious word! The wounds are deep . . . the obvious wounds in the hearts of the precious lambs, and these hidden wounds. But there is hope for healing! That is the way of our God!

Thought for the Day

Surrounding the hurting child and his family with a strong,
supportive team creates an environment
conducive to healing for all.

Lift Up Their Hands

Name Withheld
an adoptive father

The Lord GOD hath given me the tongue of the learned, that I should know how to speak a word in season to him that is weary. —Isaiah 50:4
Read Hebrews 12

Adoption is normally the realization of a precious dream that becomes a fountain of joy and blessing. But sometimes instead of stories of sweetness and joy, you may hear tales from your friends of the frustration and havoc this cute little one has brought to his new family. What is going on? You continue to experience him as a charming little man who would be any parent's delight. He appears to be a model child; in fact, he seems exceptionally well-behaved and eager to please. You begin to observe the parents relating to him in a way that does not make sense for a child who is so eager to please and so well-behaved. Are your friends making their own problems? You see them begin to restrict the child and keep him very closely supervised in social settings. Aren't they overreacting a bit?

What you may not see is that the parents wrestle with the reality of extreme two-facedness in their child: sweet and charming in surface relationships, hateful and unmanageable in close relationships. A child whose only experience of adults has been abuse and neglect is likely to use these two faces to cope with his insecurities. He may continue this pattern, sometimes to extremes, until he accepts emotionally the loss of his birth parents and begins to bond with his adoptive parents and allow them to meet the emotional needs of his heart—emotional needs he has learned to block out in order to survive the terrors of his world where adults could not be trusted.

How can the church family support those in this overwhelming situation for which they may not have been prepared? The starting point is accepting, just as the parents must, that the child who appears to be joyful and loving is actually putting on a veneer. The real child underneath who so skillfully arranges the veneer is full of anger, distrust, and fear of rejection. In fact, far from desiring a close, loving relationship, he will react with terror when presented with the opportunity. And when you think about it, what else has life taught him but to be terrified of adults?

When the parents describe what this child is like at home, believe them. They are not exaggerating. This may be difficult for you to believe if you continue to see only the veneer. But look beyond the surface and observe how he relates to his mother. To whom does he run for help with his little problems? Is he constantly seeking the attention of other adults instead of his mother? How would a securely-attached child his age act differently? If you observe carefully, you will see many little signs of a lack of trust. But be aware also that some children, while rejecting the mother at home, will actually appear very affectionate with her in public. So again, believe the parents.

And then, when you come to realize the child really does have a problem trusting his new parents, be wary of blaming his adoptive parents for the problem. They have not made the child this way, and he would likely act this way for anyone else who attempted to parent him. Neither is the child to blame. His rejection of a close relationship with a mother and father and his fierce independence are coping skills he was forced to learn in order to survive. It may take his new parents years of sacrifice and pain to bring him through the healing process of opening his heart and sorting through the overwhelming trauma he has been through. Do what you can to make this load easier for them, rather than blaming.

As you observe your friends on this journey, remember there are no easy answers. Your questions and concerns about the situation are normal. In fact, your concerns may take the form of shock and utter dismay. This, too, is normal for one who is merely observing. Rather than immediately forming conclusions, try to understand accurately the nature of the problems they are facing, just as you would want to thoroughly understand an illness before prescribing a treatment. Read books if you can, and ask questions that indicate a desire to hear and understand the struggle. If possible, talk with someone else who has helped children who had never bonded with a mother. Perhaps you can point your overwhelmed friends to someone who has had experience with such children. The parents may have much to learn about helping an emotionally troubled child, and the friendship of others who have walked the same road is immensely beneficial.

Expect less socially from your friends during this time. When Mom and Dad are burned out, they may find it difficult to maintain their normal level of social interaction. Also, while others may see only a sweet, innocent little child, the parents may be keenly aware of the threat this child could be to his playmates. He has likely been exposed to many forms of abuse, and despite his beguiling exterior, his innocence may be very corrupted. Social settings become more difficult when the child needs constant supervision. If it seems this sweet little child is always sitting beside one of his parents rather than playing with his friends, there are likely some very good reasons for it.

Remember that in the child's attempt to push away from a close relationship with his parents, he will be seeking attention in superficial relationships with others. As difficult as it may be, you will do the child and the parents a favor by being a bit distant with the child until he has bonded better with his parents. When he asks you for help with something, try telling him to go ask his mother. Then study his reaction. You will learn something about his problem.

A unified message from the church family to the child is a powerful force. Let the child know you are solidly on his parents' team. He may work hard to convince you that he is a model child who loves his parents dearly and get your emotions on his side against his parents for treating him the way they do. "Divide and conquer" is one of the survival skills an unattached child learns at an extremely young age. This requires clear communication among all adults involved, especially where a school-age or older child is in focus. It also means giving each other the benefit of the doubt and cross-checking stories before forming conclusions.

While it is necessary for the parents to learn and grow in their efforts to help such a child, don't let him succeed in getting the focus on the parents as the root of his problems. The situation may highlight immaturity or needs in the parents for which they must take responsibility in order to help their child grow. However, if the child is to find emotional healing, he will need to be held accountable for his own problems.

Pray for your friends and the child. This is a spiritual battle for the heart of the child. God uses fathers and mothers as channels for His love and healing. God needs friends and church families to hold up the hands of the father and mother in the battle. Moses in the battle needed support, not because it was so hard to lift up his own hands, but because he had to keep doing it—on, and on, and on. Remember that parents become battle-weary because of the relentlessness of the child's behavior. Be the Aaron and Hur they need to help them endure.

The parents will make many mistakes and will be forced to face their own issues that they may have succeeded in glossing over up to this point. The mother especially, as the main caretaker, faces an extreme challenge to respond lovingly in the face of constant abuse and irritation from the child. She will likely fail at times, despite her best intentions. If you see her failing, try to put yourself in her shoes and ponder whether you might also experience human limitations in those shoes. Let her know you realize the extreme pressure she is under and that you are praying for God to bless her with strength to be joyful and loving in the face of rejection.

An emotionally troubled child can stress not only the home attempting to help him, but also an entire church family. These children can act as mirrors of our own insecurities, and if we look at ourselves carefully, we may discover we are reacting to fears and problems in our own lives. Rather than allowing the stress to hinder relationships with each other, strive for patience and forbearance and consider it an opportunity from

God for growth. As God's people work together in humility and love, He can use our churches to bless and strengthen those hurting emotionally among us, and refine each of us in the process.

Thought for the Day

"Iron sharpeneth iron; so a man sharpeneth the countenance of his friend." —Proverbs 27:17

A Word Fitly Spoken

Emily Martin

A word fitly spoken is like apples of gold in pictures of silver. — Proverbs 25:11
For if ye forgive men their trespasses, your heavenly Father will also
forgive you: But if ye forgive not men their trespasses,
neither will your Father forgive your trespasses. —Matthew 6:14-15
Read Luke 11:1-4

*I*t was over a year after the death of our premature son, and we had just had another discouraging visit with an infertility specialist before leaving for a grandparent's funeral. Wondering if we would ever have more children, I was feeling a bit raw and maybe more sensitive than I would have been otherwise, but I was trying to work through my feelings and trust the future to God. It wasn't the first time I had faced this battle, and I knew the steps to take.

Malvern and I were very happy with the little boys God had given us. Our two little foster boys, Alex and Ricky, were sweet and delightful. Darian, our sturdy little Mexican son through adoption, was delightful in every way with his black sparkling eyes and contagious chuckle. They were all affectionate, lovable little boys, and in many ways were all we had dreamed of. But if the older boys had to leave, Dari would be an only child. He was almost three and big for his age, so he certainly wasn't a baby anymore. Besides, I still keenly felt the loss of our premature baby.

Maybe it was the thought of another funeral that brought back the memories so vividly. I saw again in my mind's eye Bradlyn's miniature legs as his last kicks grew slower and slower. I saw his little grave in the churchyard. I remembered the swollen milk ducts and how crying babies triggered my body's response those next several weeks after his birth. To some women it didn't seem to really matter, but I had wanted so badly to breast-feed my babies. When Dari was a baby I had nursed him, even though I'd had little milk. He had gotten frustrated at the lack of milk, and I had given up. After Bradlyn, I had the milk without the baby. Crying babies, empty arms, and my desire for another baby all jumbled together.

Many other relatives came to Grandma's funeral. I stood quietly to the side, trying to blend into the woodwork of the crowded room. Malvern and the boys were out somewhere. There seemed to be aunts, uncles, and cousins everywhere. Across the room someone was asking how many grandchildren and great-grandchildren there were. Happily the count-down began. This person had ten, that person eight . . . My ears perked up as I heard someone ask, "What about Malvern's children?"

"Well, you certainly wouldn't count the foster boys," someone said rather opinionatedly. "Who knows how long they will even have them!"

"And Darian," another voice cut in, "if he's adopted, it's not like he is actually a descendant. Is it really quite honest to count him? It's not like he's in this world because of Grandpa and Grandma or anything!"

I was so stunned I never heard the next question, but I heard the reply.

"Humph, if we started counting miscarriages, who knows where we would start and stop!"

I turned toward the window and shaded my eyes with my hand. Surely the hurt I was feeling in my heart was reflected on my face! Out of our four sons, none of them counted!

Then I recognized a third voice joining the conversation. It was a cousin whose seven healthy sons had been born to her. "Well, I think Darian should be counted. If he's adopted, then he is theirs." It was said sweetly, yet with conviction, and I wondered if she had possibly caught a glimpse of my face before I turned, or if she was just naturally kind.

I never knew whether any of our boys were counted or not. I was careful not to try to find out. That night after my husband and three sons were sleeping, I let the tears come. *Why don't our children count?* I asked. *In this huge family, are our children actually the only adopted and foster children? And how can they call Bradlyn's perfectly-formed body, even down to his eyelashes, a miscarriage?* I found a piece of scrap paper and, as I am inclined to do when distressed, I wrote how I was feeling and why it hurt. In my Bible I found verses of comfort. And I prayed, *Father, forgive them, for they know not what they do!*

My boys need never know. To me they count, every one of them—the foster sons, the adopted one, and the baby someone called a miscarriage. I asked God to forgive the people who had made the thoughtless remarks and to help me forgive them, for surely they didn't understand they were hurting anyone with their words. Sixteen years later I still feel a deep gratitude toward the cousin of kind words, but I cannot recall who the other voices belonged to.

This experience has helped me to add a kind remark if I sense someone is hurting, to forgive thoughtless words that come from someone who has not walked a similar path, and to always remember that everyone counts.

Thought for the Day

We have a choice of what we will do with other people's thoughtless remarks. To hug them to ourselves breeds bitterness; to forgive releases the hurt and lets us learn from the experience.

How Can You Help?

Name Withheld

Two are better than one; because they have a good reward for their labour. For if they fall, the one will lift up his fellow: but woe to him that is alone when he falleth; for he hath not another to help him up. And if one prevail against him, two shall withstand him; and a threefold cord is not quickly broken. —Ecclesiastes 4:9, 10, 12

Read Ecclesiastes 4

Though you may never have adopted a needy child yourself and do not feel God is calling you to do that, perhaps you'd like to support families who have done so.

As you rub shoulders with a family who seems burned out with the daily trauma of parenting a troubled child, is there anything you can do to lift up the feeble arms of these parents? There certainly is.

The most helpful thing you can do is to support, encourage, and care for *the parents* (especially the mother), who may be receiving few emotional rewards from the child they are trying desperately to help. If you have no experience with adoption or foster care or disturbed children, refrain from giving advice on how to make them behave. Don't assume that the parents are at fault if they can't manage their adopted child. We who live with deeply troubled children who are not biologically ours may become worn out with loving and caring for a child who is unable to respond with love and trust.

Sometimes we need to express our frustrations without being judged for our emotions. It is extremely difficult to love a child who can't show us any appreciation for what we do for him. In our humanness, we may sound at times as if we are at the point of giving up on the child. When we get so stressed out, we need a listening ear and some encouragement that we're doing a good job. We need to hear that God put this child in our home because He knew we'd be the best parents to help him heal from his terrible traumas. Tell us we are making a huge difference in our child's life, even if we can't see it now. Tell us you're praying for us. If you hear of organizations or information that may be helpful to us, share that, but let us decide if this is what we really need.

Do not attempt to take the child under your wing and assume that you understand his needs better than we stressed-out parents. One very common phenomenon with children who suffer from attachment difficulties is that they often respond with much more affection and warmth to people who barely know them. The people that the child should have trusted as an infant or toddler hurt him terribly or ignored or abandoned him. This child's damaged emotions tell him that the people he lives with are those most apt to be violent or uncaring. Outsiders actually seem safer to such children. An outsider doesn't know how bad and worthless the child believes he is. What child doesn't respond to attention and praise and affection from an adult who is determined to give him only positive commendation—and doesn't ever see his blackest side?

Don't imagine that if only you had this child in your care, you'd win his heart so much more easily. You have not walked in the parents' shoes, and you have not committed your life to parenting a disturbed child. Your attempts to bond with this child apart from his adoptive parents do not help the situation in the home that God gave him. If you want to make the supreme difference in a child's life, perhaps you should adopt your own troubled child. There are more children in need of understanding parents than will ever be adopted into loving, godly families.

That doesn't mean, however, that you need to be cold toward these children. We parents of adopted children love to have others show an interest in them. We lap it up thirstily when you praise our children *to us.* It is good for us to hear your appreciation for the positive things you notice in our children. When we are facing severe struggles with our child at home, it helps us to be reminded that he has some wonderful, lovable qualities, and that his future may not be doomed after all. It was especially encouraging to hear statements about my adopted daughter such as the following: "I noticed she (did a very nice thing, was very polite, showed maturity and responsibility . . . [the list goes on]), and I want you to know I think you're doing a very good job of teaching her." It is especially bonding for us when you say something like this in the hearing of the child. It is warmly bonding for parents and adopted children when an "outsider" tells a child in the hearing of his parents that he is privileged to have such loving, concerned parents.

Sometimes we need respite from the constant emotional upheaval with a troubled child. I appreciated it so much when another family asked if I'd like my daughter to join them in some family activity such as camping or a short weekend trip. (Being single and having no other children, I couldn't provide such family outings for her.) Larger families with both a mom and a dad may need a different kind of respite. The child in question may need a quieter kind of retreat with a family or single individual who is willing to keep him for several days just to give his family a break. Even if you know little about therapeutic ways to relate to the child, you might allow his exhausted family a short time to enjoy each other without the constant irritation of the child's bottomless needs. Other children in a struggling family can end up feeling neglected because their parents expend so much energy keeping the troubled child calm and secure. A few days of respite can help a family rest up. Refreshed by the short absence, they'll be able to take up the challenge again when the child returns to them. In this sense, a short separation can turn out to be a bonding experience!

Be careful, though. Your attitude must be that you are helping out the child's parents and siblings. You are not giving the adopted child an "out" from respecting or trusting or obeying his own parents. You can help immensely by constantly reaffirming to the child how much you respect and trust his adoptive parents, even while he is with you. When the child is having fun with another family (or simply having his own rest from the hard work of bonding with his adoptive family), he may complain about his own family and say things like, "I wish *you'd* be my (mom, dad, sister)." Don't listen to it. If you respond at all, make it clear to the child that although you enjoy his presence with you, you are not his family, and that *his own family loves him best of all.*

Extended family and an understanding church brotherhood can go a long way toward helping adoptive families be successful in raising children who have significant emotional problems.

Thought for the Day

"There is no brotherhood without love. Genuine brotherhood cannot
be a pretense; it cannot be acted on out of a sense of duty;
it has to come from a heart of love."

—Lester Bauman

To Stand in the Gap

Caroline Miller

And I sought for a man among them, that should make up the hedge,
and stand in the gap before me for the land, that I should not destroy it:
but I found none. —Ezekiel 22:30
Read Proverbs 1: 7-23

Are we aware that we need to lift up our parents and give them honor? Proverbs 1:8, 9 in the *Amplified Bible* says, "My son, hear the instruction of your father; reject it not, nor forsake the teaching of your mother; for they are a victor's chaplet of grace upon your head, and the chains and pendants (of gold worn by kings) for your neck." This shows us the value of guiding children to follow the teaching of their parents, particularly if they have Christian parents.

What is our response when a child tells us that he can't talk with his parents? Do we truly "listen to his heart"? Or do we think with pity, *I will rescue this child. This is how I can help him live the Christian life. It's too bad he has to struggle so hard in his home.*

If we truly listen to his heart cry, what is he saying? Is life at home so bad, or is there something he is doing that his parents do not approve of? Is the guilt he carries causing him to blame others, desiring to make himself look better? How can you know that he has told you the whole story? Sympathy will make him feel better, and if other adults seem to be taking his side it will relieve the pressure of guilt for a time, but will it help him?

Consider what it would do for the child if, rather than sympathizing, we would stand in the gap. Intercession can be a great key to the door of relationships. The child needs to know that our interest is to help him respectfully talk these things out with his parents.

Before drawing any conclusions, it may help for us to go to the parents and ask how they feel about their relationship with their child. Perhaps together you can reach his heart by considering his point of view. Open your heart to the parents as well. Listen to them. Who knows the child's heart better than his parents? Perhaps there is a side that we failed to see, a challenge that the parents have worked with for years that we are totally unaware of. Sometimes our hearts are so moved in pity for the child that we never consider that he is playing on our emotions so that we sympathize with his situation.

Alvin Miller family

Our goal should be to help the child find peace and help him through to victory rather than free him from his situation. If we teach him to honor his parents, we will be helping him. Those who seek to free him from his situation in order to influence and direct him are in for a surprise. They have not upheld Biblical principles and will find that he will not respect them either. They are stunned when he continues to do things they were not expecting from him. Then they are aghast to discover that they have helped him on his way down.

What a great reward if, instead, we can turn the heart of the child back to his parents! We stand beside them, fortifying them, and the child's heart will again be complete and at rest. Instead of helping him down, we have helped him up.

Thought for the Day

How often the Golden Rule helps us do right.

More Than We Can Handle

Emily Martin

As we have therefore opportunity, let us do good unto all men,
especially unto them who are of the household of faith. Galatians 6:10
Read Galatians 5:22—6:10

I picked up yet another pair of soiled jeans and submerged them along with the five others in the wringer washer. Tears threatened to spill as I viewed the mountains of laundry yet to be washed. Once again I determined to shake this cloud of depression that threatened to overpower me.

Why would a Christian woman, especially one with a kind and understanding husband and a house full of healthy children and the promise of another on the way, be wallowing in this valley of despair?

I remembered the days of empty arms and childlessness. *If only I could change my situation and have children to love and cherish, my happiness would be complete!* I had thought. But it was after I had learned to be happy anyway that God had granted us our quiver full. When I had gone from empty arms to five preschoolers (three were foster children) and was coping with a threatened pregnancy, I became acutely aware of the other side of the coin. Now I could feel for busy mothers in a new way.

But God is faithful always, even through times of overwhelming depression. And circumstances changed. Some children left. Some grew up.

The next time I hit an extreme low was seven years later, when I realized our former foster boys, David and Joe, would actually be staying on after their summer visit. It wasn't that I didn't love them or want them. It was just that I had been treading water, barely keeping my head above water through the summer, and was counting on catching up in the fall after the boys went home to their mother. About the time we gave permission for them to stay, I realized I was again pregnant. Here I was, a pregnant disorganized lady with ten children already—teenagers, toddlers, and seven schoolchildren, three of them hard learners. I often didn't feel well, and underneath I felt God had handed me too heavy a load. That attitude usually seemed to be the root of my depression. Does God give us more than we can handle?

Emily's family

Both times at my lowest, I was also pregnant and coping with hormonal changes. God's grace is sufficient for us to experience victory, but sometimes I think it helps to realize we won't always be in this situation. My mother used to say, "This, too, shall pass." Accepting what God is asking of us brings submission and happiness. He must know we are capable of handling more than we think we can.

Perhaps He sometimes gives us more than we can handle alone so that we reach out for help from Him and from others. This is what I needed to do. I confessed my struggles. I admitted I was about to go under. I described the fog overtaking me that I couldn't shake off. And I found a wealth of help and encouragement and love.

Slowly but surely, life got brighter again. Some of the following things really helped me:

1. **Verbal encouragement.** At least two dear friends (sisters are friends too, right?) called almost every day. They asked me how it was going and offered advice and support. They told me what I had done right that day and offered positive suggestions.

2. **Prayer.** They told me they were praying for me.

3. **A children's work chart.** My sisters helped me set up a work chart—a simple wheel chart that turned once a week for the seven schoolchildren. This covered the main tasks—dishwashing and keeping all the main rooms tidied—and kept me from having to assign so many tasks.

4. **Help with schoolwork.** One schoolteacher tried to keep homework to a minimum and even helped after school with their homework. I tried to have supper pretty well prepared before the children came home from school so I could help them with their lessons.

5. **Help with the sewing.** People gave me hand-me-down dresses for the girls, and a mother offered to mend ten garments each week. She picked them up one week and returned them the following week. It was something she could do at home and it was a tremendous morale boost for me.

6. **Help with meals.** The church women were wonderful. Entire meals were brought occasionally, and they organized a casserole shower for our freezer.

7. **Childcare help.** Several evenings we had offers to watch all of our children. When you have high-energy children, and a lot of them, an evening's break can be the tonic you need to come back and appreciate the sweet parts about each one. Also, one evening for my birthday my niece came and stayed with our children and put them to bed while my husband and I went on a moonlit walk. I told her it was the very best gift she could have given.

8. **Vitamins and herbs.** I was told of supplements I could take to sustain my health.

9. **Praying together.** It is also, even now, great tonic to pray with my husband. It spurs me on to hear him pray for me out loud. I also met on occasion for prayer with a few sisters, and we read inspiring Scriptures together. While the children were in school I listened to sermon tapes and the Bible on tape.

10. **Diversion.** I also realized I needed time for some diversion, without feeling as if I was being criticized. With all my busyness I still wrote on my computer sometimes, made cards, and read snatches throughout the day or night for a few minutes. I felt I needed those diversions to retain my sanity.

11. **Counting my blessings.** As I learned to count my blessings, I felt rich and full and loved. What a beautiful privilege to be a Christian mother; each child has a sweet special side that I love and cherish. I also have a husband who treasures me, and a church family that surrounds us with love and support.

Had my circumstances changed? Yes, somewhat, for after I admitted my struggles and the valley of despair I was in, people stepped forward to help. But mostly what changed was me and my perspective. God wants us to be grateful and give thanks to Him for His goodness. "In everything give thanks, for this is the will of God in Christ Jesus concerning you."

Thought for the Day

God never asks us to do more than we are able to do.
Maybe more than we are willing,
but never more than we are able.

Midnight of the Soul

Name Withheld

*Ye also helping together by prayer for us, that for the gift bestowed
upon us by the means of many persons thanks may
be given by many on our behalf. —2 Corinthians 1:11*
Read 2 Corinthians 1:2-24

Dear friends,

It was early Friday morning when I awakened with a snatch of tune and the phrase "midnight of the soul" going through my mind again and again. I tried to remember more and to remember the title of the song. Finally, "shall illume" came to mind.

My thoughts were drawn to you and the painful experience you are now going through and your trials of the past year. It seems to me that you must be going through a "midnight of the soul."

I also recalled what an encouragement it was when I was going through difficult times and you and others sent encouraging notes. I wish to encourage you in the same way not to go down in discouragement. We, too, had sons who deeply disappointed us, but God is faithful. My prayer is that God will answer your prayers even as He has answered ours.

Interestingly, "If On a Quiet Sea" was sung for us Sunday evening.

Blessings to you and yours,
Your brother in Christ

Thought for the Day

Sometimes an encouraging note from a friend is just what we need not to go down in despair, but rather to keep on keeping on.

If on a Quiet Sea

If, on a quiet sea, toward heaven we calmly sail,
With grateful hearts, O God, to Thee, we'll own the favoring gale.

But should the surges rise, and rest delay to come,
Blest be the tempest, kind the storm, which drives us nearer home.

Soon shall our doubts and fears all yield to Thy control;
Thy tender mercies shall illume the midnight of the soul.

Teach us, in every state, to make Thy will our own;
And when the joys of sense depart, to live by faith alone.

—Augustus Toplady

Does Anyone Understand?

Emily Martin

For God so loved the world, that he gave his only begotten Son, that whosoever believeth in him should not perish, but have everlasting life. —John 3:16

Read Isaiah 53

Jesus became a tiny, helpless newborn baby; He knows how it feels to be wet and hungry and totally dependent. *For he shall grow up before him as a tender plant, and as a root out of a dry ground.*

He was not handsome. *He hath no form nor comeliness; and when we shall see him, there is no beauty that we should desire him.*

He was raised by a man who was not his birth father; no doubt the neighbors whispered about His illegitimate birth. People turned away from Him. He was falsely accused and misunderstood. He was oppressed and afflicted. He was abused; He was shamed; His clothes were removed. He was mocked and spit on and beaten. He was judged unjustly, blamed for what He had not done, and punished for it.

He is despised and rejected of men; a man of sorrows, and acquainted with grief: and we hid as it were our faces from him; he was despised, and we esteemed him not.

He chose to suffer all of these things! He identifies with us in our pain! He knows how it feels! He cares! He even knows how it is to feel forsaken by God the Father!

My God, my God, why hast thou forsaken me? (Matthew 27:46). Surely he hath borne our griefs, and carried our sorrows: yet we did esteem him stricken, smitten of God, and afflicted. But he was wounded for our transgressions, he was bruised for our iniquities: the chastisement of our peace was upon him; and with his stripes we are healed.

Sometimes we long for another human being to understand us and our particular struggles. There is great healing in opening up and sharing with another tangible person we can see and hear, but the true Healer is Jesus Christ, the One who truly understands!

Thought for the Day

Let's take our problems and perplexities to Jesus,
the One who never misjudges
or misunderstands us.

*"Being a 'torchbearer'
is a privilege
we want to share,
to enlighten and inspire others.
As we enlarge our circles of love
we are building for eternity."*
—Marian Reinford

PART 6

With Grateful Hearts

Trusting God
With the End Results

My life is but a weaving
Between my Lord and me;
I cannot choose the colors,
He worketh steadily . . .

Our Song

Jewel Carter

And the peace of God, which passeth all understanding,
shall keep your hearts and minds through Christ Jesus. —Philippians 4:7
Read Philippians 4:4-7

*I*t began not long after I started reading books to my twin boys. To make story time more interesting for them, I started singing the nursery rhymes. I used tunes from other songs or made up my own. Somehow I began singing to our boys the story of their life, and they loved it.

Waking from their naps, they would patter out to the kitchen where I was working. I'd give them each a cookie and they'd sit down to watch me. Brady sat cross-legged on the floor, and Brett straddled his sturdy little toy semi.

"Sing our song," Brady would request. So I obliged them, starting with their birth, continuing to when they became part of our family, and on to the addition of baby Lindsay to the family. I ended the song with praise and gratitude to God for blessing us with our three precious children.

The boys would listen somberly to the song, an occasional smile quirking the corners of their mouths when their names were mentioned. Brett, our music lover, tapped his foot in time to the music. Somehow the music seemed to soften the harsh facts of their birth mother's death and their being left by a superstitious midwife and family to die at their birth mother's side. But the kindness of an aunt, who climbed into a window to rescue them, and the love and care that was given to them by mission families until a home was found for them, beautified the story.

The song seemed to have a calming effect on the boys. Where earlier in the day they might have been restless and irritable, they were now sweet and helpful.

Our song is good for me too. With the busyness of three small children, it is easy to forget that once my arms were empty. I am reminded again of how God brought these children into our home through seemingly impossible circumstances . . . of how our prayers were answered so amazingly. "Our song" reminds me again of how important it is to have enough faith to let go and let God have control of our lives.

Brett, Brady, Lindsay

I have learned and am still learning to give thanks for everything. Most especially, I have learned to thank God for allowing us to go through the blessing of infertility. No, I didn't say thank you at the time, but later I did.

What if God had allowed us to have our own way? What if Brady and Brett had never been brought into our lives? It's impossible to think of life without them! God's way is so much better than our own! I am thankful for infertility, and I am thankful for adoption. I am also thankful for the birth of our daughter Lindsay. I am so glad God has given us the privilege of experiencing both ways of adding children to our family!

Thought for the Day

Never be afraid to trust an unknown future to a known God.

—Corrie ten Boom

Sorry?

Christine Diller

The Lord shall guide thee. —Isaiah 58:11
Read Psalm 116:1, 2

"Are you ever sorry you adopted?" was the question.

Sorry? No, we're not sorry. Parenting isn't an easy road, but the joys of the journey are worth the troubles. We've faced problems, yes, and we've cried out to God. But God heard our prayers and answered. What beautiful experiences!

Sorry? I count it as a privilege. As we rejoiced in the arrival of each new child into our home, I was humbled. I thought about the birth parents. Whatever reason they had for giving up their child, they were going to miss one of life's greatest blessings, and I was sorry for them. I didn't know what made us better parents than they, other than that we had the precious blood of Jesus in our lives.

Sorry? I enjoy watching our children mature and show different interests as they grow. The different abilities of each child in our home, biological or adopted, add variety and spice to our home and make our family more complete. While we share in all the work and all the play, each child seems to enjoy one part of it more than another, and this all works out wonderfully.

Sorry? It's been a blessing. Adoption has taught us many things we may not have learned any other way. Adoption has caused us to stretch and grow in areas where we would not have been challenged except through adoption. We've grown closer to God and closer to each other. It's definitely been a blessed experience.

Sorry? No. It's been a privilege, a joy, and a blessing. I'm glad we chose to adopt.

Thought for the Day

When we feel God directing us, we can be assured that the joys and blessings of the journey will outweigh the troubles.

One Hundred Days

Emily Martin

Therefore said he unto them, The harvest truly is great,
but the labourers are few: pray ye therefore the Lord of the harvest,
that he would send forth labourers into his harvest. —Luke 10:2
Read Luke 10, especially noting verses 17-20

"Miss Emily, how long have we been at your house? Is it about one hundred days?"

I was combing Amber's hair. As usual she was full of chatter, questions, and ideas. As a very particular slip of femininity, this six-year-old preferred standing in front of the mirror so she could keep tabs on the combing project. Her big round brown eyes met mine in the glass.

"About one hundred days? It's about that. You came in March and now it's June."

My thoughts scurried on. *A bit over three months; just a hundred days. How can we get so very attached in just one hundred days!* According to the social worker, our remaining days with Amber and her sisters were numbered. It was such fun to have little girls at last—dresses to sew, hair to comb, dolls, and tea parties . . .

"Miss Emily, I think I'm getting pimples." This was said with the dramatic air of *What awful thing will happen next!* "Oh, why do I have such straight, ugly hair?"

"Oh, Amber," I assured her, "your hair is pretty. God made you, and He likes straight hair as well as curly. Think how boring it would be if everyone were exactly alike!"

Amber

God. I tried to bring Him into every conversation I could. These bright little girls had known nothing of God when they came. They were like little sponges just soaking up all we could tell them. Family devotions were a joy each evening as they listened, enraptured, to the Bible stories we told them and sang their little hearts out with all the new songs they had learned. The cassette tapes of Bible stories and children's songs were played over and over as they went to sleep, as soon as they were awake, or as they worked or played throughout the day. Lustily they sang along, starting the next song almost before the recorded voices began. Verses were recited.

One hundred days. Was I redeeming the time enough?

Nights after we tucked them into bed, they often wanted to talk a while. "I'm glad you don't have TV at your house. We saw awful things on TV. The devil and wicked creepy people who work for the devil." The thin little shoulders shuddered. "I have bad dreams from it."

"Me too."

I was upset to hear what awful things they had watched and the hideous scenes they described. It was almost enough to give *me* bad dreams, and they were just innocent little girls! They should have been thinking instead about Heaven, angels, love, and rainbow gardens. I tried to give them good things to dream about instead.

"Amber is the bad one," we had been informed. "She throws awful temper tantrums—lies on the floor and screams like one possessed." We hadn't found it to be so. The social worker seemed puzzled. "Ah, but you have given these children a quietness and peace, a tranquility like they have never experienced before. I cannot describe the difference."

One afternoon Amber and I were tidying the girls' bedroom. In confident tones she stated, "Sometimes I feel like the devil is after me. I feel like he has hold of me. I lay on the floor and scream and kick. The louder I scream, the harder he pulls. It feels like he will pull me clear through the floor. It's a horrible, horrible feeling!" She shuddered, her eyes deep pools of pain and fear. I could tell it was real and terrible to her.

"Oh, Amber," I said, "you know that God is stronger than Satan. Our whole house is filled with God. We love Him and obey Him, and He takes care of us. You do not need to be afraid of the devil when God is near."

She gave a happy little dance around the room. "Oh, Miss Emily, I was not talking about here at this house. I am not afraid of the devil at this house."

Might this explain the absence of the temper tantrums the worker had described?

The day came all too soon when, with a smile and a hug, they walked out of our home and out of our lives. But memories linger.

One hundred days. How much does a six-year-old learn and retain in one hundred days? Is it enough to help shape and mold her life? Does she remember what a Christian home is like? Is the peace and security that she experienced for a short time enough to spur her into seeking something different once she is old enough to make choices on her own?

Fifteen years have passed. We still don't know the answers to these questions. We do not need to know. God asks us to reach out and plant the seeds. The increase is up to Him.

Thought for the Day

Invest time in children, be their friend, and share spiritual truth with them. Your heart will be blessed as well as theirs.

Healing May Take a Lifetime

Name Withheld

*Pleasant words are as an honeycomb, sweet to the soul,
and health to the bones.—Proverbs 16:24*
Read Proverbs 16:16; 20-24

My story of adoption does not have a happy ending—yet. I've been single all my life, and I adopted my troubled daughter at age nine. She had been removed from her mother at age six and had worn out five foster homes during the three years she was in foster care. The agency was desperate to have Annie adopted, as they saw what she needed most was a home committed to keeping her "forever."

Annie lived with me for seven years. When she was sixteen, the court ordered her back into foster care. That was not my choice, but Annie's. My daughter had conveyed to her personal attorney her wish to "undo" the adoption. Annie had been granted this attorney, called a *guardian ad litem*—a special lawyer who represents the child's interests in custody disputes—when the courts became involved due to her problematic physical violence toward me. This attorney never interviewed me but heard only Annie's perspective on how she related to me. In his opinion, Annie would do better in another home.

But after less than a year in a new foster home, Annie became pregnant with a boy from her senior class in public high school. She ran away from the foster home and eventually moved in with her boyfriend, who helped her care for her daughter for the first four months of the baby's life. Then Annie's emotional trauma got the best of her again, and Child Protective Services removed baby Renee to the care of her boyfriend's mother, but with generous visitation rights. At the time of this writing, the custody issues are still ongoing. Annie is working hard at regaining full custody of her baby daughter; she doesn't want her children to experience the separation she experienced from her own birth mother.

Meanwhile, Annie has had a second baby girl with the same boyfriend. Then she discarded the boyfriend and found a new one. My heart aches to see how Annie seems to feel doomed to follow in her birth mother's footsteps, even though she vows she wants to be a good mother to her little girls.

For several years after Annie left my home, she resisted contact with me. Because of false allegations she made against me, I was compelled to undergo a battery of psychological tests to prove my competency as a mother. The doctor who tested me was kind and understanding, and I found myself pouring out my story. She gave me wise advice.

"Annie sounds like a wild horse," she said calmly. "A wild horse is skittish and fearful if you try too hard to catch it. What you need to do is stand still and let your daughter come to you."

This advice was hard to swallow. I wanted to storm Heaven's doors and demand that God make my daughter receptive to my love and longing. But in time I saw the doctor was right. I accepted the circumstances and thought that maybe those seven years as Annie's mother was all that God wanted of me. Perhaps I needed to lay that part of my life away forever.

But soon God opened doors for me to reach out to Annie even while she was in foster care. At every opportunity, I prayed for wisdom. I did not want to push so hard that I gave Annie a reason to resist me. But God gave me assurance that in spite of her outward reactions, Annie still needed to know that I loved her and desired a relationship with her and would never abandon her of my free will. I wrote her occasional letters, sent her birthday and Christmas gifts, and prayed for her constantly.

Just as the doctor had predicted, Annie stopped running away from me emotionally, and gradually edged closer. Over a period of years, she came back into my life again, along with her babies whom she allows me to call my grandchildren. Weekend visits with these precious granddaughters are the highlight of my life. I am so thankful I still have opportunity to influence Annie's life and theirs. The circumstances for these new little souls, while sad, are not as grim as Annie's were when she was a tiny defenseless child and her birth mother was hopeless and estranged from family supports.

Today Annie calls me several times a week. She brings her babies to visit, and she gratefully receives the help and support I love to give when I have opportunity. I see that even though she has not yet surrendered all of her life to God, she is making steps in that direction, and she is benefiting from the training she received in my home and church community.

Annie could so easily have had abortions when she discovered she was pregnant. Praise God, she didn't. Somehow she has grasped the precious value of every human life and has taken on the responsibility of mothering these baby girls, at great sacrifice to herself. "I never want my baby to think she was a mistake," Annie told me when she had her first child. And I have been able to reassure her that both babies were lovingly designed by God for a purpose, and that she did the right thing by resolving to mother them to the best of her ability.

I believe that God put Annie in my home and in my heart because He knew she needed me for a mother, and because He knew that loving and caring for Annie would draw my heart closer to His.

In the end, only God can completely heal the damage done to my daughter's wounded heart. But He continues to use me and others to communicate to her that she and her babies are loved and precious to us, and to God who created them.

Thought for the Day

He did not say, "You shall not be tempest-tossed,
you shall not be work-weary, you shall not be discomforted."
But He did say, "You shall not be overcome."

~Julian of Norwich

You Are My Best Mama

Lydia Plett

The LORD looketh from heaven; he beholdeth all the sons of men. From the place of his habitation he looketh upon all the inhabitants of the earth. He fashioneth their hearts alike; he considereth all their works. —Psalm 33:13-15

Read Psalm 33

"Do you want a boy or a girl? If the birth mother has twins, would you get them both?" My friend was genuinely interested in our upcoming adoption.

"We'll take whatever the Lord sends, a boy or a girl . . . one or two." I did not say more, but my thoughts rambled on. *Sick or healthy . . . Oh, I do not want a sick baby! I want a baby that is healthy and normal!* I hung up the phone. For the next two hours, as I was trying to take a nap, I found myself struggling intensely. *Lord, I do not want a sick baby. What would be the point of us having a child with special needs? Why does this bother me so much? Lord, are You planning to send us a baby that has something wrong with it?* After struggling against the Lord for two hours, I was exhausted. I felt almost dizzy. I was afraid to get up for fear I would fall.

Lord, thank You for the child You plan to send to our home. You choose exactly the one that will be best for us. If it is a child with special needs, I know You will walk beside us. Thank You for the strength You will provide for us exactly when we need it. With peace in my heart I drifted off to sleep.

The ringing of the phone woke me. *Is it about the baby?*

"This is from Deaconess Home, the agency you are working with for your adoption. We are wondering if you would consider taking an infant with cystic fibrosis. It is a newborn baby girl, still in the hospital."

So this was what God was preparing me for!

When I contacted my husband and shared my experience of the afternoon, he said, "God was speaking to me at the very same time about caring for a special needs child. I keep thinking, *If ye did it not to one of the least of these, ye did it not to me.* If we say no to this, will Jesus say no to us on the Judgment Day?"

Lydia Plett family

After finding out more information about the disease and receiving some counsel from family and friends, we called the agency back with our answer. "Yes, we will take her."

Damaris was a tiny baby, weighing only four pounds, and she needed to stay in the hospital for two and a half weeks before she could come home.

Damaris

She was a very fussy baby and a hyperactive toddler.

When she was two years old, my husband of twelve years died. Now I am a widow. Through all my grief and my struggle to raise the children without a daddy, I have never regretted that we said yes.

Damaris is such a comfort to me. Often she throws her little arms around my neck. "You are my best mama! Oh, I love you, Mama!"

Thought for the Day

We need not fear, for as we step forward in faith,
Jesus walks beside us and hidden blessings await us.

Favored and Chosen

Ruthie Martin

Which in time past were not a people, but are now the people of God:
which had not obtained mercy, but now have obtained mercy. —1 Peter 2:10
Read 1 Peter 2

o my nieces and nephews whom I regard with special affection:
No matter where you came from, regardless of your past, we love you. You were *chosen* to be a part of our family. Long before you were born, God planned that you would become ours. He directed the details of your life and led you to us. And I would like to tell you that we love you just as much as those who were born to us. You were born *for* us, and we for you.

I still remember the excitement as I traveled with your soon-to-be parents, sisters, and Grammy and Grandpop to meet you for the first time. Adoption was new to our family, and we were so excited! Your big, friendly smiles made it easy to love you right from the start. And then, as an added bonus, your two big brothers came to join us too. How many fond memories I have of spending time in your home as your "little aunt," singing, playing, working, and growing up together! And yes, even crying some tears together through those many adjustments and growing pains.

Later, when another of my big sisters and her husband opened their home to fostering and adoption, our hearts were enlarged still more. How

351

we delighted in each one of you! How we sorrowed and prayed over those who were sent back to live in less-than-ideal situations, especially after we had learned to love them so much. We just thank God for each of you that He allowed us to keep for always.

Recently one of you was sharing with me your memories of attending the funeral service of your biological grandfather. Tears came to my eyes as you told of how you and your siblings were asked to sing as a tribute at the funeral. Your group stood out in stark contrast to those around you. You realized anew the life you were spared. Your decision to follow God has made the difference. I am so glad you were given that opportunity—the chance to learn about God and now to have Christian homes of your own. These results are what make adoption so beautiful and worthwhile. We have all continued to learn and grow together.

I want to tell each of you again that I love you. In fact, I feel closer in heart to you than to some who are my nieces and nephews by blood, for you have chosen to follow God and we are one in the Lord. We have the same Father, and that's what truly makes us of one blood.

Thought for the Day

May we all learn to favor our heavenly Father
(to resemble Him in words, thoughts, and actions)
so we can be favored to live in His presence forever.

After Many Days

Emily Martin

Cast thy bread upon the waters:
for thou shalt find it after many days. —Ecclesiastes 11:1
In all thy ways acknowledge him, and he shall direct thy paths. —Proverbs 3:6
Read Hebrews 11:22-30

After we experienced the heartache of two of our boys running away to their birth mother at the ages of thirteen and fourteen, (See "Open Arms Leave the Heart Unprotected") we made a deliberate choice to keep in contact with them by mail and occasional telephone calls. The boys were eager to know what everyone else was doing. "Is Harmony walking yet? What new words is she saying?" When Malvern was injured in a logging truck accident three months after they left, we sent letters and pictures. The boys were full of questions and showed genuine concern.

Eight months after the boys left, our family traveled the five hours to visit them. We weren't exactly sure of our reception but we had called ahead. They were expecting us. As we neared our destination, just before reaching their home in the motel their mother was in charge of, we spied Joe perched on a large boulder, eagerly scanning the road. When he saw us, he leaped down and ran ahead, showing us where to park.

"Hi," he called out gaily as he approached the maxi van. "I've been sitting out here waiting for hours!" Shaggy blond curls framing blue eyes and a wide, welcoming grin appeared at the driver's window and peered in. "Dad, where are your crutches? Is everybody along? Your motel room is over that way. I'm not sure where David is. He's around here somewhere. I'll show you where your rooms are. Hi, Kenton and Dari and the rest. Whew! Harmony sure changed since I saw her. Drive on over this way." He hopped down and waved his hand gallantly.

Joey, age 2

Malvern grinned as he followed his bidding. "Joe hasn't changed much, has he?" he said. "Same old Joe."

David appeared a few minutes later. "Hi," he said. "Good to see you." He ran his fingers through his wiry blond hair. Tall and broad for his fifteen years, he was as princely as ever.

"Have a good trip?" He seemed a bit unsure, but after we responded warmly he continued, "How long can you stay? I hope the rooms will be okay. I know you need smoke-free rooms for Jill and all, but we didn't have any. We recently painted these rooms and aired them out, but you can still smell it a little. That smoke is hard to get rid of."

David and Joe lingered in our rooms until almost midnight. We had devotions together, and they sat on the beds visiting with us.

The next day their mother gave us permission to take the boys away for the day. We ate breakfast together, toured an old water mill that had been restored, and stopped at a park for a picnic. In Joe's letters he had told us he was sorry for how they had left. He told us he wanted to come home again more than he had ever wanted anything. We prayerfully felt our way, as we weren't sure what our response should be. That day he told us again how badly he wanted to come home. We asked him how his mother would feel about it. He was sure she wouldn't like it. We told him we would pray about it and ask advice.

I found scissors in the van and asked Joe if I could trim his hair. "Sure, I'd be glad. And Mom won't care. It's just that we don't have money for extra things like haircuts."

Both of the boys' clothes were in rather sad shape, especially their shoes. They said their mother was hoping to buy them some new clothes for school, but we knew the tight budget they were living on, so we bought them some new shoes and clothes. They were very appreciative.

Kenton, David, and Joey, 2003

We were able to talk some with their mother before we left for home, but she seemed guarded, so we didn't ask her about Joe coming back. We told Joe we would keep praying and asked him to pray too.

Two months later we asked for permission for the boys to go along to our regional fellowship meetings seven hours from home. We offered to pick them up on the way Friday evening and drop them off again Sunday night. Their mother readily granted permission for Joe, but said David had a term paper to do for school.

Joe thoroughly enjoyed the meetings. It had been almost a year since he had seen any friends from home. Everyone was kind to him. He sat and listened attentively through all the services and afterward asked for his own set of tapes of the sermons. "I loved every single message," he said, "especially Brother Solly's. I always loved when he preached at home too." On the way back to his mother's, he readily promised to do whatever we asked if he could just come home. He begged us to at least ask his mother, so we did. Her response, short and to the point, was "no." We told Joe we would keep praying. If it was God's will for him to come home again, we felt it would be with his mother's permission.

That year David and Joe were in our home for eight days from Christmas through the New Year. There was a sense of completeness and harmonious togetherness with all twelve of our children at home. The boys especially enjoyed the family gatherings and church activities. Perhaps what they had walked away from the year before was becoming more significant to them.

Joe looked around the living room after family devotions one evening and sighed deeply. He waved his hand, taking in everything. "Such peace," he said. "I can't quite describe it!" It was good to see our family through his eyes. It wasn't that our family was always without conflict, but even with the children fussing at times and problems to work through, we had a great wealth of love and caring, togetherness, safety, and yes, peace that the world just didn't have. Did we count our blessings enough?

David didn't say as much, but he appeared to enjoy being with us again. And he took pictures of everything before he left—our school, our church, our house, the sawmill, and also his own little apple tree that he had helped plant several years before.

The boys returned to their mother. Time passed.

Joe, often lonely and despondent, spent countless hours listening to story tapes, sermon tapes, and the a cappella music we sent them. We sent him a three-ringed binder where he saved the letters and pictures we mailed to him.

The summer Joe was fifteen, his mother again allowed him to stay with us, although David didn't come. When it was time for Joe to go back to his mother, who now lived in Ohio, he wanted desperately to stay with us. He had given his heart to the Lord and was growing in Christ, and we felt very sad to think of him returning to his mother. We prayed about it and talked to his mother on the phone. At first she said he could stay, but then several weeks later she said he must come home. Legally, we couldn't keep him without his mother's permission. Reluctantly, we took him the seven hours to meet her. Brookie and the two littlest girls went along. Brookie and Joe played games while we traveled. And since Joe loved having someone read to him, I read aloud *Sandi's Anchor of Hope*. I wasn't finished when we arrived at the truck stop where we were to meet his mother, so

Malvern crawled in the back and slept while I kept on reading. This was a special time for Joe and me.

"Mom," he said, blue eyes penetrating mine, "if Sandi could come through in the kind of setting she lived in, I'm sure I can make it too." When Joe's mother arrived, we transferred his luggage and encouraged him to be faithful to God.

The next summer David and Joe both came home. This time it was for Alex's wedding and for the summer. At sixteen and seventeen, they had become young men. Each weekday they went to the sawmill to work. Their muscles hardened and their stamina grew, and they were able to earn enough money for shoes and clothes and a number of things they needed. They blended smoothly into our home and the church, especially enjoying the church activities and mingling with the youth. We were able to talk about how they had left our home, and why.

"It was just a rebellious streak we were going through right then," David admitted. "We didn't want to listen to your rules. It was a stage we were in, and we had a way out. It would have been better if we had stayed. I guess I wanted my freedom. Still, it wasn't what I expected when I got to my mom's. Now we don't really have a choice."

At the summer's end, the pull again was strong to just stay, especially for Joe, but their mother said they must wait to make that decision until they were eighteen. Joe felt two years was too long to wait, and David admitted that he probably would no longer want to come by next year.

One afternoon six months later I answered the phone. "Guess what, Mom!" Joe's elated voice announced. "God is finally answering my prayers! My mom says I can come home to stay, even if I'm not eighteen yet. David lives in his own apartment, and Mom is getting married again. So she says I can come as soon as school is out. I prayed and prayed for three months straight and tried to be nice to Mom no matter what. I just can't believe God is answering like this!"

And so Joe came home to our family, our community, our church. Because we have so many little children in our home, we were advised against him actually living in our house at first. So he stayed with my sister Marian and Roy Reinford, where he was the youngest, with an uncle and aunt who loved him and cared deeply about him. From there he spent a year and a half at Shepherd's Fold, as he had agreed to do before he came home.

Joey, age 21

We are Joe's family. He is our son, even if we don't have papers to prove it. He has Christian parents, five brothers, seven little sisters, and a host of cousins and aunts and uncles. He works with his dad and brothers, and he enjoys very much the fellowship of the other Christian youth.

Joe has made remarkable strides in Christian growth and desires to live a life pleasing to his Lord. He draws closer to God by praying, reading his Bible, and counting his blessings. When he fails, he says he's sorry and tries again. He loves the men at Shepherd's Fold who helped hold him account-

able and the structured environment there that helped him redeem some of what he lost through his turbulent childhood. He has accepted God's plan for his life and agrees that God is good. In spite of all he has been through, he still loves his birth mother and prays for her salvation and for David and their two sisters.

Joe, like Moses of old, has cast his lot with the people of God.

"By faith Moses, when he was come to years, refused to be called the son of Pharaoh's daughter; choosing rather to suffer affliction with the people of God, than to enjoy the pleasures of sin for a season; esteeming the reproach of Christ greater riches than the treasures in Egypt: for he had respect unto the recompence of the reward" (Hebrews 11:24-26).

Thought for the Day

Delight thyself also in the LORD; and he shall give thee the desires of thine heart. —Psalm 37:4

A Foster Parent?

Leah Horst

A foster parent? Oh, I know
There are many who would doubt
The wisdom of pursuing this
And what it's all about.

They say, "How can you stand it?
To love and then let go?
To get attached, it'd tear us up!
It's not for us, we know!"

How many times, it's very true
Emotions are a part;
It almost seems impossible
To keep love from the heart.

Each child deserves all we can give;
When parting time appears,
Our prayers go with these special souls,
We hurt, but smile through tears.

How can we give them any less?
Their world has been unsure . . .
Through no fault of theirs they came,
Unkempt, neglected, poor . . .

Our home was open through the years.
Twenty-three children came,
Many memories come to mind,
As each one I can name.

Most stayed just a short while till
Adoptive homes were found,
Then loving arms reached out for them . . .
Their lives on solid ground.

One very special little girl
We got at three days old;
Her mother had been doing drugs
Before her birth, we're told.

The changes and withdrawal caused
Much crying night and day.
We walked the floors, it mattered not—
Her pain seemed there to stay.

Another couple wanted her;
The plans were made complete.
Our little crying bundle left,
It was with some relief.

A few days later our phone rang . . .
Case worker on the line.
Would we take this bundle back?
(Was this a special sign?)

The couple couldn't handle it—
The crying was too much,
And so our arms reached out again
This little one to touch.

She cried a lot, but gradually . . .
So slowly was the move;
How wonderful to see her change,
Develop and improve!

We marvel at God's will and plan
For making dreams come true.
We did adopt this precious girl;
How blessed we have been too!

She's grown up now, has left our nest . . .
So swift the years have flown.
She married a fine Christian man
And has a happy home.

A foster parent? Oh, I know
There's many who would doubt
The wisdom, but they just don't know
At all . . . what it's about!

Written for Esther Reinford by her sister

God Was Watching . . . He Had a Plan

(Part 1)

Emily Martin

*And we know that all things work together for good to them that love God,
to them who are the called according to his purpose.* —Romans 8:28

Read Job 42:10-17

I didn't have the privilege of holding Alex and Ricky as newborn babies, nor was I able to watch their first steps or hear them say "Mama" for the first time (See "The Prayer of Two Hearts" and "In Answer to Our Prayer"). During Alex's first year of life, I was teaching school for the third year and happily making wedding plans. Yearning over little boys somewhere that would later be my sons was far from my mind.

But God was watching, and He had a plan.

During the first two years of our married life, He was preparing me, albeit unknown to me, to be a mother to two little homeless boys. As I wept and prayed and yearned for a baby, God saw me. In His line of vision, he could also see Alex and Ricky, two sturdy little boys in a very pitiful home setting where God was not known or taught. He was watching. He had a plan.

When Alex and Ricky arrived in our home at ages two and three, it wasn't long until it felt like they belonged to the whole family.

From the beginning, my oldest sister's home, the Dan Hershey family, especially held great attraction for our boys. I remember Alex sometimes reminding the others in his rich southern drawl, "We're goin' to Jeffrey's house! Don't you want to go to Jeffrey's?" With so many big boys and interesting ideas and projects going on in the Hershey home, Alex and Ricky were sometimes reluctant to leave. During the next several years, Jeffrey, Daren, and Danette Hershey were their constant playmates. God was watching. He had a plan.

Then came the terrible day when Alex and Ricky were taken from our home (See "Can We Trust God?"). Their little cousins Daren and Danette, along with the rest of the family, watched wide-eyed as last kisses and hugs were given through our tears.

Alex and Ricky have many memories, some that reach back to even before they came into foster care and of their early life in our home, but neither Ricky nor Alex can remember anything about that awful day. The pain was apparently too much to bear. It is as if a black cloud covers it over to seal in the hurt. We clearly remember, but we didn't understand. Even so, we had no choice but to trust God. We knew He was watching. He had a plan.

God brought them back into our care after almost eight years. Much had changed during that time, but they were still our boys. When Malvern had a logging truck accident a few years later, I leaned heavily on twenty-year-old Alex for support. I realized how much our roles had changed. He spread his strong shoulders and carried more than his share as he provided stability for his brothers and helped with the little girls, rocking and comforting them and kindly disciplining them as the need arose. What a very nice young man he had become!

One Mother's Day I received a beautiful bouquet of three delicate pink roses. It was signed in manly scrawl, "Your son, Alex." That and the cards that have accompanied other such gifts have thrilled my mother heart. We continue to enjoy the openness with which Alex shares with us as his parents. He has given us the gift of himself. We have had the privilege of walking with him through many of his struggles and joys.

When Alex's love life didn't look very promising, he made big statements of how he wasn't going to bother ever getting married. "That is perfectly fine," I assured him. "I will gladly do your laundry and receive the cards and bouquets of roses. We enjoy having you here with us." But God was watching. He had a plan.

With interest we watched the budding romance unfold between Alex and my niece, Danette Hershey, his little playmate from years before.

Alex and Danette's family

Shortly before his marriage, Alex stopped in the kitchen where I was preparing supper. "You know, Mom, I was just thinking about my life and what an amazing story it is. If my dad would never have gone to prison and I would never have been in foster care, I would not have come here. I would likely not even be a Christian at all. But if I had stayed here, you would have adopted me. Danette and I would have grown up as cousins all our lives, and then I wouldn't be marrying her. I can't stand to think of that! So even though I couldn't imagine I'd ever feel this way, I'm glad my life went the way it did."

Happily we welcomed Danette into our family. It felt a bit like cheating for my first daughter-in-law to be someone I was so thoroughly comfortable with. I had been the aunt she preferred when she was a baby. I spoiled her and almost smothered her with love in her first year as we waited for children of our own—and now she has become my daughter!

Isn't it amazing? God knew it all along. He was watching. He had a plan.

Thought for the Day

God delights in our trust in Him,
especially when we don't understand.

Four brothers at Alex's wedding
Kenton, Ricky, Darian, and Alex

God Was Watching . . . He Had a Plan

(Part 2)

Emily Martin

Lo, children are an heritage of the LORD *. . .*
Happy is the man that hath his quiver full of them. —Psalm 127:3, 5
Read Psalm 127

"Hey, Mom, can you step out on the deck a minute? I have something I want to ask you." I followed my tall son out the door. Alex's eyes glistened with a happy surprise. "No way, you stay in there!" This was directed at the stair-step of curious little sisters who were mobbing the door. "I want to talk to Mom, not you."

Soon the door was safely shut, with smiling faces pasted against the glass. Alex grinned at them and then turned to face me. "I already talked to Dad, and he said he didn't think you'd mind. At first we were going to keep it as a surprise until after he is born, but now we decided to tell our parents. We thought maybe we should ask just in case. What we're wondering is . . . do you care if we name our baby Bradlyn?"

"Care? Oh, Alex, that will be so very special. I would love it if you would name him Bradlyn." My mind went immediately to the little grass-covered grave behind our church. "It would be wonderful to have another little Bradlyn."

"I didn't think you would mind." His grin reflected mine. "Anyway, don't tell anyone."

366

Now the time had come for Bradlyn to be born, complications had set in, and it had been hours since we had heard anything. It was Thanksgiving Day 2008. As our huge school building streamed with friends chatting here and there, a volleyball game was played in the gym, and little children played tag, I had come outside to find a quiet spot to ponder and pray.

O God, I prayed, *please be with Alex and Danette and the little one. This labor is dragging on endlessly, and I feel so helpless. God, I know You are watching. You have a plan . . . Please keep the baby safe. We don't want another little Bradlyn grave down at the church, unless for some reason You see that as best. And can You please show me or tell me if I should call them? I don't want to bother them needlessly. There is nothing we can do but pray. You are going to need to do the rest.*

Maybe I will call Alex again. As I looked longingly at the cell phone in my hand, it suddenly began to ring.

"Hey, Mom, this is Alex." His voice sounded years older. "We aren't sure what to do. They want to do surgery, and you know how badly we don't want that. What do you say?"

It was great comfort to talk to him. We agreed to gather into three different prayer groups to specifically pray for wisdom. They would pray, too, in the hospital. We knew God was watching. He had a plan, and He needed to show us our part. God answered. An assurance rested on them to move ahead, and surgery was scheduled. Malvern and I left our seven daughters in capable hands and headed the forty miles west. We were five minutes from the hospital when the welcome call came. "Baby is here, alert and bright-eyed and perfectly darling! All went as planned."

So this is how it feels to be a grandmother! It seems I can hardly wipe the smile from my face! Ah, such relief for mother and baby to be safe! How can God make such perfectly-formed babies, each one different, each one so unique and special? And my tall son has new fortitude from having walked beside his wife during those difficult forty-eight hours.

Enjoying our new little Bradlyn brings thoughts of our first little Bradlyn—sweet, wistful thoughts. "Uncle Bradlyn" would be turning twenty this year, had he lived. What kind of boy would he be? What would he look like? Would he be a comfort, a bulwark of strength to the rest of us? Would he be making godly choices, or would we be anguishing hours in prayer over him because of wrong choices?

The joy of knowing that one of our sons is safely in Heaven forever is much more blessed to us now than it was back on that long-ago morning when our baby stepped into the great beyond. I have long since ceased to question God as to why we needed to walk that path of sorrow. God has worked it out for good in many ways.

Several years have passed since our first grandson's birth. Alex and Danette and Bradlyn and his twin brothers, Jayson and Jaydon, live close by and come home often. Living next door to them is Alex and Ricky's birth father, Rex. It is nice to know he is no longer forlorn and alone, although his health is poor. Several years ago his sons helped him move close to them. Alex checks in on him often and takes him along to town or to the doctor or to his favorite fishing spot. There is clearly a bond between them. Rex respects our lifestyle and accepted the Bible Alex and Danette gave to him and promised to read it. Alex and Ricky have two dads and our grandsons have an extra grandpa. We are happy to have their birth father be a part of their lives.

Rex and grandchildren

We thank God for adoption and for foster care. God used it to fill our quiver full and running over. It is through foster care and then adoption that we first became parents and now grandparents. And He gave us the privilege of having biological children too. We say God must have been smiling as we prayed all those countless requests for Him to bless us with children, knowing that He was saving some to tack on at the very end.

"How many children do you have?" I remember flinching at that oft-asked question. Now I smile and remember my struggles of long ago. *Do all my children count? If all of our children had stayed, there would be twenty-two.* Aloud I say, "Twelve, thirteen—it depends how you count. And we're very glad for each one."

And if they care enough to ask for more, as mothers are inclined to do, I enumerate.

"Mom, we have lots of children," Kenton stated thoughtfully when he was ten. At that time, Alex, Ricky, David, and Joe had come back home, and new little sisters had been born—each addition stretching and blessing us a bit more. "But I guess we need every one of them, don't we?" he added.

"We sure do!" I assured him. Through the years since then, Kenton has loved tagging after his big brothers, hunting, fishing, and working together. As our only living biological son, it has only been through foster care and adoption that he has experienced the privilege of having brothers.

Melody, Harmony, Shyanne, Elva, Jill, Shari, Brooke,
Kenton, Joe, Dari, Ricky, Alex, Emily, Malvern

And although Brooke (our daughter through foster care and then adoption) was our only daughter at one time, that is certainly no longer true. We now have seven daughters as Brooke, Shari, Jill, Elva, Shyanne,

Harmony, and Melody each fill their very own special spot in our hearts and our family.

How very blessed we are, and how we have needed every one of them!

Thought for the Day

God was watching all along. He had a plan.
What a blessing to serve a God
who knows the end from the beginning!

A Circle of Love

Marian Reinford

Have not I commanded thee? Be strong and of a good courage;
be not afraid, neither be thou dismayed: for the LORD thy God
is with thee whithersoever thou goest. —Joshua 1:9
Read Joshua 1

"**I** have cancer." As I read the text message from my daughter aloud to my husband, my heart sank. *Cancer . . . what an awful word! And Melissa was only twenty-eight years old, with a family of four small children and an unborn baby.* She was so young, and so much needed.

My mind drifted back to the winsome little four-year-old who came home to stay one cold November day. Her sister Chris came with her to join their biological brothers, Mike and Chuck, in our home (See "Sisters, a Gift of God"). They added a special dimension to our family as they became part of our lives at home, church, and school.

Now our family was embarking on a new journey of walking with a loved one through the dreaded disease of cancer. We all felt a bit bewildered. Cancer is so big and so unknown. How could we best help Melissa and her husband Delbert?

As often happens when our health fails, we reach out to family. "Mom, what shall we do?" Melissa asked. "What if I die and have to leave my children and husband? How can I take chemo and take the chance of harming my baby?" We felt at a loss to know how to advise them. Again and again we gave the situation to God. Fasting became easy, and prayer was always a whisper away.

They decided to go through with a mastectomy. Oh, the comfort of pouring our hearts out before the Lord in a small prayer meeting in Delbert's living room before we left for the hospital, and knowing that God was in control! I sensed a depth of surrender and commitment in my daughter and her husband.

The surgery went well, but the reports from the doctor afterward did not sound good. "It looks like the cancer has possibly spread to the bloodstream," she said. "Chances of survival do not look good."

Family. Comfort. Hope. Peace. The circle of love around us.

"What Melissa would like better than anything else is for everyone to be together, to share, to connect, and to sing together. How many of the family can come?" Phones buzzed. Tickets were purchased and travel plans finalized. Our son Alan and his wife came with two of their children from Alaska, Chuck's family and Anya with her baby from Wisconsin, Mike's family from Ohio, and Chris from New York. Adding to the five children already in North Carolina, our family of twelve was complete. We gathered at Delbert and Melissa's house, and for two days we visited, sang, and prayed together.

Adding a special touch to our gathering was Lynn, the biological mother of our four adopted children, their sister Patti with her husband and son, and their Aunt Treva. It was a treasured experience. I had wished for years to share with our children's birth mother some special bits from their growing-up years. Now God had given me this chance. Lynn had loved these children, and had carried them, labored, and given birth. We, too, had loved these same children and had the opportunity to guide them through their growing years.

Now, together facing the uncertainty of the future, our hearts were soft and warm. Our love for Melissa and her little family drew us together in a beautiful way. One afternoon as our children sang together in the adjoining room, Lynn and I sat side by side and listened.

"And He'll hold back the sun if the need should arise.
If the mountain's too steep, He'll just lower the sky,
He'll exalt every valley when they're too rough and steep—
And between here and sunset, God will take care of me."[13]

As our eyes caressed each face, I saw and felt unashamed tears and encouraging smiles. "It was all in God's plan," I explained to Lynn. "He knew the challenges you were facing and the needs of your four young children, and He worked it out that they came to our house. It sure isn't that we have been perfect parents, but we do love every one of our children.

"As our family has grown, so has our love. Each addition has been a link in our chain, each one precious and valuable, worth more than the

Roy Reinford family, 2008

whole world. God has been so good and merciful to all of us. He loves us and cares deeply about every little area of our lives, each struggle, and each victory!"

With pleasure I watched Lynn relax and mingle with the family, even helping to sing along with the hymns. I felt richly blessed.

I joined in as they sang one of my favorite songs.

> *"So much is mine! I cannot count the treasures!*
> *My heritage, because I am an heir.*
> *A child of God through Jesus Christ the Saviour*
> *Unmerited, and far beyond compare!*
> *An inner joy abounding e'en in trial.*
> *Abiding peace while storms around me rage,*
> *Crowned with a hope of heaven with all its splendor!*
> *I have a goodly heritage!*[14]

Our Christian heritage has passed on the "torch of truth" to all of us. Being a torchbearer is a privilege we want to share, to enlighten and inspire others. As we enlarge our circles of love, we are building for eternity . . . and when we're all safely together in Heaven, oh the rejoicing, that Heaven is surely worth it all!

Six months had passed since our family had been together. Against all probability, God granted Melissa a healthy baby boy, and although there were still many unknowns, Melissa and the baby both seemed to be in good health. Ironically, over the next few months, I was the one who walked through the valley of pain, fatigue, surgery, and near death. Through this journey of Lyme disease, I distinctly felt the circle of God's love enveloping me through the church and extended family, and particularly through the loving support and comfort of my husband and children.

---

14 Words: Margaret Penner Toews © Praise Hymn Publishers. Used by permission.

I awoke in a hospital in Mexico and looked into the loving eyes of my grown children, some of whom I had thought were far away. Gentle strength. Tender massage of my excruciating extremities. Nighttime watches. Encouraging dialogue. Phone calls. Financial aid. Many miles traveled. Loving care from others for our handicapped daughter when I was unable to give it. Praying and singing together. What a tremendous blessing to be a part of this circle of love!

Thought for the Day

"I was standing aloof, alone—outside the circle.
So taking a fresh crayon,
they drew a bigger circle, drawing me in."

With Gratitude

Marian Reinford

Commit thy way unto the LORD; trust also in him;
and he shall bring it to pass. —Psalm 37:5
Read Psalm 37:1-7, 23-40

"What do you think is the first song we'll sing in Heaven?" Melissa asked. Her eyes shone in anticipation as she pondered the songs we were singing.

"Will it be about the Lamb of God?" someone suggested.

Smiling, she agreed, "That's it!" She sang two phrases, "Behold the Lamb, behold the Lamb . . ." Her voice swelled, no longer strong, but clear and sweet.

Several times in the last two days she had asked us to gather around and sing as her breathing became more difficult. The cancer was claiming more and more of her lungs, and she knew her life on earth was nearing its end.

"Mom," she had asked, "when I talk to the children and we have our family picture taken, can I go then? It would be so wonderful to be free of pain!"

My heart aching, I answered, "Yes, Melissa, when God calls, you can go! Go toward the light!"

I knew the kindest thing we can do for our loved ones is to let them go in peace . . . but oh, the struggle to give to God what we cannot keep!

Now, Melissa lay motionless on the sofa beside me, her face white and still. Her struggle for breath was over. Peace at last. Her battle was won, her victory realized. Through my tears, I felt a deep sense of gratitude to God and everyone around me. We had all fought this battle together and God was with us. He was faithful and walked with us, helping us over the hardest places.

But how could I ease the pain in my aching heart? Never again would my daughter ask me to rub her feet or back. Never again would her brown eyes beg me to find a way to relieve her pain. She was released forever from pain and heartache and doubts and fears. I thought of the last months, especially the last two weeks when she had hardly let me out of her sight. She had wanted to move closer. And for several weeks that had been enough, to live eight miles down the road, instead of eighty miles away. Almost every day I would go to massage her feet and to comfort her in any way I knew. Some days she came to our house. She said it always helped.

Melissa's fight with cancer had intensified the last two months. Her appetite and zip for life seemed dimmed by her pain. We were suspicious that cancer was spreading, and not knowing was almost worse than knowing.

But it was after their last trip to Mexico that we noticed her health diminishing. She felt panicky, especially at night when she labored to breathe. "I just want to stay at Dad's where I can breathe better," she had begged, "and I want to be with Mom." So they had done that. Delbert, Melissa, and their five little children had stayed at our house. A mattress on the floor provided a bed for Delbert and the little ones, and Melissa slept on the couch with her pillowed head propped on the armrest. In the unique way our triple-wide home is set up, I could see her from my bed through our open bedroom door. I could hear the oxygen concentrator's gentle hum and check to see whether she was peaceful or restless. Most nights I could hear her call when she needed me. Delbert helped and comforted her all he could, yet I, too, felt a desire to be there for her if she needed me.

One day as I was rubbing her feet, Melissa looked up and said, "You know, Mom, I've been thinking a lot about the children. I feel everything will be okay with them. God will take care of them, and everything will be okay with the children and with Delbert." Knowing how much this had been troubling her, it blessed me to see her trusting God with the future.

The last several days had been so incredibly precious, especially after the evening she had asked the family to gather around her. In front of everyone, she confessed that something was bothering her—some things

Delbert and Melissa's family

from the past that she wanted to clear before us and God. She thanked us for all the love and care over the years. She said that when she was growing up, she had thought we didn't really love her—the proof in her mind had been when we reproved her or punished her. She was sorry for things she had said about us and the pain she had caused us. She said that having cancer and feeling our love and care had changed those feelings, especially these last weeks. Now she realized that we had loved her all along. We assured her that she was forgiven; we had also said and done things we were sorry for, things that may have made it harder for her to feel our love. When we confess and forsake wrong, God forgives us.

This opened a subject that just Delbert, Melissa, and I discussed later. We talked about particular struggles that sometimes come with adoption. I explained about attachment challenges and bonding, and I told them I wish I had known some of this long ago. Perhaps if we had used some of the tools we know now, we could have avoided much heartache and pain. We talked about childhood memories and some of the negative times that had loomed out of proportion in her memory. The memory of that talk is priceless to me, and my heart swells in gratitude at how our heavenly Father worked out even the little details.

"Mom?" The voice almost startled me in the semi-darkness, as a few of us lingered by Melissa's body, quiet in our own thoughts. I turned toward my son-in-law.

"I just wanted to ask, was it worth it?"

I must have looked a bit perplexed. Delbert smiled.

"I mean adoption. Was it worth it?"

My mind instantly flashed to the time another adoptive mother had asked me the same question a few years ago. I had answered her, "When I think of the hills and valleys we walked, the rivers crossed and the mountains scaled, I feel weary and old, but when I think of eternity . . . and a soul being forever with God, that likely otherwise would never have known Him, I'd say a thousand times, Yes! We can't make decisions for our children, but we can give them the opportunity to find God and truth."

I looked at him and smiled, "What can I say—of course it is yes! We know worthwhile things are often not easy, yet one soul is worth more than the whole world. Yes, adoption is worth it!"

He smiled. "I was thinking the same thing. You know, in the setting Melissa was in, if she had not been adopted, the chances are she still would have died with cancer—without God, and without hope."

I had watched Delbert stand by Melissa through thick and thin, health and sickness. The deep love and commitment he had toward her was evident so often. I had watched him give tenderly and unselfishly to his wife and young children with God-given strength, and she loved him and the children deeply in return.

"If ten years ago I had understood more about adoption and some of Melissa's particular struggles, I might have responded differently," Delbert added. "But through it all, she has come through victorious."

A deep tenderness flooded my soul toward my dear son-in-law. He did understand, and life had taught him many lessons also. Through it all, he had loved and treasured his wife. And even as he looked into the lonely unknown future with five motherless children, he was focusing on Melissa's triumph—on her joy.

Melissa had requested the song "The Brevity of Life" to be read at her funeral, and that the message to her family and friends be on trusting in God, taken from Psalm 37:5. Uncle Simon told us that truly trusting God involves acknowledging Him, accepting Him, and approving of His plan for our lives. How comforting it was to realize that Melissa had grasped and accepted this concept!

Feeling the love and support of our family and friends brings a sense of healing and rest. Our prayer is that someday we will complete our circle of love in Heaven, where we will see our Saviour face to face. With gratitude we can sing together through the ceaseless ages of eternity, to the wonderful Lamb of God who washed our sins away and prepared us for Heaven.

Poem for the Day

The Brevity of Life

Did you ever stop to think about how short our life is here,
And time will never be again in a thousand million years?
How can we even compare our life beside eternity?
Our life on earth is like a drop in God's eternal sea.

How do you choose to live your life in this short span of time?
A time that's going on so fast and never will abide?
We make our plans and walk about and do our work and play;
But do we choose obedience to our God, by faith, and pray?

Did you make preparation for eternity and rest,
A rest that Jesus Christ prepared for those who pass the test?
The test is how you use your time that God put in your days,
To serve, obey, and worship Him, trust Him in all your ways.

Will you then choose the pathway of life forevermore
And walk the path the Saviour trod though it be rough and worn?

—John Esh

Remembering

Name Withheld

Weeping may endure for a night,
but joy cometh in the morning. —Psalm 30:5
Read Psalm 30

The usual clamor of the breakfast table filled Anne's ears as she moved around cutting pancakes into bite-sized pieces and filling cups with fresh milk. Mornings were always noisy and hectic until everyone settled down to eating. As they joined hands for prayer, Anne looked around and once more breathed a prayer of thanksgiving for their precious family.

We are so blessed, she thought, taking in each one of the circle. Eight-year-old Jordan was a steady little fellow. Jamin and Jared, age five, had come from an orphanage in Liberia. Their dark eyes danced with the anticipation of eating their teddy bear pancakes. *Such dear little boys, so cheerful and full of life.* Next her eyes rested on three-year-old Jeremiah. She smiled at the furrow on his brow. Making little swirls in the syrup puddles on his plate took his full concentration. He was from Honduras. Then Anne's eyes softened just a bit as they rested on her long-awaited little girl, Julie Anne, sitting in her high chair, pounding on her tray with a spoon. Julie Anne had come to them as an infant, her body racked with pain from drug withdrawal.

Anne's attention drew back to the present as Josiah admonished the boys to help pray.

Their voices arose in unison. "God is great and God is good . . ."

At the end of the prayer, Anne lifted her head to meet Josiah's smile. He had been such a good support for her, often sensing how she felt without needing words, especially during the long days and nights when Julie Anne had first come. She had screamed for hours while Anne felt helpless to know what to do. Josiah was so busy running the farm that he had little time to help.

Anne gave a little shiver remembering that time. Josiah noticed.

"What's wrong?" he asked.

"I was just thinking about when Julie Anne first came," she answered. "So much of it is just a blur. I was so tired all the time."

Josiah grinned. "But isn't she worth it?"

"Is she ever!" Anne looked over at Julie Anne, who was contentedly plastering her face with pancakes and syrup. She thought of the night when she had walked the floor for hours with the screaming bundle. She had prayed and sang and cried as she stumbled through the house. Finally around 3 a.m. Julie Anne had quieted down. Anne had sunk wearily into a chair, turning the baby to face her. Julie Anne's face had lit up with an unforgettable, beautiful smile. It was the very first responsive smile Anne had ever seen on her baby girl's face. She remembered hugging the baby to herself as she cried again, this time from sheer joy. "Thank You, thank You, God!"

"You know," Anne mused softly after the children had finished their breakfast and gone off to play, "I can't explain very well what all I went through during that time with Julie Anne. I remember being so scared those long months when she screamed so much. I had my baby girl, but she didn't want me to cuddle her or rock her! And her ability to interact was so different from our other babies. I wondered if she would ever bond." Anne's voice trailed off as memories engulfed her . . . unwashed clothes and dirty dishes, four hungry little boys . . . and then finally help from her dear friends from church.

"But just think, Anne," Josiah said, bringing Anne's attention back to the present, "we know so much more now than we did when Levi first came" (See "An Agonizing Choice" and "Not My Will").

"I know." Anne twirled her coffee cup thoughtfully. "It was so comforting to fall back on the suggestions and advice we received through our time with Levi. Things like talking to her, making eye contact, never being too rushed or too busy to connect with her."

"And carrying her everywhere in the kangaroo carrier," Josiah added.

Anne nodded. "Just like a nursing baby. I hardly let her out of my sight." She smiled as Julie Anne's giggles reached her ears. Then, with a whoop and a shout, the twins came racing through the kitchen, delightedly pushing Julie Anne on the back of their Tonka truck and chasing Jordan.

"That spontaneous giggle . . . we waited so long to hear it from her!" Anne commented. "One thing I have found so amazing about this experience with Julie Anne is how much we have learned, such as how the results of the drugs linger on, though they may not still be in the system. And because of learning this, I now can relate to her in a way that helps instead of hinders her."

"I've been wondering lately," Josiah said, pushing back his chair. "If we would get another chance at a child like Levi, would we know enough about attachment disorder to make it work?"

"We won't ever forget Levi and that sense of failure, will we?" Anne stared off in the distance. "But if our experience with him can help us in relating to our other children, then good did come from it."

"And we need to remember that we felt God leading us then too," Josiah added. "And Jordan . . . remember how afraid we were for him?" Josiah glanced fondly toward their oldest son. "He is such a good protector and big brother with his steady nature. God must have seen that it was best for him to be our oldest—just what those twins need to steady them a bit, and a sense of security for Jeremiah and Julie Anne. Oh, we have a great responsibility to direct these precious souls toward God and His love."

Thought for the Day

Each experience God allows in our lives
can be a stepping-stone for the future.

Here to Stay

Emily Martin

"Can you, will you take a baby?
We know your hands are plenty full . . .
You see, she's Joe and David's sister;
To separate them does seem cruel.
She is darling, y'all will love her . . .
I'm tempted myself to take her home,
But since I'm just a social worker,
I'll need to pass the privilege on."

"Sure, of course, we'll take the baby;
For years we've wanted a baby girl!
Could we possibly turn the chance down,
Claiming that our house is full?"

Curious neighbors, aunts and cousins,
Came to peek when she arrived.
Though dear and sweet, she was not growing.
They called it "failure to thrive."
But with love and much attention,

The only girl among our five,
It was noted with much elation,
Not only did she grow, but thrived!

For a time when she was a year old,
How scared we were that she would leave.
"Weekend visits, two times monthly."
Oh, can't you see how much we grieved?
We petitioned, asked our Father;
(We're well aware God can say "No.")
Still our faith was strong—we pleaded,
Then through our tears we watched her go.

God perhaps just planned to test us,
Our faith, submission; can we know?
He then stepped in and stopped the visits;
She never again had to go.

"God, we thank You for our Brookie.
It seems You gave her to us twice!
Does that mean we love her extra?
When she's naughty and when she's nice?

Brooke is quite an individual.
She's very hot and very cold,
Very sweet and very naughty,
Loving, hating, shy, and bold.
Seems she has no happy medium;
Can we mold her, help her grow?

But it's just this fiercely living
That endears her to us so.

Now to Brooke we have a message,
Our daughter dear in every way,
"Princess of our hearts, we love you . . .
We're so delighted you can stay."
      —*Emily Martin*

Joyfully announcing the adoption of Brooke Anna Martin
Born 4-1-91; Placed 6-27-91; Finalized 11-2-94

Brooke's adoption, 1994

An Adoptee's Prayer

Angela Detwiler

I waited patiently for the LORD; and he inclined unto me,
and heard my cry. —Psalm 40:1
Read Psalm 40

"Lord, please help my birth mother to become a Christian so I can meet her in Heaven." How many times I prayed that prayer as I grew up in my adoptive home, only God knows.

The last time I saw my birth mother was when I visited her home when I was four years old. She lived in a pitiful, wretched house, but we had a happy time together that day. "I'm going to fix up this house; then you can come to stay with me," she promised.

It was a promise that never came true. Shortly after this she was brutally wounded, and realizing the hopelessness of her condition all around, she knew there was only one thing she could do—release me for adoption. The day she signed the papers, she prayed, "Lord, take care of my little girl."

Did God answer that prayer? Indeed He did! I only wish that during those happy years I spent growing up in a Christian home, someone could have assured her that I was well—that I was secure. I heard snatches of information about my birth mother along the way. She was an alcoholic, but she stopped drinking. She married a good man and then moved to a distant state. Always my prayers followed her: "Lord, save my birth mother's soul so I can meet her in Heaven."

Did God answer my prayer? Yes, He did. My birth mother at last found the Good Shepherd, who had been following her all those rough years. And I believe that in her limited intelligence and simple faith, she tried to live up to the light she had.

It came somewhat as a surprise when, after I had been married nearly ten years, she called us on the phone one day. "I just wanted to say I'm so sorry for the way things went," she said. Only then did I realize the agony a birth mother carries for the rest of her life after she has given up a child.

I assured her that she had made the best choice for me—that I had a happy adoptive home, that I had married a kind Christian husband, and that God had been very good to me. We sent her photos of our family and of my adoptive parents.

A year later she called again. By this time she was very ill with cancer, but she wanted to assure me that she had always loved me, and she also gave a loving tribute to my adoptive parents. "Tell them I admire them for all they have done for you."

Several months later, she passed away peacefully. When we heard about her death, my husband said, "At least we have no regrets." We had not pushed her away, but had tried to relate to her as God wanted us to. Now He was giving us a beautiful ending to a sad but sweet story.

Thought for the Day

Keep praying. The mustard seed of faith grows slowly,
quietly in the darkness of long months and years.

Thank You, Mom

Martina (Reinford) Zimmerman
an adoptee

The lines are fallen unto me in pleasant places;
yea, I have a goodly heritage. —Psalm 16:6
Read Matthew 25:1-13

When I was born, I was placed directly into foster care, and at the age of fourteen months was adopted by my foster parents. My birth mom had chosen to give me up for adoption. At the time, I'm sure she had no idea how glad I would be that she made that very hard choice to give me away. Let's put ourselves in her shoes for a short time.

You carry your baby for nine months under your heart. You feel those little flutters, and as time moves on, they grow stronger. You go through the pain of childbirth, knowing you will never see that first smile, that first tooth, those first wobbly steps. But you love your little baby; you show that love by giving her a name you like.

I am that child. What a choice! I am so glad for that life-giving choice. Thank you, Birth Mom, for that life-changing choice!

When I was born, I weighed a little over six pounds, and I was put into my mom's arms at just four days old. But because of my birth mother's bad choice of taking drugs before I was born, I just cried and cried. Nobody could do anything to soothe me. I had to go through withdrawal. I cried all the time.

Thank you, Mom, for listening to me cry all those hours. Thank you for that wonderful choice of letting me be your child. You didn't know if I would be a normal or a handicapped little girl, or if I would stop crying. You didn't know if I would ever want to choose your way of life, serving the Lord.

Thank you, Mom, for putting your heart on the line for me. Now that I am all grown up and have children of my own, I realize just what all you did for me. I realize just what you gave me—lots of love. Thank you, Mom.

Let's remember that all those choices have life-changing effects on us. Let us be like the five wise virgins in the Bible and keep our lamps filled with oil. We don't know when the Lord will choose to come and take us all home.

Thought for the Day

When we choose to make right choices,
the rewards are out of this world!

Biographical
Sketches

of

Tied with Heartstrings

Contributors

*An asterisk (*) in the picture caption indicates
that writer is also an adoptee.*

Roy and Marian Reinford family, November 2012

Marian Reinford, wife of **Roy**, lives in Pantego, North Carolina. Marian is one of the compilers of this book. Roy and Marian's parenting includes biological children, adopted children, and foster care.

As of 2012, Roy and Marian have ten children and forty grandchildren. Marian writes the following about her family:

Dale and Beth have ten children.

Alan and Twila have seven children.

Dawn, born in 1976, was our special little girl with cerebral palsy who was completely helpless. Even though she couldn't walk or talk, she loved to be cuddled and talked to. She helped all of our hearts to grow wider and deeper. Our experiences with Dawn prompted us to reach out further to other children. Dawn died in December of 2012.

Anya is married to Delbert and has five children.

In 1985 we adopted a sibling group of four. The oldest is **Michael**, who was nine at the time. He is now married to Janelle and has six children.

Chuck was seven when he came to live with us and is now married to Heidi. They have six children.

Chris was six when she came to our home. As an adult, Chris has been very much involved in working with hurting children. She taught school for six years and did foster care for almost a year.

Melissa was four when she was adopted. She was married to Delbert Derstine for nine years. Melissa's story—how she passed away from cancer at the age of twenty-nine leaving behind five motherless children—is told in this book.

Our two youngest children, **Debi** and **Alex**, were born after we adopted the sibling group. Today Debi is married to Phil Graybill, and it is through them that we have experienced adoption again, this time as grandparents. Throughout the years children and teens have stayed in our home from several months to several years.

Delbert and Anya Kauffman family
2013

Anya **Kauffman** is the daughter of Roy and Marian Reinford. She lives in Sheldon, Wisconsin, with her husband **Delbert** and their five children. Anya has been a great enthusiast for *Heartstrings*. She helped much in the compiling and editing and pulling it all together. She writes from the perspective of the biological child welcoming adopted siblings.

*C*hris **Reinford**, of Lebanon, Pennsylvania, is the daughter of Roy and Marian Reinford. She writes about the comfort of her Father's everlasting arms, particularly when she faced the aching loss of her four foster children leaving her home.

*Chris Reinford, 2010

Phil and Debi Graybill family, 2012

*D*ebi **Graybill** is the youngest daughter of Roy and Marian Reinford. She is married to **Phil** and lives in Belhaven, North Carolina. Debi writes about their personal experience of relating to birth families wanting to give their babies for adoption. After working extensively with the birth families and experiencing the heartbreak of seven failed adoptions, the Graybills were rewarded with an infant son, *Josiah,* through the miracle of adoption. Debi writes about hidden blessings in this painful journey, and about her ongoing friendship with several of the birth mothers.

Malvern and Emily Martin family, 2012

*E*mily **Martin** is the wife of **Malvern** from Pantego, North Carolina. Along with her older sister Marian Reinford, she compiled this book. As of 2012, Malvern and Emily have twelve children and four grandchildren.

Alex is married to Danette, and they have four sons. Alex lived in Malvern and Emily's home as a foster son from ages 3-8. After spending eight years with his biological father, he returned to the Martin home again at age sixteen.

Ricky is one year younger than his biological brother Alex. He also lived with the Martins for five years as foster son before he and his brother returned to their birth father. Ricky was 15 when he returned to Malvern and Emily's care. The boys' birth father now lives next door to Alex, where Alex and his wife Danette help care for him in his older years.

The Martins adopted *Darian* from Mexico when he was four months old.

David was a foster child in Malvern and Emily's home from ages 3-6, then he lived with his mother for five years. He was with the Martins again from ages 11-14 with his mother's permission, and returned to his birth mother again in January of 2003.

David's brother *Joey*, also a foster child, was with the Martins from ages 2-5 and from ages 10-13. He went to live with his birth mother in January

2003 and came back to the Martins again in June of 2006 at the age of seventeen.

Brooke was two months old when she joined the Martin home as a foster child. Her adoption was finalized when she was three years old.

Mixed in and through these are eight biological children: **Bradlyn** (who died at birth), **Kenton, Sharilyn, Jill, Elva, Shyanne, Harmony,** and **Melody.** The Martins also fostered seven other children from several days to several months.

Brooke **Martin** of Pantego, North Carolina, was adopted at the age of three by Malvern and Emily Martin. Brooke contributed to _Heartstrings_ not only by writing—she also cooked and cleaned and did countless loads of laundry so that her mother could work on the manuscript.

*Brooke Martin

*Joshua Bechtel

Joshua **Bechtel** of Spruce Pine, North Carolina, entered foster care when he was two years old. He was adopted by Wilmer and Fay Bechtel from Estacada, Oregon, at the age of ten. Joshua was a counselor for several years at Fresh Start in Indiana. Josh writes from the view of an adopted child searching for his reason for being, for God's plan in placing him in the setting where he is, and for his roots as he seeks and finds his birth parents.

Phil and Connie Bear family

Connie Bear is the wife of **Phil**. They live in Parsonsburg, Maryland. In addition to their three adopted and two biological children, they did foster care for nine years and cared for twenty-four children during that time.

Phil and Connie's two oldest children, **Jeremy** and **Janelle**, are both married, and Phil and Connie have two grandchildren

Bobby entered their home as a small foster child, and they adopted him several years later.

It was while they were in mission work in Belize that **Jared** came into their home and then was returned to his birth mother. Connie writes about their experience with Jared in *Heartstrings*. Although Jared was raised by his birth family, Phil and Connie have continued to keep contact with him and have a warm relationship with him.

It was after their experience with Jared that Phil and Connie had the privilege of adopting **Diana** and **Carmen**, who are both from Belize.

Thomas and Rhoda Bontrager family, 2012

Rhoda Bontrager lives in Goshen, Indiana, with her husband **Thomas** and their four children who were adopted as newborns: *Anthony*, *Jennifer*, *Jaran*, and **Lorinda**. Rhoda is the compiler of the book *For This Child I Prayed*. She also wrote *God Gives Me a Family*. Both books are about adoption. Thomas and Rhoda are now involved in prison baby ministry.

John and Rebecca Brubaker family

Rebecca Brubaker, wife to **John**, is from Carlisle, Pennsylvania. Their parenting includes eight biological children (one died as an infant) and two daughters who were adopted as newborns. Their family circle has grown to include eighteen grandchildren.

Julia Brubaker family

*J*ulia **(Peachey) Brubaker** of Raymond, Alberta, Canada, has four adult biological children and four grandchildren. She also mothers three young Native Canadian foster children, all of whom have been in her home since birth and will likely continue as a permanent part of her family. Julia has been a single mom since 1999, during which time she has also fostered several other children.

*A*nn **J. Burkholder** is an adoptive mother who writes about the difficulties of bonding with a severely traumatized child. She and her husband struggled through deep waters, which included dealing with their daughter's baffling behavior and the criticism of onlookers who didn't understand their situation. Rejoice as you read about some of the satisfying rewards of their commitment to this very needy child.

anice Byler and her husband Wesley are from Farmington, New Mexico. Their parenting includes adoption, special needs, interracial, and foster care. Besides *Jessica,* who was their first child and the one Jan writes about in *Heartstrings,* they have adopted a sibling group

Wesley and Janice Byler family, 2010

of four Native Americans, including identical twin dwarf sons who were preemies. The twins and their younger brother came to the Byler home straight from the hospital. Recently Wes and Jan were able to adopt another little girl who had been their foster baby.

Craig and Jewel Carter family

ewel Carter and her husband Craig live at Sheldon, Wisconsin. They are parents to **Brett** and **Brady**, twin boys adopted as babies from Liberia, and two daughters, **Lindsay** and **Shaniya**, one biological and one adopted. While Jewel tells their own adoption story, she also writes with compassion and love for the many children who yet need Christian homes.

Regina **Derstine**, wife to **Trevor** of Harrisburg, Oregon, is mother to eight—one biological daughter and seven adopted children. All of their adopted children came to them first through foster care. The first set was a sibling group of five. The adoption was a very positive experience. More recently, Trevor and Regina adopted another sibling group of two.

Trevor and Regina Derstine family
2010

Luke and *Angela Dewiler family

Angela **Detwiler**, wife of **Luke**, is from Gleason, Wisconsin. Angela was adopted as a young child. She writes positively about both her birth mother, whom she remembers, and her adoptive family. Luke and Angela had three biological daughters. Then they fostered twin girls whom they eventually adopted. Recently they were blessed with their first son by birth.

Daryl and Christine Diller family, 2010

*C*hristine Diller, wife to Daryl of Doylesburg, Pennsylvania, has a love for children and writing. She is mother to nine, two of whom are adopted, and grandmother to four.

*P*hilip and Louise Hoover from Elizabethtown, Pennsylvania, are the parents of five children—*Jeffrey*, *Joshua*, *Joseph*, *Katelyn*, and *Alayna*—two of whom were adopted through foster care. The Hoovers parented a number of foster children. In this book they share the story of Sammy, a very dear little boy to them, and the

Philip and Louise Hoover family

lessons they gleaned while learning to accept God's perfect plan.

Nathan and Carol Gingerich family, 2010

Carol Gingerich, wife of **Nathan**, lives at Bloomfield, New Mexico. Their parenting includes biological children, foster children, and adopted children. Their adult daughter **Donita** has also been a foster mother. Carol writes the following:

Two of our sons, **Lyndon** and **Laramie**, came to our home as infants through foster care and then adoption. Besides them, we have had over twenty foster children in the past five years. One was a little Indian girl who passed away while in our care. **Karla** was in our home six months from the age of thirteen months to nineteen months.

God puts that special spark of interest and love for adoption in some of our hearts for some special reason. The reasons may vary between us, but mostly I think it is to prepare us for His special little ones that He desires to entrust to us.

Naoma Lee is from Aroda, Virginia, but she has lived in various Central American countries. She worked at a deaf school in El Salvador for a year and enjoys interacting with children of all ages.

John and *Anita King family, 2002

Anita King was wife to **John** of Hagerstown, Maryland. Anita had a special interest in adoption, since she grew up as a foster child and her husband John was adopted. Their parenting included three biological children—**Janet**, **Allen**, and **Jordan;** and five children they adopted from Honduras—**Donnie**, **Joshua**, **Eden**, **Julie**, and **Matthew**. Jordan passed away from drowning in his early teens. Besides the five children they adopted, Anita worked as an adoption coordinator, helping many other children find their forever families.

We enjoyed working with Anita over the time she wrote the articles for our book and were very saddened to hear that she was diagnosed with cancer in 2006 and that she passed away in 2007. It's a recognition of our mortality to realize that before we got this project finished, one of our contributors went on to be with the Lord.

We find it noteworthy that Anita's oldest daughter Janet and her husband Josue Pierre were also very involved in orphanages and foster care, both before and after their marriage while they lived in Haiti. Quite a few of the children that Janet fostered were placed in adoptive homes in the United States, and she is glad to be able to keep in contact with them.

Sarah Kraybill

Sarah Kraybill is from Dillsburg, Pennsylvania. Sarah wrote the poem "Willing to Give" for her niece, Janita Blessing Kraybill, when she was adopted by her brother and his wife. Sarah is the tenth in a family of twelve children. Before she began teaching school in 2011, Sarah frequently helped her married siblings. She fondly remembers taking her turn with the night shift in July 2005 when Janita was a baby.

James and Sharilyn Martin family

Sharilyn Martin lives in Cove, Oregon, with her husband **James** and their five children: **Melodi**, **Angela**, **Walter**, **Danny**, and **Conrad**. Two of their sons are adopted—one from Russia in 2004 and one from Belize in 2009. Sharilyn is a homemaker who does writing on the side, and James is a businessman who works in general construction and in the storage shed business. They attend the Grande Ronde Mennonite Church.

Ruthie Martin, wife of **Jason** from Lebanon, Pennsylvania, and mother of seven, writes from the perspective of an aunt to cherished nieces and nephews, hers because of the miracle of adoption.

Jason and Ruthie Martin family, 2009

Alvin and Fannie Miller family

Fannie Miller, wife of **Alvin**, is from Crossville, Tennessee. Alvin and Fannie traveled to Honduras on an electrical work project for their mission compound which included a children's home. While there, they learned of the need of two boys, ages seven and nine, who had a deep longing for a home and family. Both boys had lived at the children's home since the age of two. Alvin and Fanny felt the call to open their home to **Edwin** and **Walter**. Their family of eight made a memorable trip, traveling in a school bus to Honduras to bring Edwin and Walter home. Twenty-two years later, Fannie and Alvin are heavily burdened for their boys and the choices they have made. The family covets your prayers for the boys' souls.

Caroline Miller

Caroline Miller, from Crossville, Tennessee, is the daughter of Alvin and Fannie. She writes from the perspective of a sister of two younger adopted brothers.

Elizabeth Mullet of Pantego, North Carolina, is a licensed practical nurse with the amazing experience of having two newborn babies personally given to her at different times. She then had the sweet privilege of fostering both of them before they went to their forever homes. Elizabeth shares in this book of working with a birth mother whose baby **Kelly Rose** became her niece.

Elizabeth Mullett

Carol Peachey from Harrisonburg, Virginia, is a single adoptive mother, and grandmother to her daughter's two little girls. She writes about some of the challenges of adopting an older child and finding the supports she needed.

Harry Lee and Joanna Neuenschwander family

oanna Neuenschwander, wife to **Harry Lee** of Salem, Ohio, and their two daughters *Kristalyn* and *Janae* write about *Jarrell*, who was adopted in 2002 and passed away in 2010. Joanna also writes about the adoption of their daughter **Lashae** whom they adopted from China. Along with their two adopted children, Harry Lee and Joanna have four living biological children and two infant sons in Heaven. They also are delighted to have a recently adopted granddaughter and are looking forward to a new son, **Jadren**, joining their home through adoption. Jarrell's first request for Make-A-Wish was to have Mom and Dad get a child from Vietnam or China. Joanna writes, "While the request pierced our hearts at the time, we kept the request safely stored and accepted it as a future call."

Jadren

*L*ydia **Plett** of Lott, Texas, was married to **Larry** for twelve years. They were childless for six years. Larry passed away in 2003, almost two years after their third child was adopted. Their three children at the time of his death were two

Lydia Plett family

six-year-olds and a two-year-old. When Lydia wrote "You Are My Best Mama," she was a young widow with three children to raise. Her children are **Eunice**, who entered their home at the age of three weeks and two days; **Christopher**, almost Eunice's twin, who was four and one-half when he came to live with them; and **Damaris**, the little girl with cystic fibrosis, whom they adopted as an infant.

Bill and Carla Raley family

Carla **Raley**, the wife of **Bill,** is from Grandview, Texas. Their parenting includes seven biological children and many foster children, including three foster children whom they adopted—**Luke**, **Angel-Leah**, and **Tommy**. Carla writes about the challenge of adopting an older child and has some very good suggestions for bonding techniques that have worked well for them. The Raleys are in the process of adopting two sisters, **Cynthia** and **Selena**, who came at the ages of fifteen and five years old.

oger and Joy Rangai are from Straw-berry, Arkansas. *Joy Maria* is the adopted daughter of the late David L. and Edna Miller. Her parents had been married thirty years and had six

Roger and *Joy Rangai family

biological children ages 12 to 29 when they adopted Joy, an eight-year-old girl from a children's home in El Salvador. Joy holds her parents in high regard and is forever grateful that they were willing to adopt an older child as they were entering the sunset years of life. Roger and Joy have five children: **Steven**, **Carlos**, **Rhonda**, **Angela**, and **Edwin.**

Stan and Esther Reinford family

*E*sther Reinford is wife to **Stan** of Mt. Holly Springs, Pennsylvania. Their parenting includes biological children, foster care, and adoption. They have two biological sons and one adopted daughter. **Martina** was one of the many foster babies who came to their home straight from the hospital. Because of drugs she had been introduced to before birth, she cried excessively from withdrawal for the first several months. Martina (Reinford) Zimmerman wrote "Thank You, Mom" in tribute to her adoptive mother Esther. Adoption has been a positive experience in the Reinford family. Out of Stan and Esther's nineteen grandchildren, three grandsons are also adopted.

*M*artina Zimmerman and her husband **Darren** reside in Newville, Pennsylvania. Martina is the daughter of Stan and Esther Reinford. She was a high-risk drug baby who entered their home at 17 months old as a foster baby. She was adopted by her foster parents and became their only daughter. Darren Zimmerman and Martina Reinford were married

in 2000 and have seven children. **Ryan** and **Andrew** are theirs through adoption, and they also have four living biological children, **Jessica**, **Kimberly**, **Jeremy**, and **Anthony**. **Brent**, who died as an infant, is waiting for them in Heaven.

Darren and *Martina Zimmerman family

Charles and Kathy Rohrer family

Kathy **Rohrer,** wife of **Charles,** is from Grand Junction, Colorado. They are the parents of one adopted and five biological children. During their first eighteen months of marriage, they experienced three miscarriages. Open to the idea that perhaps God had a child for them through other options, they became foster parents. Two months later a little foster girl came to their home. Eighteen months later she became their legal daughter. As they were preparing to leave the courtroom, the judge focused her attention on Kathy and made one last remark. "Mrs. Rohrer" she said, "**Meaghan** looks just like you!" This touched the Rohrers, even though they had heard the same remark many times before. They rejoice that God revealed His plan for this dear little girl to be their first child.

*Crystal VanPelt

Crystal **Marie VanPelt** from New Holland, Pennsylvania, is the adopted daughter of Ivan and Eleanor VanPelt. Looking back on the doors God opened and closed in the past, she thanks God for the opportunities that have been handed to her as a result of someone being willing to step through those open doors. Her mother kept foster children as a single woman, and was in the process of adopting two girls from Romania, but God had other plans. When a widower asked for her hand in marriage, Crystal's mother stepped out in faith, taking her three small children with her into the marriage. Together, Crystal's parents then pursued adoption.

Has life been without struggle? No, but today, surrounded by love and the people of God, Crystal is enjoying life to its fullest and is sobered to think of what she would have missed had someone been unwilling to adopt her because of fear. Though familiar with the heartaches of watching and praying as a sibling and friends leave their heritage, she says, "It's worth it. Every time someone chooses to adopt, they shout to us who are adopted that they believe in us. They believe we can be faithful. They truly believe that one soul is worth the whole world."

Rene and Mary Ellen Rivera family, 2009

*M*ary Ellen Rivera and her husband Rene live in Annville, Pennsylvania. Rene is an evangelist and also the director of Shepherd's Fold, a Christian counseling facility, where he has been able to help many, including a great number of troubled adopted young men.

Rene and Mary Ellen had three biological daughters. They were serving as missionaries in Guatemala when a woman came to one of their fellow missionaries and asked if they knew of anyone who would want a baby. She was going to give birth and could not keep the child. When the time came, the Riveras took the woman to a clinic to give birth and brought their infant son home the next day.

Rene and Mary Ellen adopted their second son through a children's home in Guatemala City. These boys brought great joy to their home.

Even though their oldest son caused them much heartache when he chose to leave their faith and later was killed in a rodeo accident, they are still strong advocates of adoption. They believe that David had a chance and a choice to make that he would not have otherwise had. Also through this experience they have a burning desire to help other adopted boys to lives of victory and faithfulness to God.

*Marta Wagler

Marta **Wagler** of Cross Hill, South Carolina, is the daughter of Joel and Mary Catherine Wagler. She was adopted from El Salvador at the age of two. Although being a part of the Wagler family is her earliest memory, and they have been a great blessing to her, she still experienced struggles particular to adoption. She writes about a familiar question, "Do you really love me as your biological child?" and the answers she has found in seeking her true identity.

Jerry and Becky Wenger family, 2012

*J*erry and Becky Wenger live near Sacramento, California. The Wengers have four adopted children: **Bethany**, **Austin**, **Rosalie**, and **Alex.** Their first adoption was a newborn baby boy. They had a very positive experience working directly with the birth mother. Two of their children were adopted from Liberia, and more recently they adopted another little boy. Their experience includes international, interracial, and special needs adoption.

*B*renda **Weaver**, wife of the late **John** of Millmont, Pennsylvania, is the author of *Daughters of Eve, Daughters of God.* Brenda was a great enthusiast for *Heartstrings*, especially in its birthing stages. Her articles were among the first we received, and she helped us with reviewing and critiquing. Brenda's parenting experience includes biological children, foster care, and interracial adoption. She is the mother of five, one adopted. She is a grandmother and is also currently providing pediatric care as a registered nurse.

John and Brenda Weaver family, 2011

*E*lizabeth Yoder and her husband **Tobias** live at Arborg, Manitoba, Canada. Their home, which was established in 1961, has included many children. They have four biological children and three adopted children. In addition, they have had numerous foster children over the twenty-seven plus years they have been in foster care. Many of their foster children have been Native Canadians.

Tobias and Elizabeth Yoder

Tobias and Elizabeth Yoder family

Dallas and Rhoda Witmer family

*D*allas and Rhoda Witmer have resided in Colombia, South America, as missionaries since their children are grown. Their large family includes biological, adopted, and foster children, along with many grandchildren. Among their children is an older sibling group of three that they adopted from Mexico. Two of them are married and faithful in the church; the third was taken to Heaven through an accident as a young teen. We are pleased to have Dallas's introduction to our book, sharing with us some of his insights and experience about adoption, particularly relating to adopting the older child.

The Weaver

Unknown

Paul R. Martin, 2008

1. My life is but a weav - ing Be - tween my Lord and me.
2. Not till the loom is si - lent And the shut - tles cease to fly,
3. The dark threads are as need - ful In the Weav - ers skill - ful hand

I can - not choose the co - lors, He work - eth stead - i - ly.
Shall God un - roll the can - vas And ex - plain the rea - son why.
As the threads of gold and sil - ver In the pat - tern He has planned.

(vs. 1.) Oft - times He weav - eth sor - row And I in fool - ish pride,
(vs. 2.&3.) He knows, He loves, He cares, no - thing this truth can dim,

For - get He sees the up - per And I the und - er side.
He gives His ver - y best to those who leave the choice with Him.

Christian Light Publications is a nonprofit, conservative Mennonite publishing company providing Christ-centered, Biblical literature including books, Gospel tracts, Sunday school materials, summer Bible school materials, and a full curriculum for Christian day schools and homeschools. Though produced primarily in English, some books, tracts, and school materials are also available in Spanish.

For more information about the ministry of CLP or its publications, or for spiritual help, please contact us at:

Christian Light Publications
P. O. Box 1212
Harrisonburg, VA 22803-1212

Telephone—540-434-0768
Fax—540-433-8896
E-mail—info@clp.org
www.clp.org